THE LOGIC OF LOVE

T&T Clark Enquiries in Theological Ethics

Series editors

Brian Brock
Susan F. Parsons

THE LOGIC OF LOVE

Christian Ethics and Moral Psychology

Andrew J. B. Cameron

LONDON • NEW YORK • OXFORD • NEW DELHI • SYDNEY

T&T CLARK
Bloomsbury Publishing Plc
50 Bedford Square, London, WC1B 3DP, UK
1385 Broadway, New York, NY 10018, USA
29 Earlsfort Terrace, Dublin 2, Ireland

BLOOMSBURY, T&T CLARK and the T&T Clark logo are trademarks of
Bloomsbury Publishing Plc

First published in Great Britain 2023

A catalogue record for this book is available from the British Library.

Library of Congress Cataloging-in-Publication Data
Names: Cameron, Andrew J. B., author.
Title: The logic of love: Christian ethics and moral psychology / Andrew J. B. Cameron.
Description: London; New York: T&T Clark, 2022. | Series: T&T Clark enquiries in
theological ethics | Includes bibliographical references and index. |
Identifiers: LCCN 2022036237 (print) | LCCN 2022036238 (ebook) |
ISBN 9780567707130 (hb) | ISBN 9780567707178 (paperback) |
ISBN 9780567707123 (epdf) | ISBN 9780567707161 (epub)
Subjects: LCSH: Love–Religious aspects–Christianity. |
Emotions–Religious aspects–Christianity. | Christian ethics.
Classification: LCC BV4639 .C256 2022 (print) | LCC BV4639 (ebook) |
DDC 241/.4–dc23/eng/20221104
LC record available at https://lccn.loc.gov/2022036237
LC ebook record available at https://lccn.loc.gov/2022036238

ISBN: HB: 978-0-5677-0713-0
ePDF: 978-0-5677-0712-3
ePUB: 978-0-5677-0716-1

Series: T&T Clark Enquiries in Theological Ethics

Typeset by Deanta Global Publishing Services, Chennai, India

To find out more about our authors and books visit www.bloomsbury.com and
sign up for our newsletters.

To Mary-Anne:

You made this book possible,
in so many ways.
May the very long way around
represented in these pages
finally blossom into
the return of your love.

CONTENTS

Chapter 5

Part 3
CHRISTIAN REFLECTIONS IN AN ACCOUNT OF AFFECTION

Chapter 6

Chapter 7

ACKNOWLEDGEMENTS

This book has gestated from so many opportunities and serendipitous gifts that I don't know where to begin.

In the first instance, I am thankful to the Council of St Mark's National Theological Centre in Barton, ACT, Australia, for the invaluable sabbatical leave gifted to me in 2021, enabling the preparation of this book. Furthermore, without my colleagues' diligent oversight both of St Mark's and of the School of Theology at Charles Sturt University, this leave would not have been possible.

In this respect, I am especially thankful to the Rev'd Dr Jane Foulcher for shouldering several additional months both as acting director of St Mark's, and as Head of School. As will be seen in Chapter 9, I am also indebted to her scholarship in the Cistercian monastic tradition, and am thankful for her humility in never humiliating me about my ignorance of it. Another colleague, Dr Bernard Doherty, has popped up often enough in footnotes below that I realize how much I have enjoyed him as a 'corridor conversation' partner. The Rev'd Dr Andrew Errington was kind enough to read an early version, and he suggested some useful directions.

The general editors of the series, Susan Parsons and Brian Brock, have been unstinting in their encouragement to bring it to birth. Despite how long the book has taken, I have appreciated their several years of support, and Brian's years of friendship. Anna Turton, Sinead O'Connor, Sophie Beardsworth, Vishnu Prasad, and their colleagues at Bloomsbury have been unfailingly patient and professional. Several readers of various drafts have done their best to make the result slightly more bearable: Daniel Anderson; Stephen and Anna Boxwell; and especially Amy Erickson and David McLennan. I appreciate their patience and attention to detail. I have mentioned in the Preface and elsewhere my very great debt to Dr Paul Ruefli, and in Chapter 9, to Dr Micheál Loughnane.

I am also thankful to the National Library of Australia and its staff for the provision of the Petherick Reading Room, which was an all too brief haven prior to Canberra's Covid-19 lockdowns. The library network of Charles Sturt University (of which St Mark's National Anglican Memorial Library is a part) has been stupendously helpful. I thank its staff for their commitment to expanding a world-class collection of electronic resources, particularly in theology and psychology, and for their commitment to the provision of a state-of-the-art infrastructure that supports remote research.

In the original thesis on which part of the book is based, I named with thanks over fifty debts of gratitude. So much time has passed since then that I am not sure about naming them all here. But I must note my enduring debt to the Rev'd Professor Michael Banner, whose supervision first enlivened me to the wisdom of Augustine, and many other classic and modern thinkers. Archbishop Emeritus Peter Jensen encouraged my initial studies in theology, including the fateful decision to spend life-changing time in the United Kingdom. The hospitality and enduring friendship of several members of Royston Evangelical Church has been one of my life's most unexpected gifts.

I have dedicated the book to my wife Mary-Anne, who made possible all my learning in theology, but who continues to await the fruit of it in a well-lived husband. At least the Holy Spirit has sustained us, and her steadfast love, for which I am profoundly grateful.

Andrew Cameron
St Mark's National Theological Centre and
Charles Stuart University

ABBREVIATIONS AND EXPLANATORY NOTES

HH	Haidt, Jonathan, *The Happiness Hypothesis: Finding Modern Truth in Ancient Wisdom* (New York: Basic Books, 2006). See further n 127, below
MFT	Moral Foundations Theory (by Haidt and Joseph). See further n 141
NRSV	*The Holy Bible*, New Revised Standard Version (Division of Christian Education of the National Council of the Churches of Christ in the United States of America, 1989). All biblical quotations are from NRSV, unless otherwise noted
NT	New Testament
OT	Old Testament
OED	Simpson, J. A., and E. S. C. Weiner (eds), *The Oxford English Dictionary, 2nd Edition* (Oxford: Clarendon, 1989). See further n 14
LXX	The Septuagint

Where words and phrases in original quotations are emphasized, the emphasis is always original, and in the style used by that author (or their translator). Since no emphases have been added by this author to quotations, it was not thought necessary to signal that emphasis is original.

In quotations, spaced ellipsis without square brackets represents omissions made by the original author. Bracketed words or ellipsis reflect omissions introduced by this author.

For many primary sources, a generally agreed first publication date is given in brackets after the title of the work in its first footnoted reference. *Circa* should always be understood.

In the interests of readability, traditional Roman-Arabic references to Aquinas' *Summa*, and to a lesser extent, Augustine's *Confessions* and *City of God*, have generally been retained in the main text, while other references occur in footnotes. However, references to these works may occur in footnotes if details specific to some editions of the work are relevant, or if pagination seemed a more helpful referent than the traditional reference. Rather than aiming for strict consistency, I have aimed for readability as context demands.

FIGURES

PREFACE

I have been a coward all my life. I've never really had a clear opportunity to prove it, such as running from the heat of battle or failing to snatch a child from a fire. But it has been there, from when I began school a year younger than my peers, then as a result, through several years never quite getting what was going on socially, and being mocked for lack of coordination in sports. Or, when I was an eight-year-old on my father's work sites, desperately trying to master skills no child can do well, learning to mind-read and anticipate his outbursts at my errors. On top of that, my well-meaning mother taught me to be fearful of pretty much everything. Those ingredients combined with some original contributions of my own to blossom into those dark fruits of middle age – the frightened inner storytelling about my family life, my professional life, my social life – 'a script I just keep on living', as an exasperated pastor once told me.

This admission is an unconventional beginning, I concede, to a learned tome in theological ethics. It is not my intention to garner your sympathy nor to engage in 'catharcissism', as I have heard called that penchant for therapeutic public confession. It *is* my intention to elicit your adverse response to my use of the term 'coward'. After all, we are used to exonerating people, to some extent, given their origin-story; and for my experiences, there is now another, kinder word that we will encounter next.

Yet, to pause on cowardice for an uncomfortable further beat: Christian Scripture offers a disturbing denouement for people like me. 'But as for the cowardly', along with several other folk who will distract us here, 'their place will be the lake that burns with fire and sulphur, which is the second death' (Rev. 21.8). It does seem like a cruel trick to warn cowards off their cowardice by leveraging it in prospect of a lake of fire. It did not work in my case, nor did biblical exhortations not to fear. After all, we cannot command an emotion, or so it is widely believed, and so I have generally held. (I once met a good man who read Jesus' directive not to worry, Lk. 12.22, and said that in simple obedience he decided, successfully, never to do so again. I was incredulous.)

What helped me was a quasi-medical diagnosis of *anxiety*. I finally recognized my near-blackouts, and my chronic sense of total depersonalization in situations of stress (actually in all situations, at the end). Under this new label, I noticed my waking to the sound of birdsong in abject, gnawing fear at the prospect of the day ahead. Within this torrent of fear – a fear, more or less, of nothing – I had been grabbing compulsively at pleasurable moments of respite. But when *anxiety* was addressed with the modern helps of mindfulness meditation, and pharmacological and psychotherapeutic interventions, I could recognize and address the effects of a hyperactive amygdala, the nugget at the base of the brain that seems to grow in fear the more we trigger it (or so goes one neurobiological story).

In cowardice, we have as moral a term for fear as can be deployed – even a 'moralistic' term, to put morality under its pejorative hue. In anxiety, we encounter a more dispassionate description of the same experience – even a more compassionate term, by common account. The first evaluates, the second medicates. The first offers a judgment, the second makes no judgment. The first is a species of vice, the second a species, now, of mental illness.

In the Bible, Rev. 21.8 uses the reader's cowardice to throw their attention to the moral deficiency of their situation, and to their need of change. In my own case, only after passing through the belief that 'I can't help it' – a morally relieving gift of the mental illness paradigm – was I then able to see the extent to which the preoccupations elemental to my anxiety drew me away from the needs of others, and from the goodness of God. Most notably, it was my long-suffering wife Mary-Anne who bore the brunt of several bad outcomes of my anxiety and cowardice. Rev. 21.8 focuses the spotlight on its moral effects, irrespective of the coward's will, or not, to master his cowardice. But in our context, the charge of cowardice is intolerably harsh, for reasons to do with part of the story this book seeks to tell.

I have indulged in these paragraphs of 'too much Information' to highlight how an ancient and emotionally laden term of moral language, *cowardice*, seems distinct from the morally neutral emotion-term, *anxiety*. There is a story to be told about their difference, and in this book, I will attempt to tell it with Christian theology as the lens. It turns out to be a story that has previously been told, and is being retold using other lenses. But in the absence of such a story, it has become wildly problematic in the modern West to decide into which language to flip: the morally laden, or the medicalized? Was he greedy, or was he suffering from anxiety about financial insecurity? Was she jealous, or was she defending her attachment to him? Once he was regarded as lustful; now, he is addicted. She used to be content; now, she is self-actualized, or 'true to herself'. Which description best fits? Are the moral terms even needed, or are they too judgmental and hegemonic to find a place in our pluralist order?

These musings also seem an unlikely place to begin a volume entitled *The Logic of Love*. In our context, 'love' immediately sends the mind towards romantic comedies and rainbow parades. Perhaps it might extend towards our love for our children, close family, and an occasional friend. The glowing, white-hot centre of this term has become for us that centre of modern existential meaning found in authentic, intimate relationships. In our milieu, then, one would expect of my title a handbook in, say, the arts of interpersonal love. This is not that book – although as it happens, our most intense experiences of interpersonal and even erotic love will indeed offer some clues along the way.

Rather, I will be using 'love' in the most expansive sense possible. It is the kind of love that ultimately explains even my cowardice (or my anxiety). The theologians I will profile have a thing or two to say about how even such an unpleasant emotion, and the borderline and frankly immoral acts it powers in people like me, actually spring from forms of love – distorted, perhaps, but love nonetheless. We are constituted, they will say, in love. There is within us an attentiveness to what and who surround us. To put it slightly mysteriously, otherness is at the base of our soul: a primal attraction to people and objects beyond us, and a spiritual connection to God. Not only does that account for the strength of our intimate interpersonal relationships. It accounts for all our attractions, interests and desires, and for all our judgments of what matters. By extension, it accounts for our moral and ethical impulses – and even for our thoughts about what should matter in our ethical deliberations, even if this or that normative claim does not seriously matter to some of us.

If I may hazard an allusion to popular culture, I am reminded of a confession by the character Mia (played by Gemma Chan), the central character in a recent science fiction television series, *Humans*. Mia is a 'synth', a life-like artificial construct whom we would call a robot or an android. In the series, it is universally agreed that synths cannot be conscious. But Mia *is* conscious, which she seeks to prove to her human love-interest in a soliloquy that speaks also of her being constituted, somehow, in love. 'I am a synthetic. But I'm awake. Conscious. [. . .] I can think, sense, feel – care. I can like things. Like people.'[1] Such a script cannot prove much, but I am interested in the writers' intuition that not only rationality, but 'feeling' extending to 'care' and 'liking' are at the base of such soul as Mia may have.

This book began as my 2003 doctoral thesis, *The Logic of Love: A Theological Approach to the Relationship between Ethics and Emotion.* It is not that thesis, because like all such entrants to a guild, tracts of it were experiments that have no business to see the light of day. But since that project, I have found in the logic of love a helpful heuristic for understanding all manner of normative claims, and the disputes attending them. The present volume seeks to extend that project further into theological terrain.

Since that thesis, a torrent of interest and research has irrupted into this space. Even in the late 1990s, a burgeoning literature was trying to make better sense of emotion itself – motivated, I suspect as I was at the time, by a growing dissatisfaction at a kind of hyper-rationalism that had muzzled what many regarded as the beating heart of what mattered to them. (In my case, it was a version of Christian culture that mocked emotion in most of its forms, and regarded the Christian journey as one of amassing so much teaching and thinking as to effect a kind of trickle-down into behaviour – like a chemical reaction given enough reagents to maximize an outcome. This notion has long antecedents in Western philosophy.) The project of rehabilitation of emotion continues unabated in lively conversations between psychology and philosophy. But the project has been dogged, I will suggest, by structural features that excluded considerations of the moral aspects of emotion. Moreover, to track this project even within the balkanized terrain of psychology is a difficult task given the discipline's views of itself. For Svend Brinkmann:

> Psychology is essentially a contested and fragmented discipline with numerous interests in how the discipline should be designed [including proposals] that it should look more like neurochemistry (cf. certain neuroscientists),

---

1. *Humans*, 'Episode #2.3' (AMC Studios; written by Charlie Covell, Iain Weatherby and Lars Lundström; directed by Carl Tibbetts; aired 27 February 2017, Channel 4, UK), 15'30"–16'08".

computer science (cf. some cognitive scientists), biology (cf. evolutionary psychologists), sociology (cf. social constructionists), anthropology (cf. cultural psychologists), literary studies (cf. postmodernists), or political science (cf. critical psychologists).[2]

Manifold angles on emotion follow from these intramural debates in psychology. Complicating my assertion that structural features have excluded consideration of emotion's moral aspects is the emergence of a domain of thought called 'moral psychology'. Although not a new term, it now encompasses renewed attention towards interactions between psychological processes, including emotional processes, and moral life. The ancient and Christian thought we will encounter does not always map easily onto what we call 'moral', nor to what we call 'psychology'. Even so, moral psychology is the most natural modern dialogue partner for what, as we shall see, have been matters of long-standing interest to a variety of Christian thinkers. Moral psychology is also a fecund and varied terrain. According to Benjamin Voyer:

> Despite its name, moral psychology spans every discipline concerned with human interaction – from philosophy and sociology to evolutionary biology and neuroscience. [. . .] As the varied disciplines comprising moral psychology have developed, their methods have become increasingly specialized and complex.[3]

Even so, R. Jay Wallace sums up what essentially constitutes the field:

> [It views] a variety of psychological phenomena through the unifying prism of a concern for normativity. It studies the psychological conditions for the possibility of binding norms of action; the ways in which moral and other such norms can be internalized and complied with in the lives of agents; and a range of psychological conditions and formations that have implications for the normative assessment of agents and their lives.[4]

The astute reader of the quotation may notice, however, that at no point does the moral psychologist have an account of normativity itself, only of the psychological conditions for it. Brinkmann describes this mood as the 'psychologization' of

2. Svend Brinkmann, *Psychology as a Moral Science: Perspectives on Normativity* (New York: Springer, 2011), pp. 1–2, doi: 10.1007/978-1-4419-7067-1_6.

3. Benjamin G. Voyer, 'Toward a Multidisciplinary Moral Psychology', in *Moral Psychology: A Multidisciplinary Guide* (eds Benjamin G. Voyer and Tor Tarantola; Cham, Switzerland: Springer International Publishing AG, 2017), pp. 1–3 (1).

4. Cited in Alfred Mele, 'Moral Psychology', in *Continuum Companion to Ethics* (ed. Christian Miller; New York: Bloomsbury Publishing, 2011), pp. 98–118 (98).

morality[5] (and really, of everything[6]) – a mode of thought that robs us of ways to parse and inhabit the moral aspects of our lives, which are elemental to human existence. In this claim, I will go on to suggest, Brinkmann is a fellow traveller with Augustine of Hippo and Thomas Aquinas.

The series in which this book sits centres on conversation between Christian theology and other large domains of human enquiry. Like other books in the series, the current volume can hope only to intersect some Christian thought with some alternative accounts. I will proceed as follows.

In Chapter 1, I will engage with recent interdisciplinary emotion research, including some of the interminable debates about the definition of emotion and the shortcomings of the English word for it. The disciplines represented in these debates have been less comfortable than moral psychology to engage with frankly moral considerations about emotion. In an effort to shed some light on this discomfort, I will suggest in Chapter 2 that the German philosophers Immanuel Kant and Friedrich Nietzsche are the forefathers of two competing accounts of the relationship of emotion to ethics. Both thinkers clearly discern important kernels of truth. Yet they bequeathed to us competing and conflicting accounts of the relationship between emotion and ethics, and these remain strong currents in our milieu. They are opposite poles in a complex terrain.

Chapter 3 examines two very different thinkers in psychology. The first, Jonathan Haidt, represents psychology at its most morally engaged, yet still operating within the bounds of psychology's givens such as evolutionary naturalism, experimental reductions, and a highly fragmented set of almost incommensurate disciplines that all try to pass themselves off as a single discipline. Even so, Haidt's account is socially responsible, humane, and respectful of 'folk psychologies' such as are found in several religions. The second thinker, Svend Brinkmann, breaks the bonds of psychology's givens by arguing against its endemic avoidance of any substantive morality within reality. Brinkmann thinks that psychology can only function as a true account of human being when it construes itself, fundamentally, as a form of 'moral science'. Both thinkers pave the way for a more satisfying account of the relationship between our moral and emotional lives, Haidt by naming and analysing a plethora of moral emotions, Brinkman by positing that emotion is itself a fundamentally moral set of reactions to an intrinsically morally ordered world.

These chapters in Part 1 are a prelude to the theological tour of the same terrain in Parts 2 and 3. To see how Christian thought might parse these currents, I will look at two Scriptural cameos on moral psychology: the ancient notion of wisdom and the approach to desire in the Hellenistic Christianity of the New Testament (Chapters 4 and 5). St. Augustine of Hippo's account then follows (Chapter 6), because (in the West at least) he has become theology's most influential expositor of an account of desire that I call a 'logic of love'. The twelfth-century Dominican

---

5. Brinkmann, *Psychology as a Moral Science*, p. 3 n. 4; p. 11; and *passim*.
6. Brinkmann, *Psychology as a Moral Science*, p. 10 (drawing on architect Mark Jarzombek).

theologian Thomas Aquinas builds upon Augustine's insights. Esther D. Reed observes how he situates the moral life within 'a classically-framed account of the passions – as movements of the soul in response to objects seen either as attractive and thus desirable, or as evil and thus to be avoided.'[7] Reed believes we need 'reappropriation of classic discussions of "moral passion", the relationship of passion(s) to virtue, reason and the will, the role of passion(s) in the perfection of virtue, and its contextually-rooted education.'[8] I hope to offer a step towards that in my examination of Aquinas in Chapter 7. (Only the most intrepid readers may be able to traverse the vast expanses of Chapters 6 and 7, and parts of Chapter 2, although I do regard these as essential raw materials for understanding the logic of love.)

With the help of Anglican theologian Sarah Coakley, we will in Chapter 8 examine how desire itself springs from the heart of God, in contrast to some apprehensions of divine impassibility (apprehensions, I will suggest, that have misunderstood what is meant by divine impassibility, precisely as they misunderstood the nature of a passion in reference to God). This divine reality perforce supervenes the work of Augustine and Aquinas. Coakley draws our attention to how *eros* must itself spring from God's own vibrant and blazing love. Intimate relationship, then – far from being the apotheosis of meaning, purpose, and authenticity that they have become in the modern West – may in fact alert us to something more that we are missing. Springing from her insight, I will overview extensive Eastern and Western monastic practices in the moral training of emotion that terminates in new forms of participation within God's own love, refracted to us very accessibly in the work of Joan Chittister, who seeks to mediate this life to non-monastics (Chapter 9).

Before I describe the book's denouement in Chapter 10, I will pause here to make an observation arising from my recovery out of chronic anxiety. In this journey, I had the good fortune to meet Dr Paul Ruefli, a clinical psychologist with a deep background both in Jungian psychotherapy, and in the Catholic contemplative tradition (to name but two of his areas of expertise). Paul commented to me early on that good psychology ends in spirituality. This simple comment amazed me: even as a long-time Anglican priest with an informed lay-person's interest in psychology, I suddenly realized that I had been keeping the two domains highly compartmentalized. In some respects, this book also represents an effort to understand his comment and end that compartmentalization.

However, my story, and the story of the book, does not only concern personal piety and modes of introspection. While writing the book, I have been acutely aware of the stridency in civic life that is likely but the visible tip of a submerged iceberg of anxiety. Beneath all that is, I reckon, an absence of skill to recognize the moral evaluations inherent to strong emotional commitments. I cannot hope to solve all

---

7. Esther D. Reed, 'Book Review: Robin Gill, Moral Passion and Christian Ethics', *Studies in Christian Ethics* 32.3 (2019), pp. 416–17 (416), doi: 10.1177/0953946819843467d

8. Reed, 'Book Review: Gill', p. 417.

that. But Chapter 10 will make some suggestions, outlining the beginnings of a Christian moral psychology offering readers some hints to evaluate and navigate confusing terrain, and perhaps even to become a (flawed) exemplar for others of a better kind of life within it. Along the way I will also have a shot at the bankrupt modern language of values, and at lousy pelagian preaching.

An occasional reader may wonder where this book sits in relation to a previous offering, *Joined-up Life: A Christian Account of How Ethics Works*.[9] Some themes in this volume are found in simpler form in that book's earlier chapters. More curiously perhaps, not long after its publication began my near-terminal spiral into anxious dysfunction, alluded to above. I offer this information as a salutary admission that no amount of ethical expertise suffices to make a well-lived life. Other ingredients are needed, such as what Haidt argues for, and (as we shall see) what Augustine, Benedict, Aquinas, and others have long anticipated. I still stand by plenty in the earlier work; here is not the place to say where I do not. But I hope this volume is more tempered by recognitions that arise from adversity; more able to integrate the insights of Christian theology with the best truths of modern inquiry, and more attuned to practices that connect us with the inner life and love of God.

While preparing this book, I took an informal vow not to quote the prolific twentieth-century British author and apologist, C. S. Lewis. That decision meant no disrespect for him. To the contrary – the original thesis made several appeals to his work, and I have long been struck by his pithy turns-of-phrase and his depths of classical awareness. I rather felt, however, that for the purposes of this enquiry, it was important to be more current than was his milieu, and also more steeped in the classical and Christian traditions that his writing often summarizes. Even so, in the closing stages of preparing the manuscript, I had cause to revisit in *The Great Divorce*[10] that passing parade of ghosts who (like anxious me) had systematically diminished themselves by their false and fixated loves. I also reread Lewis's trenchant defence of moral realism (what he calls 'the *Tao*') in *The Abolition of Man*.[11] It struck me that any reader bewildered by my offering could equally pick up and digest these two classics, and maybe arrive at a similar destination.

Whether by those books or this, I hope we can begin to see what is entailed by a renewed love and affection for goodness, as variegated across all the forms and kinds of goodness, originating and terminating within the Triune One. I hope we will find how to have this love, how to grow it, and what inculcates the actions springing from what we name as good, in turn arising from a deeper logic of, *and participation in, love.*

---

9. Andrew J. B. Cameron, *Joined-up Life: A Christian Account of How Ethics Works* (Nottingham: IVP, 2011).

10. C. S. Lewis, *The Great Divorce: A Dream* (London: Geoffrey Bles, 1945).

11. C. S. Lewis, *The Abolition of Man: Or, Reflections on Education with Special Reference to the Teaching of English in the Upper Forms of Schools* (University of Durham, Riddell memorial lectures; 15th series; London: Geoffrey Bles, 1946).

Part 1

EMOTIONS AND MORAL PSYCHOLOGY

This part tours some recent thinking in emotion. The modern theory and practice of emotion discourse is contentious but is also fundamentally amoral. Kant and Nietzsche are offered as precursors to the modern dichotomy between languages of morality and emotion, albeit for very different reasons. The emerging field of moral psychology, however, is setting out to engage with morality using emotion-concepts, even though psychology is beset by a stance that is also substantively amoral.

Chapter 1

THE AMORAL ROOTS OF MODERN 'EMOTION'

I. Ethics and emotion: Some modern difficulties

(Tears in the kitchen:) 'Let's bandage it, and then I'll kiss it better.'
(One friend to another:) 'You make me so mad I could hit you!'
(Or perhaps instead:) 'Let's make love.'
(At the market:) 'I must have it! How much do you want?'
(In an office:) 'She'll pay – I'll destroy her.'

A brief thought about some everyday scenarios quickly reveals how intricately intertwined are our actions with our emotions. So much of what we do springs from what we *want* to do or *feel the need* to do; and so much of that wanting and feeling in the moment has some emotional tone or hue.

It would seem equally obvious, therefore, that ethical reflection might straightforwardly assess the interactions between our actions and their associated emotions. (In this book, I will use 'ethics' and 'ethical' interchangeably with 'moral', to refer broadly to considerations about right and wrong, good and evil, what to do and who to be. Some finely distinguish the 'ethical' from the 'moral'; generally, I won't.[12]) Ethical reflection might have asked and answered straightforward questions, such as the following:

- Are emotions subject to moral evaluation? If so, how?
- When should emotion help direct my action?
- When should an action ever 'go against' an emotion?
- When should an emotion straightforwardly propel an action?
- In acts highly charged with emotion, are agents always responsible?

12. The matter is of course contested and could go either way. My doctoral student, the Rev'd Mark Layson, cites Christian Smith, Jonathan Haidt, Brett Litz, and others, to conclude that whereas ethics refers to thin codes prevailing in liberal polities, morality refers to those thick and visceral norms held by individuals, families, and discrete communities. This distinction does serve to describe recent common usage. But I believe it would be prematurely stipulative to predicate anything upon it in the context of this book.

In a world as big and complex as ours, it may be that people in some places and subcultures possess well-formed answers to these questions. But this book arose because certainly throughout a lot of Anglo-American public discussion of ethics during much of the twentieth century, questions like these were not usually answered with much coherence or consensus. Indeed, they were sometimes regarded as fundamentally unintelligible, with the stuff of emotion seeming to be of a fundamentally different kind than the stuff of ethics.

Looking beyond mere actions, a related set of questions corresponds to the renaissance of virtue- and character-oriented approaches to ethics:

- Do virtues necessarily involve emotional dispositions?
- Should certain emotions be cultivated?
- Can one's desire be shaped by oneself? Can desire's emotional dimension so be shaped?

I will approach such questions initially by way of research into emotions and their connections to morality (Chapters 1–3), and eventually by means of a dive into the Christian tradition on the same subject – albeit a tradition that uses different terms than we may be used to (Chapters 4–10). But for now, we will continue to pause and ponder the relationship between our emotional experiences and our forms of ethical life (Section I). I will then look at recent attempts to find clarity in emotion terms (II); but we will find confounding effects borne of a linguistic history with a murky relationship to morality (III).

A heuristic beginning may be to consider emotion loosely as 'that which moves us'. This provisional definition would surely provide a handy, if imprecise, starting point for ethical reflection: What should be our moral understanding of that which moves us? When should we be so moved? When should we remain unmoved? The connections between emotion and movement ride a long current in Western thought (in ways that have meant it was perhaps easier for previous generations than for us to approach such questions). The early Stoics understood that literal movements of the soul within the chest caused the tuggings and sensations associated with (what we would call) emotion.[13] For Aquinas, 'passion' reflected a kind of passivity in the soul – but also a kind of movement, as the soul drew towards humanity's true end (Chapter 7). Movement is reflected in the etymology of the English word. In the handy compendium of historic usage found in *OED*, what begins as a 'moving out' becomes a physical disturbance or agitation, and then '[a]ny agitation or disturbance of the mind, feeling, passion; any vehement or excited mental state'.[14] This history of ideas is retained in the embedded '-motion'.

---

13. For a nuanced discussion of the intramural debates between Zeno and Chrysippus, see Richard Sorabji, *Emotion and Peace of Mind: From Stoic Agitation to Christian Temptation* (Oxford: Clarendon Press, 2000), pp. 31, 34–40.

14. *Oxford English Dictionary* (Oxford: Oxford University Press, 2nd edn [CD-ROM, v. 4.0.0.3], 2009), s.v. 'emotion'. It should be noted that this clear etymological sequence is

Even when the emphasis within the word is on motions conceived as internal, only a hairsbreadth separates 'I'm moved' from 'I'm moved to action'. A body of literature debates intricately whether external actions and internal feelings are respectively causes or effects of the other. But lay observers of this debate, at least, are assured that plenty of emotions give rise to plenty of actions.

While actions have been elementary to reflection on morality and ethics, it may come as a surprise to find that these *wellsprings* of action have not always been the subject of sustained ethical enquiry. (More accurately, they *were* the subject of lively enquiry for much of Western history until, roughly, the late nineteenth century; and a minority strain of ethical reflection continued the attempt to make sense of emotions within morality.) The legacy of a Kantian account has been the widespread view that morally sound decisions to action should not, on the whole, be touched by emotion: they were not considered a relevant consideration for serious analysis of morality. (Even if younger cohorts have largely repudiated this kind of approach, older cohorts are likely to have vivid personal recollections of some version of this account, such as my recollection above of the Christianity of my formative years.)

Reciprocally, a parallel minority view (represented by the thought of the 'emotivist' C. L. Stevenson) tried to sustain a view that morality consisted *only* in 'extrascientific'[15] emotive utterances, conveying only attitudes of approval or disapproval. In the emotivist account, the 'extrascientific' was whatever could not be tested by then-canons for the verification of propositions. Hence attitudes were a kind of black box that could not be meaningfully tested or morally philosophized about.

In the first kind of view, a rift lay between ethics and emotion: to think about ethics was deliberately to marginalize reflection upon emotion. In the second kind of view, the rift lay between ethics and reason: to think reasonably entailed a failure to be able to think about ethics, if ethics was primarily some kind of expression of emotion.

Both views relied upon the notion of a basic chasm between reason and emotion, a long-standing conceit in the West. This conceit, which has come under sustained attack of late from several quarters and will also be challenged in this book, still regularly grounds the various pejoratives deployed to render some ethical claims and arguments suspect. Thus, in popular parlance, to deride an ethical argument (or any argument) as 'emotive' is, by enthymeme, to expect it to be regarded as invalid and unsound. Equally, arguments that are called

more evident in the 2009 version of the dictionary's Second Edition, whereas a later version of the Second Edition significantly reworks the entry: *Oxford English Dictionary Online* (Oxford: Oxford University Press, 2nd edn, with prospective 3rd edn revisions, 2021), online at: https://www.oed.com. Even so, both entries indicate a Latin origin mediated via French, with concepts of movement a key component.

15. Charles L. Stevenson, *Ethics and Language* (New Haven, CT: Yale University Press, 1944), p. 21.

'rationalizations' are allegedly driven by an irrational – that is, an emotional – impetus, which is to be unmasked and condemned. Both kinds of mockery are observed in Michael Banner's memorable first-hand description, during the Alder Hey scandal, of denizens within the medico-legal establishment who regularly tried to marginalize the dismay of parents – parents whose deceased children's body parts had *repeatedly* been sequestered in secret for teaching and research, without parental consent:

> To very many of these actors and commentators, the parental wishes were evidence of mere confusion, error, sentimentality, or emotionalism; they had to be reckoned with or managed, to be sure, but they couldn't be understood and didn't need to be genuinely respected.[16]

Both forms of pejorative would seem clearly to evidence the post-Kantian rift, where only 'reasonable' utterances are welcome. Concomitant to this negative account of emotion in relation to ethics, and underlying the background conceit about the chasm between reason and emotion, is a conception of emotions' *unruliness*. Herein lies a suspicion that has ancient antecedents and a long lineage in Western thought. Our assumptions about the mode and magnitude of this unruliness predicates optimism or pessimism about the possibility of emotional control (or some related idea), and dictate how we navigate the rifts on view.

It is worth pausing here to observe that if my impressions so far turn out to be warranted in the chapters that follow, the warrant will be found exclusively within texts written by men. We may already have a sneaking suspicion that the conceits and notions named thus far were heavily gendered, with educated beneficiaries of the patriarchy setting many of the cultural rules on the relevance of emotion to ethics. Some feminist thinkers have offered welcome relief to the inertia created by these approaches, and have done so without committing us to any essentialisms about the emotional lives of men and women. I am too inexpert to do justice to their thought, albeit that we will glimpse some able women thinkers. But suffice for the moment simply to note, in what I have alluded to so far, its male lineage.

Even so, what I regard as the Kantian legacy has not entirely held sway. A very different legacy, inaugurated in modern times by Friedrich Nietzsche, also lays claim (somewhat subversively) to ancient antecedents. It celebrates the unruliness, and even seeks to assert excellence as intrinsic to it. Negative accounts of emotion for ethics are challenged on this account, and Nietzsche's polemic has arguably triggered a sea-change against the older negativity. A famous quotation by the Scottish philosopher David Hume is often adduced as a slogan for this kind of approach. ('Reason is, and ought only to be the slave of the passions, and can

16. Michael Banner, *The Ethics of Everyday Life: Moral Theology, Social Anthropology, and the Imagination of the Human* (Oxford: Oxford University Press, Kindle edn, 2014), loc. 5827 (ch. 8).

never pretend to any other office than to serve and obey them.'[17]) But I will deploy Nietzsche as its more voluble and extensive proponent.

Accounts arising from this newer legacy seek to affirm the place of emotion in ethics and do not seek to close the rifts we have mentioned. Rather, they declare as fictive all and every conception of this landscape as fissured at all. For Nietzsche, the fiction extended to morality itself (that it was a mere invention of the weak's will to power, to hoodwink the strong). His heirs do not go quite so far, preferring to retain various forms of morality while celebrating the generative power of emotional experience for action.

Given this turbulent and contradictory recent history, it has become difficult for moderns to articulate the interconnections between emotion and ethics. Consider the following advice, in a journal grappling with the intersection of public policy, legal responsibility and anthropology. Sidney Callahan argues for (what we might call) a recursive relationship between (what he calls) the 'tutoring roles' of reason and emotion. Of interest is the high level of complexity involved in joining these two realms during moral deliberation:

> If one would decide wisely and well, the best strategy would include both trusting and skeptical awareness of all of one's capacities and reactions. An individual is far too complex and personal consciousness (and pre-consciousness) operates too instantaneously, for simple linear processing. It is essential to engage in fully extended, fully inclusive, circular, parallel processing of the dynamic interplays of consciousness.

> While I am assessing my reasoning and arguments by rational criteria, I should pay attention to emotions, even those fleeting negative feelings that may be most in danger of defensive suppression. In the same process my emotional responses are in turn being rationally and emotionally assessed for appropriateness, or for their infantile or qualitative characteristics. Deficits and numbness should also be considered. As rational argument proceeds I can seek to enrich the process with emotional intuitions and associations, imagined moral scenarios, and the testimony of the wise and good. Can these emotions become universal, can they produce good consequences, are these feelings consistent with my other best emotions? Communication about my feelings with others would be a further test. Certainly, I should also continually compare my rational arguments to the critical reasoning of reflective experts, as found, say, in analytic articles or ethical guidelines. New ideas, arguments, or emotions should be continually checked and mutually adjusted.[18]

---

17. David Hume, *A Treatise of Human Nature* (Vol. II; London: J. M. Dent and Sons Ltd, 1911), p. 127 (Bk II, 'Of the Passions'; Part III, 'Of the Influencing Motives of the Will').

18. Sidney Callahan, 'The Role of Emotion in Ethical Decisionmaking', *Hastings Center Report* 18 (1988), pp. 9–14 (13).

This advice helpfully envisages an expansion of moral imagination and attention to *something* relevant in the emotions. But we may wonder if reason largely holds court; and nor are we closer to finding *why* some emotions have relevance, and others serve to trump them. Most striking is the sheer complexity of the task of 'fully extended, fully inclusive, circular, parallel processing of the dynamic interplays of consciousness'. A similar example is found in the work of Gerald L. Clore:

> Current emotions provide feedback about the consequences of particular actions in particular situations. On the basis of such experiences, we can subsequently anticipate the emotional consequences of similar actions in related situations. When contemplating such actions in the future, twinges of anticipated affect can then alter our choices to maximize positive outcomes.

> The process of deciding is the attempt to find the better option among alternatives, and we depend on some minimal positive affective reaction to announce the better option when it is encountered. Indeed, people usually feel comfortable exiting the decision-making process only when thinking about an option yields more positive affect than negative affect. And people tend to reconsider the options again and again when none of the alternatives elicits positive affect or related experiences of cognitive fluency. Does such a process lead to a 'rational' outcome? It does appear to be a process that would lead to decisions that are both coherent and satisfying.

> Moreover, a virtue of this account is that it allows an integration of the cognitive and affective factors that we know to be involved in decision-making without forcing one to decide whether people are rational or irrational. Good decision-makers are people who are both emotionally and intellectually intelligent in that they are attuned to the affective reactions that foreshadow productive and unproductive lines of thought and action. By focusing on feelings, they can be motivated to recast the problem or reconsider available options to avoid both self-contradictory and self-defeating choices.[19]

The pastoral wisdom in these ways of seeing interconnection between ethics and emotion cannot be doubted. But are both authors perhaps saddled with undue complexity arising from cumbersome modern thought? Even within these worthwhile attempts to parse the matter, we see how modern attempts to reunite thought, emotion and ethics can almost run aground. A clue to a different way forward can be found in Aner Govrin's plea for 'Why we need a new psychology' (his chapter title):

---

19. Gerald L. Clore, 'Psychology and the Rationality of Emotion', in *Faith, Rationality, and the Passions* (ed. Sarah Coakley; Chichester: John Wiley & Sons, Ltd, 2012), pp. 209–22 (214–15).

[N]umerous theories in moral psychology from Kohlberg to Haidt deal with the question of morality by reference to only one axis, namely cognition versus emotion. In doing so, the tradition assumes, falsely in my view, that the study of moral psychology is forced to choose between cognition and emotion. [. . .] [I]t is more plausible that body, emotion, conscious reasoning and unconscious mental operations form one continuous mutually informing field of moral judgment. Since all these components interlock, we should perceive moral judgment as a whole system. In this sense, most moral psychologies erred when they assumed these components are isolated and bounded.[20]

I am hoping, in the present book, to show some examples of how theology has us inhabiting 'one continuous mutually informing field of moral judgment'.

II. The recent quest for foundational clarity

But my account so far is merely an impressionistic rendering of a landscape, and I can easily imagine some growing frustrations. Depending, perhaps, on one's background, various questions and objections can reliably be expected:

- 'What, even, do you mean by "emotion"? It could entail anything ranging from fear and/or sexual desire through to patriotism and/or awe. And will you include itchiness or hunger – are *they* emotions? They are at least feelings that prompt actions!'
- 'It is all very well to speak generically of "emotion" in this way, but what *particular emotions* do you have in mind? The relevance to ethics of joy or compassion or kindness surely each demands discreet discussion, as also for envy, anger, grief, or fear.'
- 'Hasn't your discussion so far failed to take into account the way empirical psychology and neurobiology is noticing several kinds of emotions and thoughts refracting through our brains, prompting us in multiple ways?'

There may be others! But I have framed these questions to allude to three sprawling areas of research and discussion that have burgeoned over the past several decades. The subject of the third objection will be the substance of Chapter 3. The remainder of the current chapter will précis some developments in relation to the first two.

The first two broad questions (which emotions, and in what consists an emotion) may be characterized as a quest for foundational clarity. If we could but pin down, so the story goes, the nature of these entities, it will become easier to study them with some clarity.

---

20. Aner Govrin, *Ethics and Attachment: How We Make Moral Judgments* (Milton: Taylor & Francis Group, 2018), p. 21.

In 1984, the *International Society for Research on Emotion* (ISRE) was formed by an interdisciplinary group of emotion researchers. The Society's flagship journal *Emotion Review* was launched in 2009.[21] Its first editors, James Russell and Lisa Feldman Barrett, describe the complexity of emotion, 'one of the great mysteries of life', and their goal for the *Review*:

> Scholars in the natural sciences, social sciences, and humanities study emotion. Emotions have been defined as brain states, bodily states, behaviors, feelings, cognitions, social roles, cultural practices, or any combination of the above. Some scholars believe that emotions are what make us human. Others believe emotions are vestiges that interfere with our rational thought. Others believe that emotions are what link us to our animal cousins. Still others say that emotions link us to our immediate surroundings and cultural heritage. For humans to understand their place in the world, we need to understand the nature of emotion. [. . .] We must work toward a common language and understanding.[22]

Several early special editions of the *Review* highlighted important areas and figures in the field. Volume 1.4 of the journal was a special issue on the history of emotion and its terms of conceptualization, an area of considerable scholarly interest. Volume 2.1 was a special edition dedicated to the late Robert Solomon, a US philosopher who pioneered much recent reappraisal of emotion concepts. Volume 3.4 was a discussion of the now-contested concept of 'basic emotions' (outlined below). Volume 4.4 included twelve contributions 'On Defining Emotion', although the contributors found no consensus.

Contributors to another influential work have also sought to hammer out some foundational clarity, beginning in 1993 with the first edition of the influential *Handbook of Emotions,* now in its third edition.[23] The authors of the *Handbook*'s seminal forty-nine chapters include several regular contributors to *Emotion Review.* Although other literatures on emotion can be found, I will concentrate on these sources as representative of the state of emotion research.

To orient us to this field and to these authors' debates on the question of what, actually, *is* an emotion, I will risk another impressionistic summary. As we shall see in Chapter 2, Kant warned about the inadvisability of basing moral law upon something as imprecise and subjective as feeling. His view could, arguably, be vindicated by the sheer volume and extraordinary range of twentieth-century attempts at a definition, as indicated above by Russell and Feldman Barrett.

Some argue that emotions are a kind of experience that is primarily feelingful, while for others they are a complex kind of judging-thought that is not a feeling;

---

21. 'About ISRE', online at: https://www.isre.org/page/ISRE101 (accessed 7 July 2021).

22. James A. Russell and Lisa Feldman Barrett, 'Editorial', *Emotion Review* 1.1 (2009), p. 2, doi: 10.1177/1754073908097174.

23. Michael Lewis, Jeannette M. Haviland-Jones, and Lisa Feldman Barrett, *Handbook of Emotions* (New York: Guilford Press, 3rd edn, 2008).

and a spectrum of views prevails between these poles. The difficulties of definition are summarized in Robert C. Solomon's introductory essay in the *Handbook of Emotions*:

> It would be a mistake [. . .] to put too much emphasis on the term 'emotion', for its range and meaning have altered significantly over the years, due in part to changes in theories about emotion. So too, the word 'passion' has a long and varied history, and we should beware of the misleading assumption that there is a single, orderly, natural class of phenomena that is simply designated by different labels in different languages at different times. The language of 'passion' and 'emotion' has a history in which various feelings, desires, sentiments, moods, attitudes and more explosive responses enter and from which they exit, depending not on arbitrary philosophical stipulation but on an extensive network of social, moral, cultural and psychological factors. Thus we will often find that the focus is not an emotion as such, but rather some particular class of emotion and its role in the manners or morals of the time.[24]

The *Handbook* highlights the degree to which the study of emotion is strewn across the academy. Each contributor enunciates the intellectual space of their discipline for emotion theory, and in its second edition, one offers this helpful overview:

> [I]n primacy of interest, disciplinary seemliness, and volume of empirical work, psychologists 'own' the topic of emotions. Yet, given the scope, span, and ramifications of emotion phenomena, many other disciplines are also legitimately concerned with affective life. Physiologists link emotions to anatomical structures and processes; anthropologists tie emotions to particular cultural logics and practices; historians trace emotions of today to emotions of the past; ethologists seek what is phylogenetically given as well as distinctively human in emotions; and sociologists examine how emotions are triggered, interpreted, and expressed by virtue of human membership in groups.[25]

The ownership of emotion by psychology was actually a sprawling century-long tussle among various competitors. This landscape is surveyed by William Lyons[26] and by Robert C. Solomon.[27] Lyons observes Descartes' effect upon modern

---

24. Robert C. Solomon, 'The Philosophy of Emotions', in *Handbook of Emotions* (eds Michael Lewis and Jeannette M. Haviland-Jones; New York; London: Guilford Press, 3rd edn, 2008), pp. 3–16 (4).

25. Theodore D. Kemper, 'Social Models in the Explanation of Emotions', in *Handbook of Emotions* (eds Michael Lewis and Jeannette M. Haviland-Jones; New York; London: Guilford Press, 2nd edn, 2000), pp. 45–58 (45).

26. William Lyons, *Emotion* (Aldershot: Gregg Revivals, 1993), pp. 1–52.

27. Robert C. Solomon, *The Passions: Emotions and the Meaning of Life* (Indianapolis, IN: Hackett, 2nd edn, 1993).

psychology. 'From the seventeenth century to roughly the end of the nineteenth century, the Cartesian theory was the orthodox theory',[28] according to which the emotions are hidden within an immaterial soul. Then, as Solomon puts it, a nineteenth-century 'hydraulic model' emerged (under the influence of Freud). On this view, each emotion is a wild, alien force that presses up against thought, like steam against the valve containing it. The model generates words such as 'repression', 'energy', 'overwhelmed' and so on. Psychologists and philosophers moved away from the private, mentalist nature of the Cartesian view, and at the end of the nineteenth century, William James shifted the locus of the emotion from the hiddenness of the soul to the body's physiological disturbances. The core of James's 1884 theory (which, after being independently propounded by Carl Lange, came to be known as the James-Lange thesis) is that 'bodily changes follow directly the perception of the exciting fact, and [. . .] that our feeling of the same changes as they occur is the emotion. Common-sense says, we lose our fortune, are sorry and weep [. . .] The hypothesis here to be defended says [. . .] that we feel sorry because we cry'.[29]

According to the James-Lange thesis, emotions arise from their physiological correlates. It is only a short step to twentieth-century behaviourism, where emotions are *only* the observable behaviours they generate. Behaviourism was interested solely in physiological changes, and forbade reference to inner states. The behaviourists exclusively measured physiological and behavioural responses, and behavioural psychology was at best agnostic, and at worst hostile, to the feelingful inner world of what it disparagingly called 'folk psychology'. 'The "emotions" are excellent examples of the fictional causes to which we commonly attribute behaviour', declared eminent behaviourist B. F. Skinner in 1953;[30] and for behaviourist George Mandler, any attempt to define emotion was 'obviously misplaced and doomed to failure'.[31] This unrealistic scepticism, and the extreme unreality of behaviourist approaches to emotion, led in turn to a 'cognitive revolution' in psychology.[32]

More recently then, the ownership of emotion is now jointly held with neuroscience, after brain-imaging and other studies have observed regions within the brain operating as substrates for emotional processes and experiences. It remains unclear precisely how these substrates convey our experiences to us, and even what constitutes them. For Joseph LeDoux, emotional responses represent a kind of whole-of-brain networking;[33] while for Jaak Panksepp, there are certain

28. Lyons, *Emotion*, p. 2.

29. Cited in Lyons, *Emotion*, p. 13.

30. Cited in Jaak Panksepp, *Affective Neuroscience: The Foundations of Human and Animal Emotions* (New York; Oxford: Oxford University Press, 1998), p. 9.

31. Cited in Panksepp, *Affective Neuroscience*, p. 25 n 14.

32. Panksepp, *Affective Neuroscience*, p. 10.

33. This material is summarised in Joseph E. LeDoux and Elizabeth A. Phelps, 'Emotional Networks in the Brain', in *Handbook of Emotions* (eds Michael Lewis and

domains of emotion that congregate around various parts of the brain,[34] so much so that he once regarded various emotions as 'natural kinds'.[35]

How might we untangle this complexity? In a valuable summary of recent scientific research into emotion, Dylan Evans begins by listing the set of 'basic emotions' said to be found in all the people of the world: disgust, joy, surprise, anger, fear, and distress.[36] The classification of basic emotions is based on the ground-breaking fieldwork of Paul Ekman, in turn arising from observations by Charles Darwin, and has been highly influential for emotion research. (Even this notion, and the findings upon which it is based, is hotly contested on various grounds.[37]) But some emotions are not so basic: examples might include 'patriotism', 'schadenfreude', 'nostalgia' or 'spite'. Therefore, various schemata have been proposed to parse in more detail the terrain generally covered by the portmanteau word 'emotion'.

For philosopher Paul Griffiths, emotion is a term that covers three quite different domains of experience. These three, roughly, are autonomic bodily reflexes (such as fear); strongly expressed personal concerns (such as lust, longing, ambition, or outrage); and social performances (such as patriotism or indignation).[38] Similarly, Evans distinguishes 'higher cognitive emotions' such as romantic love, guilt, shame, embarrassment, pride, envy, and jealousy, all of which are fundamentally social.

Some basic emotions can be co-opted for social purposes (e.g., disgust; Chapter 3 describes how social psychologist Jonathan Haidt makes much of this co-opting). Higher cognitive emotions can include experiences that are recognizable to us, but which are better described in another language, for example, Japanese *amae* (a pervasive feeling of social well-being and belonging).[39]

Jeannette M. Haviland-Jones; New York; London: Guilford Press, 3rd edn, 2008), pp. 159–79; and at a more popular level, in Daniel Goleman, *Emotional Intelligence: Why It Can Matter More Than I.Q.* (London: Bloomsbury, 1996), pp. 13–29; 297–300; 12–14; 39 n 7.

34. Jaak Panksepp, 'The Affective Brain and Core Consciousness: How Does Neural Activity Generate Emotional Feelings?', in *Handbook of Emotions* (eds Michael Lewis and Jeannette M. Haviland-Jones; New York; London: Guilford Press, 3rd edn, 2008), pp. 47–67.

35. Jaak Panksepp, 'Emotions as Natural Kinds within the Mammalian Brain', in *Handbook of Emotions* (eds Michael Lewis and Jeannette M. Haviland-Jones; New York; London: Guilford Press, 2nd edn, 2000), pp. 137–56.

36. Dylan Evans, *Emotion: The Science of Sentiment* (Oxford: Oxford University Press, 2001), p. 7.

37. For a useful survey of complaints, see Andrea Scarantino and Paul Griffiths, 'Don't Give Up on Basic Emotions', *Emotion Review* 3.4 (2011), pp. 444–54, doi: 10.1177/1754073911410745.

38. Paul E. Griffiths, *What Emotions Really Are: The Problem of Psychological Categories* (Chicago, IL: University of Chicago Press, 1997), pp. 14–17 and *passim*. (The examples given in parentheses are mine.)

39. Evans, *Emotion*, pp. 1–3, 27–30.

In a subtle but important distinction, there also exist 'culturally specific emotions' – emotions specific to certain cultures, such as 'being a wild pig' in New Guinea. This emotion is specific to newly married and indebted young men, who are viewed with pity as they tear up the camp and lightly attack random others. Their debts are usually forgiven.[40]

If we presume to map these two taxonomies onto one another, we have:

- basic emotions (Evans) or autonomic bodily reflexes (Griffiths);
- higher cognitive emotions (Evans) or strongly expressed personal concerns (Griffiths); and
- culturally specific emotions (Evans) or social performances (Griffiths).

Each range begins at what is more innate, and ascends to the less innate. Each also ranges from emotions that are fastest to appear, through to those that gestate for much longer before they appear.[41]

In noting a cognitive revolution in psychology, anyone who cares about the feelingful aspect of emotion may regard the label 'cognitive' as not a very promising one. To speak of an emotion as being cognitive may, or may not, be to smuggle rationality into the centre of emotion, so displacing it, or feelingful elements of it; we will return to this concern below. In the main, however, a cognitive account of emotion refers to the view that each emotion is a complex and feelingful judgment about affairs in the world. That is, our thoughts and feelings are interwoven into complexes we name as various emotions. The biblical scholar Matthew Elliott exemplifies a cognitive view of sorts when he asserts that '[r]ightly understood, our emotions are connected to what we focus on, what we know, what we value, and what we believe. What we *think* and how we *feel* work together to point us to the truth.'[42]

Cognitive theories of emotion have a very useful central feature that behaviourism could not offer – that often, something about an emotion is immediately and obviously thinkable and articulable. In other words, emotions have their own logic. Contrary to the 'hydraulic model' (where hot emotions press against cooler thoughts), each emotion is an interwoven package of thought and feeling.

For Robert C. Roberts, this 'family of views' holds in common that 'an emotion is an intrinsically intentional mental state' (against James's nonintentional view) and that 'an emotion's object is constitutive of the emotion'.[43] Roberts describes emotions as 'focused actualizations, episodic versions of [. . .] prior dispositional

40. Evans, *Emotion*, pp. 17–20.

41. Evans, *Emotion*, p. 30.

42. Matthew Elliott, *Feel: The Power of Listening to your Heart* (Carol Stream, IL: Tyndale House Publishers, 2008), p. 117.

43. Robert C. Roberts, 'Emotions Among the Virtues of the Christian Life', *Journal of Religious Ethics* 20 (1992), pp. 37–68 (48).

concerns [or] perceptual instances of [. . .] respective cares.'[44] They are, in his main catchphrase, 'concern-based construals'.[45]

A useful if older example of a cognitive approach is offered by Lyons.[46] He takes specific occurrences of emotion to be the paradigmatic unit of consideration (sidestepping, that is, emotions as considered dispositionally, such as in the case of a mood). These occurrences involve an *evaluation* that brings about significant *physiological change*. These two facets of an emotion are, he believes, necessarily constitutive to it; and the evaluations usually have a personal twist – that is, they relate specifically to the person doing the evaluating. That an evaluation is involved delineates emotional experiences from other physiological experiences. That a physiological change is involved delineates emotional thought from other forms of thought. Different emotions can be discerned by their different evaluative aspects. An emotion's central evaluative aspect brings about emotional behaviour, because the evaluation rationally expresses some desire.

Therefore, on the cognitive view, denunciations of an emotion as irrational simply miss the mark, because evidently, the detractor neither shares nor understands the rationality of the one who emotes. That it all happens in a moment in no way detracts from the emotion's rationality. As Lyons sees it, 'a cognitive theory of emotion is one that makes some aspect of thought, usually a belief, central to the concept of emotion and, at least in some cognitive theories, essential to distinguishing the different emotions from one another.'[47] Critics point to difficulties in ascribing judgments to those who know their emotion to be irrational – with, say, a phobia of insects, or an aggressive moment towards a wounding tin opener, or ongoing affection towards an abusive partner.[48] Nevertheless, the cognitivist claim that emotions have their own kind of logic is hard to refute. (An 'irrational' anger towards a tin opener reflects a profoundly rational moment towards my thumb; phobias might sometimes concern what could happen; and love for abusive partners might include forlorn hopes for what could be in a relationship.)

However, there is variance among cognitive theories in the degree to which they admit emotions as feelingful. The matter is a storm-centre of dispute. Cognitive approaches can become fallaciously reductive. '[W]hile emotions can be said to be unreasonable, unjustified or inappropriate, feelings cannot, therefore emotions are not feelings.'[49] This 'therefore' forgets that equally possibly, emotions could

44. Roberts, 'Emotions Among Virtues', p. 39.

45. Roberts, 'Emotions Among Virtues', p. 48. See also Robert C. Roberts, 'What an Emotion Is—a Sketch', *Philosophical Review* 97.2 (1988), pp. 183–209.

46. Lyons, *Emotion*, pp. 52–69.

47. Lyons, *Emotion*, 33.

48. Rosalind Hursthouse, 'Virtue Ethics and the Emotions', in *Virtue Ethics* (ed. Daniel Statman; Edinburgh: Edinburgh University Press, 1997), pp. 99–117 (109–10). Hursthouse names these as two critiques among many, and without necessarily agreeing.

49. Lyons, *Emotion*, p. 8.

both incorporate and *be more than* feeling. Moreover – and in implicit agreement, oddly, with behaviourism – the claim simply begs the question of whether bodily feelings are a genus of which emotional feelings are species. The claim trades upon feelings that are not emotions (such as itchiness), to make a claim against those that might be (such as sadness).

Michael Stocker tells of his correspondence with 'a respected philosopher who has done considerable work on emotions', who insisted that he played with children, made love, and engaged in community activities – all without feelings. This philosopher thought that feelings were not necessary for a good life, and are unnecessary to an account of emotion. He did not mean that he had no momentous feelings, but no feelings at all. Yet, on meeting the philosopher, Stocker found him to be friendly, outgoing and personable.[50] Suffice here to say that persuasive rebuttals exist against views that emotions are essentially feelingless.[51] As Stoker cites of cultural anthropologist Richard Shweder, 'Three-year olds, Ifaluk islanders, and psychoanalysts (in other words, almost everyone, except perhaps the staunchest of positivists) recognize that emotions are *feelings*.'[52]

These are murky waters for lay persons who simply wish to think, feel, and do well. We may perhaps conclude this section with Michael L. Spezio's adroit summary[53] of the twists and turns in the emergent consensus within affective neuroscience, wherein emotions are also cognitions. This body of research has found that affect and cognition are not served by independent neural circuits, and that the old phylogenetic view of the triune brain (divided into supposed reptilian, paleomammalian, and neomammalian subcomponents) is no longer tenable. But its now-favoured dual processing models (where conscious and unconscious processes tussle within us), he goes on to argue, may only repristinate the old dichotomy between reason and emotion. He finds that 'a renewed interest in integrationist approaches, which seek a unified conceptual system where emotion is constitutive of reasoning, is now gaining momentum.'[54] 'Rather than dichotomous, opposing systems, what is emerging is a complex interconnection of circuits in which emotional signals cannot be separated from adaptive reasoning and decision making when such judgment and action are relevant for oneself and

---

50. Michael Stocker, *Valuing Emotions* (Cambridge: Cambridge University Press, 1996), p. xvii.

51. David Pugmire, *Rediscovering Emotion* (Edinburgh: Edinburgh University Press, 1998), p. 104 and *passim*; Stocker, *Valuing Emotions*, pp. xvii, xix, 17, 25 and *passim*; cf. Justin Oakley, *Morality and the Emotions* (London: Routledge, 1992) for a survey.

52. Cited in Stocker, *Valuing Emotions*, pp. 17–18.

53. Michael L. Spezio, 'The Neuroscience of Emotion and Reasoning in Social Contexts: Implications for Moral Theology', in *Faith, Rationality, and the Passions* (ed. Sarah Coakley; Malden, MA: Wiley-Blackwell, 2012), pp. 223–40 (229–36).

54. Spezio, 'The Neuroscience of Emotion and Reasoning in Social Contexts', p. 234.

others [...] A morally virtuous person is one who is "not a double psyche, a person of two souls."[55]

Spezio's conclusion here supports Govrin's suggestion, above. It may be that this 'complex interconnection' is theology's logic of love.

III. Linguistic complications

If defining emotion is basically impossible, studies of the evolution of the term may suggest why. It is a concern that has burgeoned into an academic historical subdiscipline, 'emotion history', both within English, and also for other languages. In Anastasia Scrutton's summary of the term, emotions are non-definable and elusive, a group of phenomena with only family resemblances, so that 'the search to define emotions in terms of necessary and sufficient conditions has proved fruitless.'[56] Sharper still is Paul Griffiths's complaint against the incommensurate phenomena the word tries to encapsulate. He regards emotion as merely a false categorization, an obsolete and inappropriate word for incommensurate domains. To refer to all these as emotion is as false a grouping as the 'superlunary objects' of ancient astronomy (where everything beyond the orbit of the moon was held to be of the same kind).[57]

A related complaint is found in the influential and pioneering work of Thomas Dixon.[58] Dixon found that emotion colonized twentieth-century psychology, after William James (and others) displaced a more overtly Christian eighteenth-century psychology. That lively Christian discourse of 'soul science', steeped in Christian theology and anthropology and espoused (among others) by Jonathan Edwards and Isaac Watts, preferred to talk of passion and affection, understood within a Trinitarian and soteriological framework. In that milieu, emotions simply referred to disturbances within our bodies (in continuity with much older usage). The serious semantic work was done using the language of passion, affection, and

55. Spezio, 'The Neuroscience of Emotion and Reasoning in Social Contexts', p. 236, quoting Bonhoeffer.

56. Anastasia Scrutton, 'Emotion in Augustine of Hippo and Thomas Aquinas: A Way Forward for the Im/passibility Debate?', *International Journal of Systematic Theology* 7.2 (2005), pp. 169–77 (170), citing A. S. Reber, R. Corsini, and Robert M. Gordon.

57. Griffiths, *What Emotions Really Are*, pp. 14–17.

58. For his detailed account, see Thomas Dixon, *From Passions to Emotions: The Creation of a Secular Psychological Category* (Cambridge: Cambridge University Press 2003), pp. 45–61 and *passim*. Summaries of his position can be found in Thomas Dixon, 'Theology, Anti-Theology and Atheology: From Christian Passions to Secular Emotions', *Modern Theology* 15.3 (1999), pp. 297–330; Thomas Dixon, '"Emotion": The History of a Keyword in Crisis', *Emotion Review* 4.4 (2012), pp. 338–44, doi: 10.1177/1754073912445814; and Thomas Dixon, '"Emotion": One Word, Many Concepts', *Emotion Review* 4.4 (2012), pp. 387–88, doi: 10.1177/1754073912445826.

virtue.[59] To glimpse this discourse first-hand, I will for a moment sidestep from Dixon and his place in emotion history research.

A passage from the eighteenth-century New England pastor and preacher, Jonathan Edwards, illustrates what Dixon contends and highlights several features he identifies within the earlier discourse. *The Religious Affections* (1746) is primarily a treatise on what dispositions constitute authentic Christian faith, as opposed to several ecstatic or culturally conventional practices the author regards as mere social affectations that ape faith. Near the start of the work, Edwards offers thumbnail definitions that illuminate Dixon's argument.

The passage that follows presumes an account of 'soul' as what operates our 'bodily fluids' and 'animal spirits' – a literally hydraulic mechanism that was supposed to trigger physical movement in humans and animals (long since replaced by our conceptions of a central nervous system that triggers contracting muscle fibres). At the same time, the soul presages what elsewhere Edwards assumes in concord with Christian tradition: a person's core personal and spiritual essence, the hinge that makes possible a relationship between God and each human (via the Holy Spirit):

> In every act of the will for or towards something not present, the soul is in some degree inclined to that thing; and that inclination, if in a considerable degree, is the very same with the affection of desire. And in every degree of the act of the will, wherein the soul approves of something present, there is a degree of pleasedness; and that pleasedness, if it be in a considerable degree, is the very same with the affections of joy or delight. [. . .] Such seems to be our nature, and such the laws of the union of soul and body, that there never is in any case whatsoever, any lively and vigorous exercise of the will or inclination of the soul without some effect on the body, in some alteration of the motion of its fluids, and especially of the animal spirits. And on the other hand, from the same laws of the union of the soul and the body, the constitution of the body and the motion of its fluids may promote the exercise of the affections. But yet it is not the body, but the mind only, that is the proper seat of the affections. The body of a man is no more capable of being really the subject of love or hatred, joy or sorrow, fear or hope, than the body of a tree, or than the same body of a man is capable of thinking and understanding. As it is the soul only that has ideas, so it is the soul only that is pleased or displease with its ideas.[60]

Those final claims suggest for us a highly contestable dichotomy between the operations of body and mind, where bodies are somehow not the seat of the

---

59. I have added the term 'virtue' to this account given the work of Gertrude Himmelfarb, *The De-Moralization of Society: From Victorian Virtues to Modern Values* (New York: Knopf, 1995). I will touch on 'virtue', too briefly, in Chapters 6, 7 and 10.

60. Jonathan Edwards, *The Religious Affections* (1746; Edinburgh; Carlisle, PA: The Banner of Truth Trust, 1961), p. 26.

soul's affections. Edwards continues that while movements of bodily fluids and animal spirits are concomitant with affections, they are nonetheless distinct from affections. It follows that 'an unembodied spirit may be as capable of love and hatred, joy and sorrow, hope or fear, or other affections, as one that is united to a body.'[61] It is important to note, though, that this dichotomy it is not the same dichotomy as we have seen between reason and emotion. The point may seem oversubtle, and here is not the place to defend it; suffice simply to note that Edwards thinks affection to lie at the base of the operation of mind – even though *passion* can overmaster mind, as the quotation following will attest. His next comment highlights the distinction between affection and passion, while also conceding that even in his milieu, the language does not always work in bright, clear lines:

> The affections and passions are frequently spoken of as the same; and yet in the more common use of speech, there is in some respect a difference. Affection is a word that, in its ordinary signification, seems to be something more extensive than passions, being used for all vigorous lively actings of the will or inclination; but passion for those that are more sudden, and whose effects on the animal spirits are more violent, and the mind more overpowered, and less in its own command.[62]

'More extensive' in this quotation makes a distinction connoting how affections can exist in an unembodied, spiritual entity; whereas passions are more closely connected to the body. We will see variations on this theme in the older thinkers to follow, alongside the same acknowledgement that while passion and affection have differing 'centres of gravity', as it were, the line between them is not always clear.

Whatever we make of Edwards's claims, the passage offers a vignette of the sort of thought-world Dixon believes predated twentieth-century psychology. Dixon argued that this earlier discourse had four distinctive characteristics: the absence of a reason/passion dichotomy; a distinction between passion and affection; a moral (and social) contextualization of the passions and affections (as seen in the opposition of Butler, Shaftesbury, Hutcheson and Smith to Hobbes and Mandeville – figures whom we will touch on in Chapters 2 and 3); and the importance of the soul.[63] But as psychology was secularized over the course of the nineteenth century, a plethora of psychological theories and psychotherapeutic approaches

---

61. Edwards, *The Religious Affections*, p. 26.

62. Edwards, *The Religious Affections*, pp. 26–27.

63. If these four distinctives are not all immediately apparent in the passage from Edwards, they are certainly evident overall in *The Religious Affections*. Edwards goes on to exemplify the moral and social contextualisation of affection when he argues that true religious affections take the form of virtues (pp. 266–85), a point I will return to briefly in Chapter 10. It should also be noted that Edward's dichotomy between body and mind is not strictly the same as a dichotomy between reason and passion or reason and emotion.

stripped it of any theological and moral referents, so that emotion blanketed previous distinctions.

Dixon's work signalled a massive resurgence of interest in the history of emotion[64] (or, more accurately, in the terminologies and conceptualizations over time in those human experiences that *we* like to label as emotions). This now-enormous field of enquiry is, to over-simplify, social-constructionist and anti-universalist in mood, arguing by induction from sources to the conclusion that people in different places and ages have named, framed and conceptualized (what we would call) emotions in particular ways that defy easy generalization. A comment by Olson and Boddice is representative: 'Even if there is a basic biological backdrop that delimits the range of what can happen, the meaning of emotions is theoretically infinite and tied to circumstance.'[65] They go on to suggest that thinkers in this domain generally disagree with any monolithic or essentializing psychological theory, including the concept of transcultural basic emotions, outlined earlier in this chapter. (I would also wager that, like all historians, some will take exception

---

64. To indicate a few of many initiatives in history of emotion research, we should add, first, a recent massive multi-author work: Juanita Feros Ruys, Michael W. Champion, and Kirk Essary, *Before Emotion: The Language of Feeling, 400–1800* (Routledge Studies in Medieval Literature and Culture series, Vol. 14; New York: Taylor & Francis; Routledge, 2019). Also, the *Emotions in History* series (https://global.oup.com/academic/content/ series/e/emotions-in-history-eih), published by Oxford University Press and edited by Ute Frevert and Thomas Dixon, now runs to twenty volumes, and deals with emotions in several geographical areas and eras. Frevert directs the work of the *Centre for the History of Emotions* at the Max Planck Institute, Berlin (https://www.mpib-berlin.mpg.de/research /research-centers/history-of-emotions. Dixon and others oversee the *Queen Mary Centre for the History of the Emotions* (https://projects.history.qmul.ac.uk/emotions). The work of the *ARC Centre of Excellence for the History of Emotions* (www.historyofemotions.org .au); its associated *Society for the History of Emotions*; its journal *Emotions: History, Culture, Society* (published by Brill); and several other associated publications, represents in sum a significant Australian project. One of its leading thinkers offers an excellent overview of recent thinking: Katie Barclay, 'State of the Field: The History of Emotions', *History* 106.371 (2021), pp. 456–66, doi: 10.1111/1468-229X.13171. In the US context, it is hard to overstate the impact of Peter and Carol Stearns, whose pioneering paper [Peter N. Stearns and Carol Z. Stearns, 'Emotionology: Clarifying the History of Emotions and Emotional Standards', *American Historical Review* 90 (1985), pp. 813–36] triggered a cascade of related work that is analysed and celebrated by Stephanie Olsen and Rob Boddice, 'Styling Emotions History', *Journal of Social History* 51.3 (2018), pp. 476–87, doi: 10.1093/jsh/shx067. These sources are so prolific that a short student-oriented article may assist to offer a helpful overview of field: Liam Greenacre, 'An Introduction to the History of Emotions', *The York Historian: The University of York Student History Magazine* (4 November 2019), online at: https:// theyorkhistorian.com/2019/11/04/an-introduction-to-the-history-of-emotions (accessed 26 January 2022).

65. Olsen and Boddice, 'Styling Emotions History', p. 481.

to my attempt in the chapters following to make normative claims from historical archaeologies of the language of Augustine and Aquinas. However, my attempt will have more interest in their general theological framework than in specific uses of their own language.)

Therefore, Dixon graciously suggests that this scholarship has 'moved on dramatically' since his work, offering 'several much more expert answers than mine to the historical question of the meanings of affective terms', especially 'in Augustine and Aquinas',[66] which observation will have some bearing on my own Chapters 6 and 7. Even so, I will return repeatedly to Dixon's general thesis (if not its every detail) since it remains a serviceable and helpful entrée for moderns into the complexities of ancient emotion language. That decision has to do with his own special reference to emotion terminology in theological language; and if I am honest, also because it was Dixon who first opened my eyes to the issues. He remains an elder statesman within the field.

Dixon's commentary on passion and affection deserves pause. His account has been critiqued within history of emotions research as overdrawn in terms of historical word usage, and as too focused on history of thought within the United Kingdom. But I think his conceptual clarifications give us lenses by which to notice how older language operates differently to modern language (as we have noticed in Jonathan Edwards). In short, Dixon contended that in traditional Christian psychology, the passions formed only a *subset* of those phenomena that move us. There also exist our *affections* – voluntary movements of the soul that were a crucial second half of the traditional Christian picture.[67] Affections were regarded as those morally commendable attractions to the good that motivated good action, and ultimately, praiseworthy character.

However, when late nineteenth- and twentieth-century behaviourist approaches and their associated theories of emotion (commencing with James) re-emphasised the body, notions of soul were excised. What followed, thinks Dixon, was a corresponding elision of the *moral* nuances of feelingful experiences. '[I]nvoluntary appetites, passions and commotions of animal nature as well as moral sentiments and voluntary affections, were all lumped together under the undifferentiated concept of "emotions".'[68] In other words, twentieth-century approaches collapsed passion and affection into the single, anthropologically self-referential notion of emotion, and in this way our emotions were shorn out of any moral context. Then, the cognitivist project poorly 'reinvent[s] the richer and more balanced view of the passions and affections that was lost as a consequence

66. Thomas Dixon, 'Preface', in *Before Emotion* (eds Juanita Feros Ruys et al.; New York: Routledge, 2019), pp. xi–xvi (xii).

67. Dixon, 'Theology, Anti-Theology and Atheology', p. 303.

68. Dixon, 'Theology, Anti-Theology and Atheology', p. 302. Dixon traces rise of 'emotion' from Thomas Brown's 1820 lectures through Bain and Darwin, and culminating in James' seminal 1884 article. In this way, emotions became bodily manifestations understood simply as a part of our animal heritage (pp. 305–09).

of the predominance of a narrow scientific view during the period between *c.* 1850 and *c.* 1930.'[69]

Ancillary to this observation is that today, passion no longer connotes a morally suspect operation within us. The word confounds us, spanning the moral spectrum. The ten senses supplied by *OED* for 'passions' include 'an eager outreaching of the mind towards something; an overmastering zeal or enthusiasm for a special object; a vehement predilection'.[70] This sentence would seem to describe what we have when our awe is inspired. But if passion is also 'an outburst of anger or bad temper', then sometimes it is a form of vice. Yet, passion can sometimes be value-neutral, describing '[a]ny kind of feeling in which the mind is affected or moved; a vehement, commanding, or overpowering emotion' – which is to say, a broad initial description of feelingful experience. None of these definitions enable us to settle whether or not passion is a moral category. To complicate matters further, the *Oxford Dictionary of English* settles on the most common modern meanings: 'strong and barely controllable emotion'; 'a state or outburst of strong emotion'; 'intense sexual love'; 'an intense desire or enthusiasm for something'; or 'a thing arousing great enthusiasm'.[71] Our minds carry much equivocation when we encounter passion in various literatures, whether in its moral or non-moral uses.

It is worth acknowledging that twentieth-century developments were motivated by defensible scientific aims. Human motivation and behaviour, like any other aspect of the material order, can be observed for regular patterns, and theories then formed. The best aspects of psychology arise from observations and analyses of thoughts, feelings and acts that fall into regular bounds. But Dixon alerts us to how, since the beginning of the twentieth century, this feelingful aspect began to be observed and analysed as a set of phenomena in its own right, without reference to moral implications. There is a rainbow of discrete emotions, but the modern development has been the capacity for ongoing attention to emotion itself as a set of morally neutral phenomena.

It has followed that today people think it odd to ask whether a given emotion is good or bad. We judge goodness or badness almost solely on the basis of actions and outcomes. We also tend to be '"mood purists," [. . .] people who [say they] would never try to change a mood since, in their view, all emotions are "natural" and should be experienced just as they present themselves'.[72] Conversely, an older generation (particularly, perhaps, of Christians) with a 'hydraulic' view will be suspicious of just about all emotions, and depend on rationality to force emotions down so as to act well.

---

69. Dixon, 'Theology, Anti-Theology and Atheology', p. 311.

70. *Oxford English Dictionary*, s.v. 'passion'. The quotations are meanings 10, 7 and 6a respectively (2009 edn.).

71. Angus Stevenson (ed.), *Oxford Dictionary of English* (Oxford: Oxford University Press, 3rd edn, 2015), s.v. 'passion'.

72. Goleman, *Emotional Intelligence*, p. 58, citing Diane Tice.

IV. Conclusion

If I have succeeded in showing that emotions have something to do with ethics, we are none the wiser as to how they may be related. All we have seen is that some connection is apparent; that there is a long history of thought about it; that some recent developments have tried to make better sense of the connection than do some older conceits; but that the language we use for such enquiry is muddled.

I have hinted that theology has a logic of love, which may assist to resolve some of these confusions and difficulties. But before going there, it will be helpful to look more closely (in Chapter 3) at moral psychology, and one of its coherent exponents, to see the best sense that this field can make of the connection between ethics and emotion. We will also visit a thinker who believes psychologies should be more explicit about the overtly and primarily *moral* object of psychology's study – someone who, we may say, urges the discipline to reach earlier than the twentieth-century developments Dixon surveys. If he is correct, that would put us within striking distance, at least, of a theological account.

Before doing so, however, Chapter 2 will outline two competing accounts of the relation of emotion to ethics, from the perspective of ethics. Their claims and counterclaims have also left us confused about the relation.

Chapter 2

COMPUTERIZING ETHICS OR SATIATING VORACITY?

We have begun to see how the notion of emotion has become estranged from ethical concepts. Recent moral psychology has sought to redress that estrangement, as we shall see in Chapter 3. However, I also made the claim in Chapter 1 that modern ethical reflection has been heir to competing legacies. This chapter sets out to offer some substance to that claim in relation to Kant (I), then Nietzsche (II), with some conclusions (III).

It is difficult to prove claims in the history of ideas, so this chapter can only succeed to offer such lenses as give us recognition of some ideas commonly held in daily Western life. These lenses can only succeed as far as they give a meta-language to describe what we live with; what follows cannot name every nuance of what we experience in moral reflection and deliberation. Even so, Kant and Nietzsche have been influential in our cultural history, and whether or not modern thought can be directly attributable to them, their ideas serve to highlight some elements of ethical thought that remain with us. Their relevance to this study is insofar as they name two competing approaches to the relation between ethics and emotion. In the case of Nietzsche, who post-dated Kant and was his polemical opponent, the competition was overt and intentional.

On Kant's view, emotions have no place in ethical deliberation, although I will also argue that Kant respects emotion, and cannot hold his view with complete consistency. Conversely Nietzsche rejects Kant's approach, thinking that excellences are intrinsic to passion and that emotions energize and enhance life – so much so that attempts morally to evaluate emotion are decadent. Emotions should be allowed free expression in a caste society ranked by excellence, irrespective of any claims for justice.

I. The Kantian legacy

In the preface to his *Groundwork of the Metaphysics of Morals* (*Groundwork*), Immanuel Kant announces his intention 'to work out for once a pure moral philosophy, completely cleansed of everything that may only be empirical and that belongs to anthropology', since 'that there must be such a philosophy is clear of itself from the common idea of duty and moral laws'.[73] It will transpire that for Kant, anything we might regard as a moral emotion belongs to this empirical, anthropological realm. Kant's excision of emotion from morality will have a lasting influence on Western conceptions of morality.

The language of emotion in *Groundwork* are terms translated as 'inclinations' and 'impulses of sensibility'. Kant uses this language in a discussion of the 'hardened scoundrel', who serves as a test-case for the relevance of emotions to moral deliberation. Anyone – even, *a fortiori*, a scoundrel – can see that good moral emotions are good. But good moral emotions cannot, it is claimed, be self-generated:

> There is no one – not even the most hardened scoundrel, if only he is otherwise accustomed to use reason – who, when one sets before him examples of honesty of purpose, of steadfastness in following good maxims, of sympathy and general benevolence [. . .] does not wish that he might also be so disposed. He cannot bring this about in himself [. . .] because of his inclinations and impulses; yet at the same time he wishes to be free from such inclinations, which are burdensome to himself.[74]

We might question whether the scoundrels we know have such a sense of burden surrounding their errant desires, and yearn for a better way. But that is not the point. Kant wishes to demonstrate that ethical insight arises from 'an order of things altogether different' than the realm of moral emotion. He continues:

> Hence [the scoundrel] proves, by this, that with a will free from impulses of sensibility he transfers himself in thought into an order of things altogether different from that of his desires in the field of sensibility, since from that wish he can expect no satisfaction of his desires and hence no condition that would satisfy any of his actual or otherwise imaginable inclinations (for if he expected this, the very idea which elicits that wish from him would lose its preeminence); he can expect only a greater inner worth of his person.[75]

That is, implicit in his wish to be honest, steadfast, and benevolent is the recognition that betterment of the 'inner worth of his person' would prevail against his wants and desires. It must follow, thinks Kant, that this insight arises other than from

73. Immanuel Kant, *Groundwork of the Metaphysics of Morals* (1785; eds Mary J. Gregor and Allen W. Wood; trans. Mary J. Gregor; Cambridge: Cambridge University Press, *Cambridge Edition of the Works of Immanuel Kant: Practical Philosophy*, 1996), p. 44 (AK 4:389). The *Cambridge Edition's* cross-references to the Berlin Academy Edition of Kant's works are shown here as 'AK volume: page number'.

74. Kant, *Groundwork*, p. 101 (AK 4:454).

75. Kant, *Groundwork*, p. 101 (AK 4:454).

the scoundrel's existing emotional topography. Fundamental to this account is a distinction between an intelligible world of understanding, and a world of sense:

> This better person, however, he believes himself to be when he transfers himself to the standpoint of a member of the world of understanding, as the idea of freedom, that is, of independence from *determining* causes of the world of sense, constrains him involuntarily to do; and from this standpoint he is conscious of a good will that, by his own acknowledgements, constitutes the law for his evil will as a member of the world of sense – a law of whose authority he is cognizant even while he transgresses it.[76]

In other words, perhaps, this highly philosophical scoundrel can do no other than to evaluate moral betterness from a higher, non-emotional standpoint, thus proving that even in the worst case of the scoundrel, humans *think* their way to moral truth on the basis of reasoning about what would work if everyone went with their desires.

Kant's claim is a continuation, for practical reason, of his project in the first *Critique* (published four years earlier) to knit together the epistemologies of empiricism and rationalism. 'Inclinations' and 'impulses' (and elsewhere, 'desires') are uncontroversially a part of the world of sense; and any resignation to the world of sense is a capitulation to heteronomy, and thus unacceptable, given the freedom Kant understands to be distinctive to rational agents.[77] Even the scoundrel knows as much when he steps in and out of the intelligible world:

> The moral '*ought*' is then his own necessary '*will*' as a member of an intelligible world, and is thought by him as 'ought' only insofar as he regards himself at the same time as a member of the world of sense.[78]

To put it crudely: when he thinks, he is autonomous and free, knowing and willing the good. It is only when he feels that this good forecloses against him, unpleasantly, as an ought.

This discussion offers a cameo of some persistent themes in the *Groundwork*. Once Kant introduces his formidable claims for the universality of any true moral, it was never likely nor possible for the emotions to be considered part of its ambit, with Kant regarding them as too particular to be of use to rational moral reflection. The universalizability of maxims, and so the categorical imperative, is founded upon the absolute equality of all persons; thus, there can be no place for vague and varied feelings. (The 'categorical imperative' we might loosely gloss as 'that which is always objectively necessary, and applicable unconditionally to everyone in similar situations'.) Therefore, it follows that the emotions are at best irrelevant:

---

76. Kant, *Groundwork*, p. 101 (AK 4:454–55).
77. Kant, *Groundwork*, p. 99 (AK 4:452).
78. Kant, *Groundwork*, p. 101 (AK 4:455).

To be beneficent where one can is a duty, and besides there are many souls so sympathetically attuned that, without any other motive or self-interest they find an inner satisfaction in spreading joy around them and can take delight in the satisfaction of others so far as it is their own work. But I assert that in such a case an action of this kind, however it may conform with duty and however amiable it may be, has nevertheless no true moral worth but is on the same footing with other inclinations [. . .].[79]

Kant goes on to imagine the philanthropist overcome by grief, in whom all sympathy is extinguished. '[S]uppose that now, when no longer incited to it by any inclination, he nevertheless tears himself out of this deadly insensibility and does the action without any inclination, simply from duty; then the action first has genuine moral worth.'[80] The implication of this 'first' is that it has not had much moral worth when done with and from joy and delight. Only such a view, Kant believes, can render intelligible the scriptural command to love the enemy, since:

love as an inclination cannot be commanded, but beneficence from duty – even though no inclination impels us to it and, indeed, natural and unconquerable aversion opposes it – is *practical* and not *pathological* love, which lies in the will and not in the propensity of feeling, in principles of action and not in melting sympathy; and it alone can be commanded.[81]

That such love 'lies in the will' relies upon Kant's premise that '[i]t is impossible to think of anything at all in the world, or indeed beyond it, that could be considered good without limitation except a good will.'[82] This 'will' is the fundamental locus of Kant's good, and operates in league with the intellect to bring human action into the conflicted world of sense.

Kant's extreme separation of feeling from thought has not come from nowhere. Twenty-three years prior to the *Groundwork*, Kant held to a moral sense theory, where goodness is apprehended directly, as a feeling. We shall visit such theories in Chapter 3. Suffice for now to observe that just as Kant's philosophical enquiries represented a mediation between rationalism and empiricism, so also do his ethical enquiries represent an arbitration within an eighteenth-century crucible of ethical disagreement about the source of moral knowledge. He is thought to have been influenced towards his earlier view by the Scottish philosopher Frances Hutcheson,[83] a protagonist in a lively dispute among Britons who assumed the affections to be centrally significant for ethics, but who could not agree over whether

---

79. Kant, *Groundwork*, p. 53 (AK 4:398).

80. Kant, *Groundwork*, p. 54 (AK 4:399).

81. Kant, *Groundwork*, p. 54 (AK 4:399). Gregor glosses *pathologische* as 'dependent upon sensibility' (note j).

82. Kant, *Groundwork*, p. 49 (AK 4:393).

83. Allen Wood, introduction to Kant, *Groundwork*, pp. xiii–xiv.

human affections are either primarily selfish and constituted fundamentally within self-interest; or disinterested, and arising fundamentally from benevolence towards others. Kant was initially attracted by the impetus of those moral sense theorists who found a moral law arising from benevolence, independent of self-interest. That his initial sympathies lay with Hutcheson (who argued for fundamental benevolence) underlines his antipathy to Hobbes and Mandeville (who assumed the primacy of self-interest), and is retained in Kant's trenchant hostility to all forms of utilitarianism. But the moral sense theorists' shared presumption – that the good is accessed by affection – is ultimately jettisoned by Kant. Just two years after his initial endorsement of moral sense theory, Kant begins to back away from any moral sense kind of solution, precisely *because* the British dispute about the nature of affection – self-interested, or benevolent – highlighted how feelings are not uniform and no agreement about them can be reached.[84] This intractable antinomy causes him to look elsewhere for the source of moral truth.

Modern readers of Kant tend now to be scandalized by the exclusion of emotion from the calculation of moral worth. For such readers, his clarification of the moral sense issue (near the end of the *Groundwork*) is an unexpected, even a pleasant, surprise. An appropriate set of feelings, which he denotes as 'interest' and even 'pleasure', might follow from duteous enaction of the moral law, even if it must insistently be denied that any explanation can be offered for this experience, or that a heteronomous morality can be derived from it:

> The subjective impossibility of *explaining* the freedom of the will is the same as the impossibility of discovering and making comprehensible an *interest* which the human being can take in moral laws; and yet he does really take an interest in them, the foundation of which in us we call moral feeling, which some have falsely given out as the standard for our moral appraisal whereas it must rather be regarded as the *subjective* effect that the law exercises on the will, to which reason alone delivers the objective grounds.

> In order for a sensibly affected rational being to will that for which reason alone prescribes the 'ought', it is admittedly required that his reason have the capacity to *induce a feeling of pleasure* or of delight in the fulfilment of duty, and thus there is required a causality of reason to determine sensibility in conformity with its principles. [. . .] But it is quite impossible to see, that is, to make comprehensible *a priori*, how a mere thought which itself contains nothing sensible produces a feeling of pleasure or displeasure [. . .] [F]or us human beings it is quite impossible to explain how and why the *universality of a maxim as law* and hence morality interests us. This much only is certain: it is not *because the law interests* us that it has validity for us (for that is heteronomy and dependence of practical reason upon sensibility, namely upon a feeling lying at its basis, in which case it could never be morally lawgiving); instead, the law interests us because it is valid for

---

84. This summary of Kant's journey is distilled from Allen Wood's introduction to Kant, *Groundwork*, pp. xiii–xiv.

us as human beings, since it arose from our will as intelligence and so from our proper self; but what belongs to mere appearance is necessarily subordinated by reason to the constitution of the thing in itself.[85]

There is convolution here, in that emotional sensibility is never permitted to be prior, yet it is nonetheless deeply consonant with what Kant regards as 'reason'. More simply perhaps (and unlike a tempting caricature of his position), here Kant is perceptive of how emotional dispositions may become allied to ethics. We wonder if he even hopes for that in people, recalling his famous and more personal manner of regarding morality with awe. 'Two things fill the mind with ever new and increasing admiration and reverence, the more often and more steadily one reflects upon them: *the starry heavens above me and the moral law within me*.'[86] But he is genuinely mystified by that alliance, believing himself to know only that it can form no sound basis for ethics. As in the *Groundwork*, so in the final emphasis of the second *Critique*: 'though admiration and respect can indeed excite enquiry, they cannot supply the want of it.'[87]

Even in his discussion of the scoundrel, 'sympathy' is slipped in among that which was set before the scoundrel as morally upright. We may wonder, finally, if even Kant can keep watertight the distinction between morality and feelings that he seeks to assert – 'thus calling into question', according to Solomon, 'the harshness of his ruthlessly divided self'. Solomon also observes how Kant's supposedly rationalist notions of human dignity 'are sometimes suggested to be matters of feeling as well as of reason'; how the *Critique of Judgment* celebrated 'intersubjective' feeling; and Kant's own utterance that 'nothing is ever done without passion'.[88]

Kant has retained a commanding position in modern ethics, not in that the majority of modern ethical analysis is Kantian, but certainly in that the majority of nineteenth- and twentieth-century ethics adopted his strategies against intuitionism and emotivism to sideline matters of emotion. The view may be rapidly eroding, at least formally, under the weight of several kinds of criticism. But perhaps it still emerges materially in those quotidian moments of moral reasoning that pejoratively sideline feelingful arguments as 'emotive' or 'irrational'.

The post-enlightenment split between fact and value (from which the so-called 'naturalistic fallacy' in ethics derives[89]) seems largely to *consist* in the Enlightenment

---

85. Kant, *Groundwork*, pp. 105–06 (AK 4:459–460).

86. Immanuel Kant, *Critique of Practical Reason* (1788; trans. Mary J. Gregor; Cambridge: Cambridge University Press, *Cambridge Edition of the Works of Immanuel Kant: Practical Philosophy*, 1996), p. 269 (AK 5:162).

87. Kant, *Critique of Practical Reason*, p. 270 (AK 5:162).

88. Solomon, 'The Philosophy of Emotions', p. 8.

89. It is beyond our scope to pursue here, but the supposed distinction between fact and value has been challenged by several thinkers, particularly once emotional reaction is admitted as some kind of primary moral datum. For an introduction to such critique,

distillation of emotion from reason. Kant and Stevenson (Chapter 1) represent opposing rationalist views on the place of emotion in ethics, ultimately because both are bewildered by emotion.

I call Kant's legacy a 'computerizing' of ethics because the conceit within Kant's moral rationalism and his denigration of emotionally motivated action was that moral truth could be derived from a kind of mental algorithm that delivered the same result in every time and place. The merit within Kant's quest for universalizability in ethics was to protect against a morally nihilistic relativism, and to set the expectation that ethical deliberation considers deeply the needs of others while being duly cognizant of the distorting effects of the self's needs. But Kant's failure to have any meaningful account of emotion within ethics arguably sets the scene for his major rival, whose influence over our own time is at least as great as Kant's. Friedrich Nietzsche completely rejected the rationalist approach that I have outlined, along with any of its Christian underpinnings.[90]

II. The Nietzschean legacy

In Nietzsche's alternative approach to the relationship between ethics and emotion, excellences are intrinsic to passion, and emotions energize and enhance life. Therefore, emotions should be allowed free expression. These themes have made Nietzsche the darling of thinkers who wish to rehabilitate the role of the emotions, even if they do not go so far as Nietzsche. (Few are quick to endorse his attempt to establish that morality itself is decadent; or to aspire to his caste society ranked by excellence, irrespective of justice – which he also regards as decadent – as the ideal social order.) Nietzsche's notoriously unsystematic style calls for a more discursive approach, which will resolve itself into a series of themes that bear directly upon our concerns.

see Ruth A. Putnam, 'Perceiving Facts and Values', *Philosophy* 73 (1998), pp. 5–19, and her further works noted there. For a succinct summary of some twists and turns over millennia that dichotomized 'fact' and 'value', see Oliver M. T. O'Donovan, 'Deliberation, Reflection and Responsibility', in *The Grandeur of Reason: Religion, Tradition and Universalism* (eds Peter M. Candler and Conor Cunningham; London: SCM Press, 2010), pp. 29–46 (31–34). The psychologist whom I will examine in Chapter 3 also offers an important statement in Brinkmann, *Psychology as a Moral Science*, pp. 79–93.

90. Kant's indebtedness to Christian theological conceptions in ethics is well-explored in the literature but is beyond the scope of this book. For a useful study (from the perspective of competing secular and Christian resources to meet the 'gap' between moral aspirations and endemically flawed moral performances), see John E. Hare, 'Augustine, Kant, and the Moral Gap', in *The Augustinian Tradition* (ed. Gareth B. Matthews; Berkeley; London: University of California Press, 1999), pp. 251–62; and John E. Hare, *The Moral Gap: Kantian Ethics, Human Limits, and God's Assistance* (Oxford: Clarendon Press, 1996).

Much of Nietzsche's polemic is overtly directed against a Kantian-style deontology:

> A word against Kant as a *moralist*. A virtue has to be *our* invention, *our* most personal defence and necessity: in any other sense it is merely a danger. What does not condition our life *harms* it: a virtue merely from a feeling of respect for the concept of 'virtue', as Kant desired it, is harmful. 'Virtue', 'duty', 'good in itself', impersonal and universal – phantoms, expressions of decline, of the final exhaustion of life, of Königsbergian Chinadom. The profoundest laws of preservation and growth demand the reverse of this: that each one of us should devise *his own* virtue, *his own* categorical imperative. A people perishes if it mistakes *its own* duty for the concept of duty in general. An action compelled by the instinct of life has in the joy of performing it the proof it is a *right* action: and that nihilist with Christian-dogmatic bowels understands joy as an *objection* [. . .].[91]

('Königsbergian Chinadom' is a double insult, against Kant's home town – now Kaliningrad – and stereotypical East Asian emotional reserve.) In this quotation, we see a precursor to the modern insistence that the central datum for morally meaningful action resides in one's heart, or passion, or identity. Nietzsche's engagement with science is very ambivalent, unlike his trenchant dismissal of Kant's rationalism. But in one key respect, he is unimpressed with science for the same reason as grounds his contempt for Kant:

> [W]hen we view it physiologically [. . .] science rests on the same base as the ascetic ideal: the precondition of both the one and the other is a certain *impoverishment of life*, – the emotions cooled, the tempo slackened, dialectics in place of instinct, *solemnity* stamped on faces and gestures (solemnity, that most unmistakable sign of a more sluggish metabolism and of a struggling, more toiling life).[92]

The rise of scientific consciousness, then, depreciates humanity. 'Gone, alas, is [humanity's] faith in his dignity, uniqueness, irreplaceableness in the rank-ordering of beings'.[93] But there is ambivalence, because the 'physiology' in this complaint,

---

91. Friedrich Nietzsche, *The Anti-Christ* (1895; ed. Michael Tanner; trans. Reginald J. Hollingdale; London: Penguin, *Penguin Classics* edn, including *Twilight of the Idols*, 1990), p. 134 (§11).

92. Friedrich Nietzsche, *On the Genealogy of Morality* (1887; trans. Carol Diethe; Cambridge: Cambridge University Press, *Cambridge Texts in the History of Political Thought* edn, 1994), p. 121 (§III.25).

93. Nietzsche, *On the Genealogy of Morality*, p. 122 (§III.25). Cf. 116–17 (§III.23) where scientific consciousness is variously described as an 'abyss, a *hiding place*' for 'ill-humour, unbelief, nagging worms' and 'bad conscience', 'a means of self-anaesthetic', in view of its lack of passion.

which figures widely in Nietzsche's thought, is the scientific basis upon which he will revalue all values. '[E]very table of values, every "thou shalt" known to history or the study of ethnology, needs first and foremost a *physiological* elucidation and interpretation, rather than a psychological one; and all of them await critical study from medical science.'[94]

The comment is prescient, for as we shall see in Chapter 3, the physiological (and emotional) correlates to morality have indeed become fecund data for moral inquiry. Nietzsche also believed that science serves to kick the struts out from under dogmatic Christianity, whose scrupulous morality – its 'confessional punctiliousness', as translated into 'intellectual purity at any price' – founded science. This is 'Europe's bravest and most protracted self-overcoming'; but it is to continue into the overthrow of Christian morality.[95]

How is this ambivalence to be understood? Probably in terms of the 'history of an error' – Nietzsche's genealogical story of the notion of the 'real world'.[96] The access to the real world supplied by classical wisdom was wrested from it by Christianity, which promises the real world to all, but only in the eschaton. Kant's transcendently metaphysical real world that follows – that is, the intellect, and a pure will – is the Christian ideal 'grown sublime, pale'. Kant is in turn supplanted by positivist scepticism, the consciousness of science, for which the impetus is a real world unattained and unknown. But even this gives way to that place where 'all free spirits run riot', where the real world, and then even the apparent world, are abolished – and Zarathustra (which is to say, Nietzsche's phenomenological consciousness, based in the passionate self) begins. Within this history, the virtue of science is in its liberations; but its corresponding vice is a superficial timidity.

Throughout these complaints and stories, Nietzsche's demand on behalf of the emotions is simply to let them be, since they are about what we purpose; and what we purpose concerns our deepest instincts for life. The point of the objection to Kant and to science is their failure so to permit the emotions. Even seriously negative moods are to be reckoned along these lines, with German philosopher Arthur Schopenhauer (1788–1860) used as Nietzsche's exemplar:

> [W]e must not underestimate the fact that Schopenhauer [. . .] *needed* enemies to stay cheerful; that he loved wrathful, bilious, bitter-black words; that he got angry for the sake of it, passionately; that he would have become ill, a *pessimist* (– because he was not one, however much he wanted to be) without his enemies [. . .].[97]

94. Nietzsche, *On the Genealogy of Morality*, p. 37 (§I.17, concluding note).

95. Nietzsche, *On the Genealogy of Morality*, pp. 126–27 (§III.27); cf. Nietzsche, *The Anti-Christ*, p. 48 (§48) for God's own 'fear' of science.

96. Friedrich Nietzsche, *Twilight of the Idols* (1889; ed. Michael Tanner; trans. Reginald J. Hollingdale; London: Penguin, *Penguin Classics* edn, including *The Anti-Christ*, 1990), pp. 50–51.

97. Nietzsche, *On the Genealogy of Morality*, p. 80 (§III.7).

Thus emotions, whatever their hue, can energize and enhance us. Any attempt, then, to police or codify or otherwise morally to evaluate emotion, will represent decline, decadence, or sickness. Moreover, the attempt will likely be towards some ulterior motive, which will resolve itself as some perverse exercise of the critic's will to power. Emotions are so ceaselessly active, and so energizingly powerful, that physiology makes intelligible certain phenomena that have been generally overlooked until Nietzsche. Emphatically *unlike* Schopenhauer,

> every sufferer instinctively looks for a cause of his distress [. . .] for a living being upon whom he can release his emotions, actually or in effigy, on some pretext or other: because the release of emotions is the greatest attempt at relief, or should I say, at *anaesthetizing* on the part of the sufferer, his involuntarily longed-for narcotic against pain of any kind.[98]

The problem Nietzsche seeks here to pillory is not the negativity of the emotion. Rather, it is the attempt to anaesthetize or sublimate it in a sickly manner. The same passage continues:

> In my judgment, we find here the actual physiological causation of *ressentiment*, revenge and their ilk, in a yearning, then, to *anaesthetize pain through emotion* [. . .]. The sufferers, one and all, are frighteningly willing and inventive in their pretexts for painful emotions; they even enjoy being mistrustful and dwelling on wrongs and imagined slights: they rummage through the bowels of their past and present for obscure, questionable stories which will allow them to wallow in tortured suspicion [. . .].[99]

Here would seem to reside an accurate description of our dominant culture in the Twitterverse! (*Ressentiment* in Nietzsche's discourse is, roughly, the seething and chronic envy of the powerless towards the privileged, able, and strong.) But Nietzsche's final target will become the Christian priest, who learns 'to detonate this explosive material [i.e. *ressentiment*] without blowing up either the herd or the shepherd',[100] by changing its object from anyone near the sufferer to the *self* of each sufferer. Nietzsche considers the Christian account of sin to be fictive ('not a fact, but rather the interpretation of a fact, namely a physiological upset'[101]). Likewise, he holds Christian conceptions of love merely to represent the avoidance of pain ('The fear of pain, even of the infinitely small in pain – *cannot* end otherwise than in a *religion of love*'[102]). A better way would be to let these emotions simply be, and

---

98. Nietzsche, *On the Genealogy of Morality*, p. 99 (§III.15).

99. Nietzsche, *On the Genealogy of Morality*, p. 99 (§III.15).

100. Nietzsche, *On the Genealogy of Morality*, p. 99 (§III.15).

101. Nietzsche, *On the Genealogy of Morality*, p. 100 (§III.16); cf. Nietzsche, *The Anti-Christ*, pp. 177–78 (§49).

102. Nietzsche, *The Anti-Christ*, p. 154 (§30).

nobly to accept pain, with no search for any culprit. The attack by a noble upon an enemy,[103] like any reflexive outburst of emotion to prevent pain or loss,[104] is fundamentally healthier. To allow this kind of beastliness will prevent us becoming bestial.[105]

As a necessary aside, it is of course hard to see how this last claim coheres with Nietzsche's florid celebration of prowling nobles, 'exultant monsters' who commit 'murder, arson, rape, and torture', each one a 'magnificent *blond beast*' who is convinced that bards will sing of his exploits.[106] Modern commentary tends to regard that compliant as a cheap shot against Nietzsche's flourishes. But after the twentieth century, his desiderata are at least a little stomach-turning:

> Look at the epochs in the life of a people during which scholars predominated: they are times of exhaustion, often of twilight, of decline, – gone are the overflowing energy, the certainty of life, the certainty as to the *future*. The preponderance of the mandarins never indicates anything good: any more than the rise of democracy, international courts of arbitration instead of wars, equal rights for women, the religion of pity and everything else that is a symptom of life in decline. [. . .] No! – open your eyes![107]

Philippa Foot cites Thomas Mann's rueful 1947 comment: 'How bound in time, how theoretical too, how inexperienced does Nietzsche's romanticizing about wickedness appear [. . .] today! We have learnt to know it in all its miserableness.'[108] Foot weighs the usual defences of Nietzsche alongside his passages that deride tyranny and affirm gentleness. Notwithstanding, she simply concludes that 'Nietzschean teaching is inimical to justice.'[109]

III. Conclusion

Much more could be said about Nietzsche, who has served as the inspiration for several modern thinkers' attempts to rehabilitate the place of emotion in our moral reasoning. Much could also be said in defence of his entertaining and often highly insightful attacks on various instantiations of Christianity, and more in reply. It suffices though for us to notice this aggressive rejection of Kant's marginalization

---

103. Nietzsche, *On the Genealogy of Morality*, pp. 24–25 (§§I.10–11).

104. Nietzsche, *On the Genealogy of Morality*, p. 99 (§III.15).

105. Nietzsche, *On the Genealogy of Morality*, p. 69 (§II.22).

106. Nietzsche, *On the Genealogy of Morality*, p. 25 (§I.11).

107. Nietzsche, *On the Genealogy of Morality*, p. 121 (§III.25).

108. Mann, as cited by Philippa Foot, 'Nietzsche's Immoralism', in *Nietzsche, Genealogy, Morality: Essays on Nietzsche's Genealogy of Morals* (ed. Richard Schacht; Berkeley, CA; Los Angeles; London: University of California Press, 1994), pp. 3–14 (7).

109. Foot, 'Nietzsche's Immoralism', p. 13.

of the emotions as a source of moral truth, and its persuasive appeal in honouring how emotions convey to us the real meaning and value of things. Indeed, the rise of our modern term of art for ethics – our values – can in large part be granted to Nietzsche's influence. (I will have more to say on this in Chapter 10.)

However, our next chapter will overview the way a whole body of experimental thought has sought to sidestep the Kant–Nietzsche argument, to measure inductively and then theorize about the extent to which our emotions frame and ground our moral thinking. I will use the work and thought of Jonathan Haidt as an ambassador for this domain, and then the work of Svend Brinkmann to suggest that psychology, therefore, must regard itself as fundamentally a moral exercise. These thinkers set the scene for investigating theology's logic of love.

Chapter 3

PARSING THE SOUL

SOME DIRECTIONS IN MORAL PSYCHOLOGY

Philosophers have traditionally held sway in the discourse of morality, and psychologists more recently in the discourse of emotion. A more recent entrant to the intersection between these domains has been, broadly, the practices of empirical ethics and neuroethics, and more specifically the attention to moral psychology in the work of social and positive psychology. In this chapter, I will review some recent work in modern moral psychology to catch its mood.

Psychologist Svend Brinkmann, whom I will introduce later in this chapter, represents a direct throwdown against Kant's conceits, somewhat in the mood of Nietzsche but without his concomitant diatribe against morality *per se*:

> Qualitative moral events ought always to be the starting point for our theoretical investigations. In our everyday lives we are much more certain of the correctness of the belief that we ought to try and save a drowning child, for example, than of any theory we can invoke to back that belief.[110]

Primary attention to 'qualitative moral events' is a welcome facet of moral psychology. It will turn out that there is also something further in Brinkmann's challenge than what moral psychology delivers. That 'something further' is, I will suggest, of a piece with the long-standing concerns of theology. But there is a little way to go before we get to that.

Somewhat cheekily, the chapter heading denotes recent activity in moral psychology a 'parsing' of 'the soul'. Almost no modern psychologist would countenance the notion of an immaterial soul in the sense meant by Descartes, nor in the sense that most people expect (perhaps wrongly) is meant by Christian theology. (I glossed the term in Chapter 1, in relation to Jonathan Edwards.) The naturalistic givens of many sciences, and an associated drift to neuroessentialism or neurocentrism,[111] have left no room for *that* kind of soul, or so it is thought. I

---

110. Brinkmann, *Psychology as a Moral Science*, p. 3.

111. For nuanced accounts of this intellectual fashion, see Peter B. Reiner, 'The Rise of Neuroessentialism', in *The Oxford Handbook of Neuroethics* (eds Judy Illes and Barbara J.

will retain the term though, with a view towards later chapters conveying its more subtle uses.

Some recent developments in moral psychology have been ably summarized by Neil Messer, who focuses mainly upon the work of neuroscientist Joshua Greene.[112] Messer surveys how this style of enquiry into morality and moral behaviour began with the puzzle (for evolutionary theorists) of the existence of altruism.[113] He briefly notes social psychologist Jonathan Haidt's and others' dual-process model of moral cognition, where a fast intuitive system functions alongside a slower cognitive system.[114] (Haidt's synthesis will be outlined below.) Messer observes that literature in evolutionary psychology tends to deploy conceptions of intuitions and emotional predispositions as coterminous with morality. Rational moral reflection comes later, 'but it is the existence and form of the moral sentiments that call for evolutionary explanation.'[115] Messer alludes to a few issues here, one of which may be that despite the evolutionary narrative's consistent recourse to just-so stories positing the emergence of moral traits under various conditions, these stories only come part-way (if at all) in describing humanity's turn to the actual *qualia* of moral experience and its significance.

Even so, there is much to appreciate in modern moral psychology's attention to the *fact* of moral emotion, especially given forms of scepticism about the moral aspects of emotion seen in previous chapters. This chapter, then, will consider modern moral psychology through the integrative work of social psychologist Jonathan Haidt, and the radical revisionism of qualitative psychologist Svend Brinkmann. The significance of their thought for theology, and theology's significance for their own accounts, will be suggested at the end of the chapter.

I. Historical antecedents

To survey the terrain of modern moral psychology, some further background noted by Messer deserves pause. Modern literature in moral psychology, he suggests, is conceptually indebted to 'eighteenth-century debates involving moral-sense theorists like Shaftesbury, Hutcheson, Smith and Hume about the place of reason and the passions in moral judgement and action', albeit that the modern

---

Sahakian; Oxford: Oxford University Press, 2011), pp. 306–29; and the more pointed work of two loyal opponents in Sally Satel and Scott O. Lilienfeld, *Brainwashed: The Seductive Appeal of Mindless Neuroscience* (New York: Basic Books, Kindle edn, 2013).

112. Neil Messer, *Theological Neuroethics: Christian Ethics Meets the Science of the Human Brain* (*T&T Clark Enquiries in Theological Ethics* series, New York: T&T Clark/ Bloomsbury, 2017), pp. 39–69.

113. Messer, *Theological Neuroethics*, pp. 40–43.

114. Messer, *Theological Neuroethics*, pp. 43–44.

115. Messer, *Theological Neuroethics*, p. 43.

literature 'does not always distinguish as clearly between emotions and intuitions as the philosophical literature'.[116]

The eighteenth-century debate, or at least Kant's reaction to it, was briefly noted in Chapter 2. Paul McReynolds grasps the milieu within which moral sense theorists such as Hutcheson found themselves:

> Hutcheson lived in an age when there was tremendous interest in ethical questions. The moral superstructure that had lent stability throughout the long medieval period had lost its effectiveness some time before, and the need in his time was to discover, or to develop, a new and more stable moral paradigm. Though a number of systematic proposals, including that of Hutcheson, were put forth, none of these, as it turned out, gained general acceptance – nor indeed, have any of the metaethical systems developed since that time, and the moral crisis that we face today is fundamentally a part of the same crisis that confronted Hutcheson's era.[117]

On this account,[118] disputants such as Hobbes and Mandeville (and perhaps Locke) argue pragmatically that social order is founded upon the cooperation of desires among selfish and self-interested agents. Mandeville's *Fable of the Bees* is representative:

> Vast Numbers thronged the fruitful hive;
> Yet those vast numbers made them thrive;
> Millions endeavouring to supply
> Each other's lust and vanity [. . .]
> Thus every part was full of vice,
> Yet the whole mass a paradise;
> Flattered in peace and feared in wars
> They were the esteem of foreigners [. . .].[119]

But this notion – that the cumulative effect of self-centred desires is to create a community of 'knaves turned honest' – was opposed by the Third Earl of

---

116. Messer, *Theological Neuroethics*, p. 43 and n 12.

117. Paul McReynolds; in Frances Hutcheson, *An Essay on the Nature and Conduct of the Passions and Affections: With Illustrations on the Moral Sense* (1742; ed. Paul McReynolds; Gainsville: Scholars' Facsimiles and Reprints, 1969), p. ix.

118. See also the illuminating older account of W. R. Sorley, 'Berkeley and Contemporary Philosophy', in *The Cambridge History of English Literature* (eds Adolphus W. Ward and Alfred R. Waller, Vol. 9; 18 vols; Cambridge: Cambridge University Press, 1907–27), pp. 279–304 (296–302).

119. Bernard Mandeville, 'The Grumbling Hive (1705)', online at: https://mandevillesbees.weebly.com/the-fable-of-the-bees.html (accessed 21 July 2021), lines 31–34 and 155–59.

Shaftesbury (Anthony Ashley Cooper), Bishop Joseph Butler, and Frances Hutcheson, all of whom argued for a human nature that includes natural social affections from which morality derives. The dispute between these eighteenth-century moral sense theorists turned on whether the beneficiary of the affections was the self (egoism) or the other (altruism). Even so, despite their disagreement about the focus of moral emotions, they shared a contention that moral intuitions and affections lie, somehow, at the root of human moral reasoning and indeed of human society.

Their debate is an instance, then, of the notion of intuitionism in moral theory. (Other representatives of moral intuitionism include W. D. Ross;[120] Robert Audi;[121] and [perhaps] Ruth Anna Putnam.[122]) Philosopher Alasdair MacIntyre once quipped 'that the introduction of the word "intuition" by a moral philosopher [. . .] is always a signal that something has gone badly wrong with an argument.'[123] But the quip can no longer pass so easily uncontested.

The psychologists noted in this chapter observe what seems to be the fundamental role of some emotions in moral processing, and the fundamentally moral nature of some emotions. Moral intuitionism, in its various forms, agrees with Charles Taylor's assertion that ontology should be discerned through whatever account can best retain, for example, courage or generosity; for such terms are substantive features of the real world, enabling deliberation and personal assessment.[124] 'My perspective is defined by the moral intuitions I have, by what I am morally moved by. If I abstract from this, I become incapable of understanding any moral argument at all.'[125]

II. Haidt's 'synthesis' and 'foundations'

Within the burgeoning recent literature on emotions and moral psychology, the social psychologist Jonathan Haidt offers a valuable representative interlocutor. His 'social intuitionism' is an interesting contribution to ongoing debate about the merits of moral intuitionism. He is attentive to and respectful of previous debates in moral psychology and moral philosophy, such as Messer recalls. Furthermore,

120. W. D. Ross and Philip Stratton-Lake, *The Right and the Good* (*British Moral Philosophers* series, Oxford: Clarendon Press, 2002).

121. Robert Audi, *The Good in the Right: A Theory of Intuition and Intrinsic Value* (Princeton and Oxford: Princeton University Press, 2004); Robert Audi, *Moral Perception* (Princeton and Oxford: Princeton University Press, 2013).

122. E.g. Putnam, 'Perceiving Facts and Values'.

123. Alasdair MacIntyre, *After Virtue: A Study in Moral Theory* (Notre Dame, IN: University of Notre Dame Press, 3rd edn, 2007), p. 69.

124. Charles Taylor, *Sources of the Self: The Making of the Modern Identity* (Cambridge: Cambridge University Press, 1989), p. 69.

125. Taylor, *Sources of the Self*, p. 73.

regarding his account as a species of a 'New Synthesis' in moral psychology, his articulation of that synthesis usefully introduces us to the complexities of modern moral psychology.

Haidt has described moral psychology as consisting in a cluster of competing stories, all embedded within 'a larger competition between two historical narratives about modernity: one featuring individuals, and the other featuring groups and institutions.'[126] Locating himself within the modern (US) liberal-progressive tradition,[127] Haidt has nonetheless made a study of ancient and religious wisdom, and throughout his work sought a proper account of 'parts of the moral domain held dear by most of the world's inhabitants',[128] such as moral systems that 'regulate selfishness by binding people into larger collectives, such as families, guilds, teams, and congregations [with] virtues of cohesiveness, interdependence, and limitations on choice and acquisitiveness.'[129]

a. 'Social intuitionism' within the 'New Synthesis'

A short article on the history of modern moral psychology[130] offers an illuminating guide to the complexities of the discipline and its philosophical assumptions. His 'visual history of moral psychology', reproduced in Figure 1,[131] alludes to more than can be recounted here. But its y-axis 'represents (very roughly) the degree to which each line takes reasoning and deliberation to be the major phenomena of moral psychology', from which may be inferred the degree to which the highly influential figures of Piaget and Kohlberg were indebted to a Kantian account of moral deliberation. Figure 1 also illustrates the surge of more recent interest in less overtly cognitive processes, with approaches emphasizing emotional processing appearing lower on the y-axis.

The diagram also prominently displays Haidt's own contribution to the field as a proponent of the New Synthesis. At its core is an emerging consensus, as Haidt sees it, around the existence of fast, phylogenetically ancient modes of evaluation ('intuition'), and more recent (on an evolutionary timescale) modes of thoughtful, articulate deliberation ('reasoning'). The New Synthesis embraces manifold discoveries in empirical psychology and general neuroscience, and their specific application to morality (such as Messer has summarized of Greene). Rather than

126. Jonathan Haidt, 'Morality', *Perspectives on Psychological Science* 3.1 (2008), pp. 65–72 (65), doi: 10.1111/j.1745-6916.2008.00063.x.

127. Jonathan Haidt, *The Happiness Hypothesis: Finding Modern Truth in Ancient Wisdom* (New York: Basic Books, 2006), p. 210.

128. Haidt, 'Morality', p. 71.

129. Haidt, 'Morality', p. 70.

130. Cited above, n 126.

131. Reproduced from Haidt, 'Morality', p. 68.

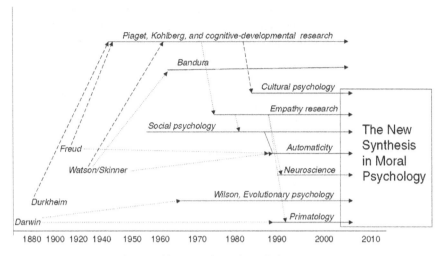

Figure 1 Jonathan Haidt's visual history of moral psychology.

rehearsing these lines of evidence,[132] it is perhaps more instructive to stay with Haidt's account of how modern moral psychology regards the nature of emotion and cognition.

It is important, he insists, *not* to map the distinction between (evolutionarily ancient) intuition and (more recent) reasoning onto a simplistic disjunction between feelingful emotion versus rationalistic cognition:

> It must be stressed that the contrast of intuition and reasoning is not the contrast of emotion and cognition. Intuition, reasoning, and the appraisals contained in emotions are all forms of cognition. Rather, the words intuition and reasoning are intended to capture the contrast made by dozens of philosophers and psychologists between two kinds of cognition.[133]

> [M]any have objected to the contrast of 'affect' and 'cognition', which seems to imply that affective reactions don't involve information processing or computation of any kind. [. . .] [T]he most useful contrast for moral

132. Haidt handily summarizes many lines of evidence: Jonathan Haidt, 'The Emotional Dog and Its Rational Tail: A Social Intuitionist Approach to Moral Judgment', *Psychological Review* 108.4 (2001), pp. 814–34 (819–28), doi: 10.1037/0033-295X.108.4.814. This article is Haidt's most sustained and concise articulation of his trademark 'social intuitionism' (outlined below), and its distinctives in comparison to other models in moral psychology. Another useful summary of this evidence can be found in Christopher Suhler and Patricia Churchland, 'The Neurobiological Basis of Morality', in *The Oxford Handbook of Neuroethics* (eds Judy Illes and Barbara J. Sahakian; Oxford: Oxford University Press, 2011), pp. 99–145.
133. Haidt, 'The Emotional Dog', p. 818.

psychology is between two kinds of cognition: moral intuition and moral reasoning. Moral intuition refers to fast, automatic, and (usually) affect-laden processes in which an evaluative feeling of good-bad or like-dislike (about the actions or character of a person) appears in consciousness without any awareness of having gone through steps of search, weighing evidence, or inferring a conclusion. Moral reasoning, in contrast, is a controlled and 'cooler' (less affective) process; it is conscious mental activity that consists of transforming information about people and their actions in order to reach a moral judgment or decision.[134]

Haidt's distinction, therefore, opposes the old hydraulic notion that thought controls emotion. It probably also opposes the schemas of both Kant and Nietzsche. But the exemplary conceit he opposes is from Plato, who (as Haidt sees him):

> [. . .] presents a charming myth in which the gods first created human heads, with their divine cargo of reason, and then found themselves forced to create seething, passionate bodies to help the heads move around in the world. The drama of human moral life was the struggle of the heads to control the bodies by channelling the bodies' passions toward virtuous ends.[135]

The distinction between intuition and reasoning (as opposed to that between emotion and cognition) defends the view that emotions have their own inherent logic; that moral emotions have their own inherent moral logic; and that a cognitive account of emotion has more to it than mere reversion to cognition – all in concert with the (confusingly named) cognitive accounts of emotion outlined in Chapter 1.

But these insights and their supporting data have arisen largely in respect of individuals. Haidt's social intuitionist account of moral psychology shares E. O. Wilson's sociobiological underpinnings, where 'groups that develop norms, practices, and institutions that elicit more group-beneficial behavior can grow, attract new members, and replace less cooperative groups.'[136] Haidt boosts this social emphasis in two further dimensions. First is the recognition, based on empirical studies, that in the main and despite occasional private changes of moral mind, 'most moral change happens as a result of social interaction.'[137] (Recursively with intuitionism, 'reasoned persuasion works not by providing logically compelling arguments but by triggering new affectively valenced intuitions in the listener.'[138])

---

134. Jonathan Haidt, 'The New Synthesis in Moral Psychology', *Science* 316.5827 (2007), pp. 998–1002 (998), doi: 10.1126/science.1137651.

135. Haidt, 'The Emotional Dog', p. 815.

136. Haidt, 'The New Synthesis', p. 1001.

137. Haidt, 'The New Synthesis', p. 999.

138. Haidt, 'The Emotional Dog', p. 819.

Second, his own research has focused upon how socially intuitive morality may entail more aspects that the liberal-progressive tropes of justice, altruism and harm-avoidance:

> [T]here are also widespread intuitions about ingroup-outgroup dynamics and the importance of loyalty; there are intuitions about authority and the importance of respect and obedience; and there are intuitions about bodily and spiritual purity and the importance of living in a sanctified rather than a carnal way.[139]

Social intuitionism is an interesting hybrid and convergence of two schools of moral thought long held to be in conflict. Its intuitionism finds empirical grounds to propose that we possess immediate and primal emotional reactions to things moral.

> Intuitionism in philosophy refers to the view that there are moral truths and that when people grasp these truths they do so not by a process of ratiocination and reflection but rather by a process more akin to perception [. . .] Intuitionist approaches in moral psychology, by extension, say that moral intuitions (including moral emotions) come first and directly cause moral judgments.[140]

The adjective 'social' notices how these reactions are then harnessed and conscripted by cultures to 'construct' moral narratives and practices. Tangled into this account is, on the one hand, an implicit moral realism, the view that a consistent and transcultural moral order exists (somehow) beyond our constructions of it; and on the other hand, that various social constructions of morality are not unimportant and are locally variable.

In other words, primal emotionally ethical responses shared by all people through evolution are also leveraged to become socially constructed ethical emotions. The account (i) decisively challenges hyper-rationalist approaches to ethics; (ii) in some respects vindicates emotivist accounts of morality; yet (iii) dislodges moral relativism albeit with interesting accommodations to social constructivism. The cultural traction provided by these features is amplified, in our context, by its philosophically naturalist provenance. Haidt is in this synthesis both a fellow traveller with and a formidable alternative to theological accounts of morality and emotion.

b. 'Moral foundations theory'

Haidt and others have proposed a 'Moral Foundations Theory' (MFT), according to which morality rests upon five innate 'foundations'.[141] The authors' introduction

---

139. Haidt, 'The New Synthesis', p. 1001.
140. Haidt, 'The Emotional Dog', p. 814.
141. Jonathan Haidt and Craig Joseph, 'The Moral Mind: How Five Sets of Innate Intuitions Guide the Development of Many Culture-Specific Virtues, and Perhaps Even

to it extends upon the basic notion of emotionally mediated intuitions that become woven into cultures.

> We have long been searching for the foundations of intuitive ethics – the psychological primitives that are the building blocks from which cultures create moralities that are unique yet constrained in their variations. [. . .] We identified five sets of [transcultural] concerns, each linked to an adaptive challenge and to one or more moral emotions, as the best candidates for the psychological foundations of human morality. The five foundations we identified are harm/care, fairness/reciprocity, in-group/loyalty, authority/respect, and purity/sanctity.[142]

These 'five foundations of intuitive ethics' are each taken to map onto some evolutionary challenge; a 'proper domain' of very ancient concerns; and an 'actual domain' of triggering moral concerns. Each has respective characteristic emotions, and attendant virtues. Their summary schema is reproduced in Figure 2.[143]

	Harm/Care	Fairness/Reciprocity	In-group/Loyalty	Authority/Respect	Purity/Sanctity
Adaptive challenge	Protect and care for young, vulnerable, or injured kin	Reap benefits of dyadic cooperation with non-kin	Reap benefits of group cooperation	Negotiate hierarchy, defer selectively	Avoid microbes and parasites
Proper domain (adaptive triggers)	Suffering, distress, or threat to one's kin	Cheating, cooperation, deception	Threat or challenge to group	Signs of dominance and submission	Waste products, diseased people
Actual domain (examples of modern triggers)	Baby seals, cartoon characters	Marital fidelity, broken vending machines	Sports teams one roots for	Bosses, respected professionals	Taboo ideas (communism, racism)
Characteristic emotions	Compassion	Anger, gratitude, guilt	Group pride, belongingness; rage at traitors	Respect, fear	Disgust
Relevant virtues (and vices)	Caring, kindness, (cruelty)	Fairness, justice, honesty, trustworthiness (dishonesty)	Loyalty, patriotism, self-sacrifice (treason, cowardice)	Obedience, deference (disobedience, uppitiness)	Temperance, chastity, piety, cleanliness (lust, intemperance)

Figure 2 Haidt's and Joseph's schema for the 'Five Foundations of Intuitive Ethics'.

Modules', in *The Innate Mind, Volume 3: Foundations and the Future* (eds Stephen Stich, Stephen Laurence, and Peter Carruthers; New York: Oxford University Press, 2008), pp. 367–92, doi: 10.1093/acprof:oso/9780195332834.003.0019. For a summary and critique, see Christopher L. Suhler and Patricia Churchland, 'Can Innate, Modular "Foundations" Explain Morality? Challenges for Haidt's Moral Foundations Theory', *Journal of Cognitive Neuroscience* 23.9 (2011), pp. 2103–16, doi: 10.1162/jocn.2011.21637. For their response, see Jonathan Haidt and Craig Joseph, 'How Moral Foundations Theory Succeeded in Building on Sand: A Response to Suhler and Churchland', *Journal of Cognitive Neuroscience* 23.9 (2011), pp. 2117–22, doi: 10.1162/jocn.2011.21638.

142. Haidt and Joseph, 'The Moral Mind', p. 381.

143. Reproduced from Haidt and Joseph, 'The Moral Mind', p. 382.

'The five foundations are, to propose an analogy, the innate "taste buds" of the moral sense.'[144] That is the core of the theory, although the authors accept that other candidate foundations may exist, and have much more to say about the mind's modularity (or not) in moral processing, and about the role of narrative in the cultural editing of emotions to become virtues. MFT also therefore gives reasons for the authors seriously to commend ancient and recent virtue theory, with attention to each virtue's emotional undertones.[145] Critics Suhler and Churchland pause to note the distinctive contribution of the theory:

> [Moral intuitions are] flashes of approval, disapproval, or other emotions upon detecting some pattern in the social world. These intuitions, in turn, are what actually drive our moral judgments, beliefs, actions, and the like. This is an important point of divergence between MFT and views of morality historically accepted in philosophy (e.g., Kant) and psychology (e.g., Kohlberg), which have tended to focus on reason as the sole driver of moral judgment.[146]

Suhler and Churchland appreciate the attention to emotion and intuition in moral behaviours and judgment; the rejection of any single mechanism as an account of morality; the attention to non-Western moral cultures; and the contribution to an evolutionary narrative.[147] Several complaints they go on to make are beyond our scope, but apposite for our purpose is their challenge to MFT's moral taxonomy (with its seemingly arbitrary inclusions in and exclusions from the five foundations), and in the allocation of this or that emotion to each foundation. In common with much moral discourse, their challenges are *ad hominem* and mischievous (e.g., 'liberals also make substantial use of the purity/sanctity system'[148]). After a foray into some neurobiological intricacies, they conclude that 'MFT seeks to explain morality by connecting evolution, psychology, and development. Although we applaud the project's ambition, the overall execution is disappointingly insensitive to the height of the evidence bar.'[149] The specifics of Haidt's rebuttal are also beyond our scope. However, his parting comment is worth quoting: 'Morality is tough stuff to work with [. . .]'.[150]

Suhler and Churchland are correct to observe the ambition of MFT. Its scope is somewhat breath-taking. It seeks to make sense of morality in *every* culture, using an array of empirical research, with close attention to mediation by the

---

144. Haidt and Joseph, 'The Moral Mind', p. 385.

145. Haidt and Joseph, 'The Moral Mind', pp. 386–88.

146. Suhler and Churchland, 'Can "Foundations" Explain?', p. 2104 (their references omitted).

147. Suhler and Churchland, 'Can "Foundations" Explain?', pp. 2104–05.

148. Suhler and Churchland, 'Can "Foundations" Explain?', p. 2108.

149. Suhler and Churchland, 'Can "Foundations" Explain?', p. 2111.

150. Haidt and Joseph, 'How Moral Foundations Theory Succeeded in Building on Sand', p. 2121.

emotions in our moral processing, and all in dialogue with various theories of ethics. Nor is it hard to challenge what seem to be oversimplifications in MFT's moral taxonomy: morality is not only tough stuff to work with – its discourses and concerns are endlessly nuanced, and feature in every nook and cranny of our lives. But an even more ambitious synthesis has emerged from Haidt's thought about psychology and morality.

c. A further synthesis: The Happiness Hypothesis

The Happiness Hypothesis[151] *(HH)* is Haidt's most expansive and popular development of his account. The synthesis in *HH* is far more ambitious than even the New Synthesis or MFT. He positions this work within the wider movement of positive psychology, the approach to psychology that actively seeks out what conduces to human flourishing. Haidt integrates as much as he can from across psychologists' and neurobiologists' findings on morality and its emotions (including his own early research into moral emotions such as contempt and disgust,[152] and awe or 'elevation'[153]), with as many nuggets of ancient wisdom as he can muster. It is a robustly naturalistic account of morality, but one that does not seek to displace the immanent aspects of religious and philosophical morality, even while offering no succour to their metaphysical claims. It somewhat confounds both apologists for and polemicists against religious and philosophical ethics. In many respects, it is an admirable piece of work.

Haidt begins *HH* with a discussion of human dividedness, what ancient Greeks called *akrasia*. The chapter begins with an approving quotation from St Paul: 'For what the flesh desires is opposed to the Spirit, and what the Spirit desires is opposed to the flesh; for these are opposed to each other, to prevent you from doing what you want' (Gal. 5.17).[154] The quotation illustrates Haidt's respectful, if eclectic, appropriation of Christian Scripture and other sacred and traditional texts. His defining narratives are philosophical naturalism and evolutionary anthropology. No allowance is made, for example, for 'Spirit' as a Person of the Godhead. Even so, Haidt remains open to the wisdom that cultural traditions other than that of science can and do contribute to moral psychology.

His account of dividedness observes our human condition as consisting in four modes of dividedness.[155] First, 'mind versus body' describes the way the operations of our conscious mind do not always cohere with, literally, our gut. 'Left versus right' describes the curious operations and interactions of the two hemispheres of

---

151. Haidt, *The Happiness Hypothesis* (see n 127 above).

152. This work is reprised in Jonathan Haidt, *The Righteous Mind: Why Good People are Divided by Politics and Religion* (London: Allen Lane, 2012).

153. Haidt, *The Happiness Hypothesis*, pp. 200–06.

154. Haidt, *The Happiness Hypothesis*, p. 1. For completeness it should be noted that the quotation includes a typographical error, referencing 'Galatians 5:171'.

155. Haidt, *The Happiness Hypothesis*, pp. 5–17.

our brains, which perform different tasks and yet are in constant communication. (Haidt subscribes to the now common view that the language centres in the left often function to narrate *ex post facto* justifications for actions that arise from impulses hidden to us.) The third mode of dividedness is 'new versus old', where anciently evolved reactions do not always cohere with relatively more recent ways of being thoughtful. Finally, 'controlled versus automatic' summarizes our instantaneous reactions versus our more voluntary moves.

Haidt's controlling metaphor of how we navigate this inherent dividedness pictures the human person as a three-million year evolved, instinctive, intuitive 'elephant', directed by a 100,000 or 200,000 year evolved reasoning 'rider'. (Again, intuition and reasoning do not simply map to emotion and cognition.) Using this evocative image, Haidt examines several domains of our psychological lives.

Interventions such as cognitive-behavioural therapy, medication and meditation are considered alongside ancient wisdom about cognitive reframing, and modern research into negativity bias (where the elephant is primed to be more sensitive to threat), and affective styles.[156] But these approaches risk perpetuating the conceit that we are existential lone rangers, so to speak; therefore, Haidt also tours extensive research showing how attuned we are to the demands of reciprocity[157] – while at the same time blind to our own constitutional propensity towards selfish bias and self-justification, and our converse tendency to blame, judge and demonize others, all well proven in research.[158] Discussing our pursuits of happiness, Haidt surveys how the positive psychology movement highlights the importance of environment and of satisfying activities for happiness. This research causes him to demur from the Buddha's council of unattachment, even though for Haidt, the research does confirm the Buddha's (and the Preacher's, of Ecclesiastes) awareness that acquisition does not finally satisfy.[159] We do, however, need social attachment.

The turn to attachment causes Haidt to examine love.[160] Beginning with behaviourism's absurd conceit that human children did not really need love, Haidt outlines the development of attachment theory, including its application to adult couple love (where Mk 10.7-9 is given honourable mention, and so by extension also Gen. 2.24).[161] The contrast between short-lived passionate love, and longer-lasting companionate love, is examined; from which Haidt concludes that Buddha and the Greeks were wrong to denigrate the central necessity of attachment, or in the case of Jesus, to omit mention of it.

---

156. Haidt, *The Happiness Hypothesis*, pp. 23–44.

157. Haidt, *The Happiness Hypothesis*, pp. 45–58.

158. Haidt, *The Happiness Hypothesis*, pp. 59–80.

159. Haidt, *The Happiness Hypothesis*, pp. 81–106.

160. Haidt, *The Happiness Hypothesis*, pp. 107–34. Compare p. 45: 'When the sages pick a single word or principle to elevate above all others, the winner is almost always either "love" or "reciprocity."'

161. An excellent exposition of the attachment needs of adults is Sue M. Johnson, *Hold Me Tight: Seven Conversations for a Lifetime of Love* (New York: Little & Brown, 2008).

The benefits of adversity then receive some attention,[162] although perhaps surprisingly, without noting the Bible's many interpretations of it (e.g., Job 23.10; Ps. 66.10; Isa. 48.10; Heb. 12.11; Jas 1.2-4; 1 Pet. 1.6-7). Similarly, an introduction to virtue seems unaware of extensive New Testament reliance on virtue language in its moral parenesis;[163] rather, a circuitous description of the West's loss of character categories in favour of procedures deontological (Kant) or utilitarian (Bentham) then turns to a commendation of virtue, via positive psychology's 'discovery' of six universal virtues in a taxonomy that overarches twenty-four more.[164]

The penultimate chapter of *HH* concerns spirituality, or 'divinity with or without God',[165] in an account that must cleave to the givens of evolutionary naturalism while also noticing the psychological benefits of awe, 'transcendence' and 'elevation', and the significance of their centrality in non-Western cultures. (A short coda evaluates the US culture war in terms of the left's respect for autonomy as against the right's respect for community.[166]) Haidt finally concludes that although he remains agnostic about any ultimate, trans-natural meaning or purpose, it is found 'in between' – in our quotidian transactions and relationships, and in ways that can and should be informed by what matters more in non-Western cultures.[167]

d. Haidt's contribution

Four outcomes of Haidt's overall work – his contribution to the New Synthesis, his Moral Foundations project and the grand synthesis of *HH* – are worth closer consideration, discussed here in what I consider to be an ascending order of significance.

First, by corralling extensive research in moral and general psychology, and by comparing and contrasting it to ancient and non-Western wisdom, Haidt seeks to burst the jejune constraints of Western moral assumption. He is an often astute and caustic observer of questionable tales that have long dominated late modern Western thought and practice in relation both to morality, and to emotion. He amply demonstrates renewed interest within psychology at the intersection between emotions and morality, and illustrates a moral psychology that firmly relegates several fads within nineteenth- and twentieth-century moral philosophy, and psychology, to ancient history. He has been a voice within moral psychology of the need to expand the terms of reference for morality:

---

162. Haidt, *The Happiness Hypothesis*, pp. 135–53.

163. For a full list, see Chapter 10.

164. Haidt, *The Happiness Hypothesis*, pp. 155–79.

165. Haidt, *The Happiness Hypothesis*, pp. 181–211.

166. Haidt, *The Happiness Hypothesis*, pp. 208–11; reprised in Haidt, *The Righteous Mind*.

167. Haidt, *The Happiness Hypothesis*, pp. 219–39.

One of the distinctions that has been most important in the study of morality, but also most problematic, is that between 'moral' and 'conventional' judgments. [. . .] Moral rules are those related to justice, rights, and harm/welfare (e.g., don't hit, cheat, or steal), and they can't be changed by consensus because doing so would create new classes of victims. In contrast, all those other rules children encounter (e.g., don't call adults by their first names, do place your hand over your heart while saying the Pledge of Allegiance) are matters of tradition, efficiency, or social coordination that could just as well be different if people in power, or if people in general, chose to change them.

In Western societies in which people accept a version of contractualism as the basis for society, this distinction makes sense. But in most cultures the social order is a moral order, and rules about clothing, gender roles, food, and forms of address are profoundly moral issues. [. . .] We take as given (at least at the beginning of analysis) that what people think are their moral concepts are, in fact, moral concepts – rather than dividing them into 'moral' and 'conventional' concepts at the outset.[168]

This expansion of perception of the moral field is significant, and arguably consonant with Christian theological conceptions of ethics and morality.

A second observation on Haidt's work, then, may follow. Western academic and practical culture since the Enlightenment floats upon a sea of Christendom.[169] Although Haidt attempts to touch upon that influence, it is not his expertise or main emphasis. The attempt deserves appreciative respect, since learned effort to step beyond one's guild should be applauded. It is revealing, though, that Haidt's short history (in Figure 1) only begins in the late nineteenth-century – precisely that timeframe when Dixon believes a secularized psychology wrested the story of emotion and its moral evaluation (or not) from a more theologically informed

---

168. Haidt and Joseph, 'The Moral Mind', pp. 371–72.

169. The impact of two-millennia of Christian thought and practice upon of daily lives, at least in the West, has been made severally in various contexts. Examples include (to choose just one relevant work among several by each of the following authors): Taylor, *Sources of the Self* (see n 124 above); Michael C. Banner, *Christian Ethics: A Brief History* (Chichester: Wiley-Blackwell, 2009); William T. Cavanaugh, *Theopolitical Imagination: Christian Practices of Space and Time* (Edinburgh: T&T Clark, 2003); Oliver M. T. O'Donovan, *The Desire of the Nations: Rediscovering the Roots of Political Theology* (Cambridge; New York: Cambridge University Press, 1996); Hare, *The Moral Gap* (see n 90 above); Tom Holland, *Dominion: The Making of the Western Mind* (London: Little, Brown, 2019); Rodney Stark, *For the Glory of God: How Monotheism Led to Reformations, Science, Witch-hunts, and the End of Slavery* (Princeton: Princeton University Press, 2003); and Robert D. Woodberry, 'The Missionary Roots of Liberal Democracy', *The American Political Science Review* 106.2 (2012), pp. 244–74, doi: 10.1017/S0003055412000093. These thinkers exemplify a vibrant discourse across several disciplines, reminding Western moderns of how their intellectual and social momentum often arose from overtly Christian theology.

milieu. For centuries, this milieu generated far-reaching and serious attempts to make sense of human being in terms of our emotional and social lives, and in terms of what gives us purpose and meaning. Moral psychology deserves a more extensive consideration of those attempts.

Third: in the main and in common with much psychological punditry on morality, his narrative pivots on evolutionary prehistory (and its just-so stories) to make sense of us. A casualty of the account is any joyful expectation of an integrated, whole, complete, or perfected human person. The synthesis is of a fundamentally divided set of entities that comprise, first, each human, and then, each community. The approach capitulates to a story of inherent fragmentation in the human person.[170] If the evolutionary and naturalist narrative is true, then so be it; we are in a serious sense tragic, and are asked to mourn any more coherent account of human being, along with unicorns or an earth-centric universe. Here is the best portrayal Haidt can give of our constitution and the inhabitation of our lives:

> We were shaped by individual selection to be selfish creatures who struggle for resources, pleasure, and prestige, and we were shaped by group selection to be hive creatures who long to lose ourselves in something larger. We are social creatures who need love and attachments, and we are industrious creatures with needs for effectance [sic], able to enter a state of vital engagement with our work. We are the rider and we are the elephant, and our mental health depends on the two working together, each drawing on the other's strengths.[171]

It remains to be seen if psychology's attempt to parse our soul as the balancing of myriad competing inner entities, most of which require of us rat-cunning to unmask and nudge, can suffice for us to inhabit our lives well. Wherever we fall on metaphysics – hard naturalism, christological theism, or somewhere else – it at least remains of interest to see whether those earlier attempts at moral psychology, developed within the Christian tradition, offer as much or more on how to navigate our lives. But perhaps the starkest point of difference between naturalistic moral psychology and a Christian account of such things is with the naturalist insistence that we are fundamentally divided, a 'kluge' of unrelated systems bundled together by evolutionary accident. Contrast this Christian perspective, from a work to be further investigated in Chapter 9 (and here interpreted by the former archbishop of Canterbury, Rowan Williams):

> It is Diadochos of Photike who [. . .] gives one of the most suggestive accounts of what the Fall effects. We discover, says Diadochos, in the course of our

---

170. The title of a popular book in the same discourse aptly names this way of seeing humanity: Gary F. Marcus, *Kluge: The Haphazard Construction of the Human Mind* (London: Faber, 2008).

171. Haidt, *The Happiness Hypothesis*, p. 238.

growth in illumination by the Spirit, that human sensation is primitively one and undivided. In unfallen humanity, the variations of bodily sensation among the five senses are due only to the varying needs of the body – that is, they are diverse aspects of a single disposition of receptivity [. . .]. The body's receptivity is not separate from that of the intelligence. But in the fallen state, perception has become divided. This division is not, it seems, simply a division of body from soul or sensible from intellective, but a division between self-oriented and other-oriented perceiving. Both bodily sense and intelligence are split between their natural openness to things as they are [. . .] and the compulsion to obscure this true perception through selfish will, through the 'passionate' consciousness that replaces the reality with a simulacrum, a passion-laden perception that is designed to serve the self's agenda.[172]

Williams' and Diadochos' comments are redolent of concepts to be introduced via Augustine (Chapter 6) and Aquinas (Chapter 7) (and the sense of 'passion' in this quotation will turn out not to be what it seems to the modern mind). Suffice though here to note the contrast between a naturalist account that finally rests in inherent dividedness, and an alternative that does not. Each account invites Charles Taylor's test, where if actual life falls outside of a given account of human life, then the account is not making the best sense of life:

> What better measure of reality do we have in human affairs than those terms which [. . .] make the best sense of our lives? 'Making the best sense' here includes not only offering the best, most realistic orientation about the good but also allowing ourselves best to understand and make sense of the actions and feelings of ourselves and others. For our language of deliberation is continuous with our language of assessment, and this with the language in which we explain what people do and feel. [. . .] What are the requirements of 'making sense' of our lives? These requirements are not yet met if we have some theoretical language which purports to explain behaviour for the observer's standpoint but is of no use to the agent in making sense of his own thinking, feeling, and acting.[173]

Haidt's account (and some others like it) does qualify as a *good* account, for it (and some others) take seriously several significant elements of human life. Taylor judges that 'various theories of moral judgments as projections, and the attempts to distinguish "value" from "fact", fall afoul of this [best account] principle',[174] since we regularly deny such distinctions in practice. Haidt's work, it should now be clear, edges away from such inadequate accounts.

---

172. Rowan Williams, *Looking East in Winter: Contemporary Thought and the Eastern Christian Tradition* (London: Bloomsbury, Kindle edn, 2021), p. 15.
173. Taylor, *Sources of the Self*, p. 57.
174. Taylor, *Sources of the Self*, p. 58.

It should also, therefore, be clear that my purpose is not to level polemic. In reading Haidt, I recognize (with sadness) much that I have missed in myself, in Christian culture, and in my close relationships. In seeking to commend Christian accounts of moral psychology in the chapters that follow, we would be fools to think that modern moral psychology is not, like much other human wisdom, rightly seeing what is too easily missed. Jockeying for mastery of the metanarrative all too easily becomes yet another sad exercise in the beating of tribal drums.

But whether his is the best account remains to be seen. Another reason for wondering so – in addition to that commitment to a fundamental human dividedness – is, *prima facie*, its prevarication on its relationship to frankly moral discourse, a fourth outcome of Haidt's work that is of central significance. For *HH* in particular is clearly an exercise in morality, grandly understood. It is a statement of the nature and purpose of humanity, with several strong, if interesting, suggestions on how we should proceed:

> The final version of the happiness hypothesis is that happiness comes from between. Happiness is not something that you can find, acquire, or achieve directly. You have to get the conditions right and then wait. Some of those conditions are within you, such as coherence among the parts and levels of your personality. Other conditions require relationships to things beyond you: Just as plants need sun, water, and good soil to thrive, people need love, work, and a connection to something larger. It is worth striving to get the right relationships between yourself and others, between yourself and your work, and between yourself and something larger than yourself. If you get these relationships right, a sense of purpose and meaning will emerge.[175]

These statements are overtly normative, and arise from a substantive account of human being and purpose. This paragraph, with all of *HH*, reflects an overtly eudemonistic ethic. Even though happiness cannot directly be pursued, it is in some sense the human *telos*, not to be pursued directly yet always to be pursued out of the corner of the eye, as it were.

In Haidt's version of the discipline, psychology reveals itself to have turned full circle. Once setting out to examine humans as freed of the constraints of dogma, now it tells us who we are and how to live. Psychology thereby reveals itself as in some way fundamentally a moral exercise, and an exercise in morality (widely construed). At the same time, it trades in the 'psychologization' of all of life. These are the claims Svend Brinkmann puts to psychology, outlined below.

Not only do these charges point to the potential for hegemonic conceit in the psychological enterprise. If modern psychology is *inherently and fundamentally* engaged in morality – beyond, even, its subdomain of moral psychology – then there is no reason to think it should not be expected to make account of itself

---

175. Haidt, *The Happiness Hypothesis*, pp. 210–11.

alongside theology which, for all its faults and all the doubts about it, has at least had a thing or two to suggest about morality.

III. Brinkmann's challenge

Danish psychologist Svend Brinkman is a leading commentator on the philosophy of psychology in his context. His role as head of the Centre for Qualitative Studies at Aalborg University signals his interest in a psychology that makes better sense of the phenomenology and *qualia* of human experience, including as it pertains to morality. Among his several projects, of interest for our purposes is his challenge to psychology *in toto* to accept that fundamentally, it is a 'moral science'. His view presupposes moral realism, the approach to morality that regards it as inherent to reality itself, not only to our perceptions and constructions.

> What is a good reason is not up to me, but is a matter of the structure of the space of reasons. Often, our reasons and evaluations are implicit in our reactions, feelings, and intuitions – in our 'moral know-how' – rather than in formulated moral views and theories. But like explicit propositions, these reactions, feelings, and intuitions can still be more or less correct and morally legitimate, according to the moral realist. The realist claim is that what is morally good and right is not good and right because someone happens to like it. Rather, we ought to like what is morally good, and likewise detest what is morally bad. Indeed, we have moral reasons to like what is morally good, and detest what is morally bad. This is the view that I shall try to defend.[176]

Hence psychology, insofar as it deals in observing reactions, feelings, and intuitions, needs also to accept that it is also dealing with how humans engage with patterns of normativity that exist beyond each person.

> [P]sychology and its phenomena (human perceiving, acting, feeling, thinking, learning, and development) cannot be understood if the moral normativity of the human world is ignored or left out. Psychological phenomena are saturated with morality. The point can be put even stronger: The scientific project of exorcizing morality from psychology leaves no genuine psychological phenomena behind, for psychological phenomena are constituted by normative moral orders.[177]

Brinkmann thinks that when the strategy of psychologization presents feelings, preferences, and modes of reasoning as being all there is to human moral functioning, it hides an implicit moral anti-realism. On such a view, one's values may present as facts susceptible to scientific research, but moral norms themselves

---

176. Brinkmann, *Psychology as a Moral Science*, p. 95.
177. Brinkmann, *Psychology as a Moral Science*, p. 3.

are not. Yet, such anti-realism is not accepted among psychologists as it pertains to other mental operations, such as logic.[178]

In addition to his moral realism, Brinkmann offers an account of personal moral processing that he denotes as 'interpretative-pragmatic':

> [M]oral judgment in practice necessarily involves situational interpretation and judgment, and cannot be understood as a mere application of moral rules. [. . .] [T]he validity of moral judgments, rules, and concepts is to be evaluated by their effects in practical action. [. . .] Being alive as a human being is, from the interpretive-pragmatic perspective, an interpretive process of inquiry that is subject to normative appraisal. Psychological phenomena and moral phenomena are, in a broad sense, conversational.[179]

Such an approach (to morality and its psychology), which Brinkmann refuses to claim as a comprehensive theory of morality, is in contrast to 'emotivist, subjectivist, and relativist theories' (here naming various sociobiological and social-constructionist theories of morality), and to 'various kinds of formalism and proceduralism' (such as neo-Kantian theories).[180] He goes on to show and refute

---

178. Brinkmann, *Psychology as a Moral Science*, pp. 95–96. To illuminate the problem of psychologization, I note also Michael Spezio's summary of what he calls 'psychologism': 'the doctrine that normative logic and ethics/morality are subsets of descriptive, causal theories of mental processes' and that such descriptions *determine* what thoughts are true, and what judgments morally proper (Spezio, 'The Neuroscience of Emotion and Reasoning in Social Contexts', p. 224). To be fair, Spezio observes, its proponents regularly issue caveats around the limits of measurement and statistical analysis of these mental processes, and around the application of results. (A useful compendium of several measurement and experimental design issues in brain-imaging studies can be found in Satel and Lilienfeld, *Brainwashed*, pp. 13–20, a work that challenges ill-advised applications of such research.) More overtly problematic, however, is the breath-taking question-begging that psychologism hides in plain sight. For Spezio, 'the current methods of neuroscientific investigation into reason and moral action depend utterly on the very normative distinctions that psychologistic proponents seek to replace.' (Spezio, 'The Neuroscience of Emotion and Reasoning in Social Contexts', p. 225.) In other words, for example, Greene's studies of the brain processes that deliver utilitarian conclusions rely upon an already normative concept, 'utilitarian'. This and other such categories 'are given to neuroscience and are not generated by it.' (Spezio, 'The Neuroscience of Emotion and Reasoning in Social Contexts', p. 225.) Spezio adduces clear exceptions to this intellectual mistake, but names several more well-known examples of it. He includes the work of Jonathan Haidt, although I suspect that the sheer ambition of Haidt's project implicitly strains the psychologism of his guild, becoming as it does a quest for some more substantive account of morality.

179. Brinkmann, *Psychology as a Moral Science*, p. 2.

180. Brinkmann, *Psychology as a Moral Science*, p. 2.

three common stances on morality within the psychologists' guild: strategies of reductionism (to biology or social construction); of narrowing morality into sets of rules; or of its complete avoidance.[181] The basic stance echoes Taylor:

> The terms we select have to make sense across the whole range of both explanatory and life uses. [. . .] Just as physical science is no longer anthropocentric, so human science can no longer be couched in the terms of physics. Our value terms purport to give us insight into what it is to live in the universe as a human being, and this is a quite different matter from that which physical science claims to reveal and explain. The reality is, of course, dependent on us, in the sense that a condition for its existence is our existence. But once granted that we exist, it is no more a subjective projection than what physics deals with.[182]

Brinkmann cites a related thought by Alan Costall: 'When physical science had promoted its methodology (of atomism, mechanism, and quantification) to an exclusive ontology, psychology (so conceived) was a pretty obvious mistake just waiting to happen – an essentially derivative science modelled on physics, yet having as its subject the very realm that physics rendered utterly obscure.'[183]

We noted above how for Charles Taylor, ontology needs to be discerned through an account that can make the best sense of (for example) courage and generosity. They are features of the real world that enable deliberation and personal assessment.[184] 'My perspective is defined by the moral intuitions I have, by what I am morally moved by. If I abstract from this, I become incapable of understanding any moral argument at all.'[185] Brinkmann makes clear that psychologization is precisely such an abstraction. In this mistake, moral normativity is regarded as 'a resulting *epiphenomenon* of psychological operations.'[186] Attributing the origins of the mistake in part to Hume's subjectivism on passion, in part to Rousseau's elevation of an 'inner voice', and in part to fetishisms of research method, Brinkmann concludes: 'The result has been that the human capacity for moral action has been ignored at best, or reduced away at worst, for a mind that is recreated in the light of value-neutral methods can hardly see itself in moral terms.'[187]

---

181. Brinkmann, *Psychology as a Moral Science*, pp. 11–13.

182. Taylor, *Sources of the Self*, pp. 58–59.

183. Alan Costall, 'From Darwin to Watson (and Cognitivism) and Back Again: The Principle of Animal-Environment Mutuality', *Behavior and Philosophy* 32.1 (2004), pp. 179–95 (184); cited in Brinkmann, *Psychology as a Moral Science*, p. 26.

184. Taylor, *Sources of the Self*, p. 69.

185. Taylor, *Sources of the Self*, p. 73.

186. Brinkmann, *Psychology as a Moral Science*, p. 3.

187. Brinkmann, *Psychology as a Moral Science*, p. 34.

IV. Psychology, moral psychology and theology

Polish scholar Vaiva Adomaityte has suggested that 'emotions are not morally neutral, but on the contrary, they are essential, value-laden elements of morality. [. . .] [E]motions not only signal values, but also enable one to access a particular moral situation in its fullness.'[188] Her conclusion arose in part from a study of Thomas Aquinas, whom we will consider in Chapter 7, and illustrates how theology has much to say about the fundamentally moral nature of emotion, and by extension, of psychology.

Brinkmann broadly construes psychology as a cultural form that 'has infiltrated our social imaginary'; and in its more narrow disciplinary form as a fragmentary and contradictory set of disparate ideas and theories that unite either around various projects of metrication, or various quests for personal change.[189] However, he invites psychology 'to look more like moral philosophy than anything else',[190] and aims 'to direct psychologists' attention to certain moral aspects of human experience that we simply cannot ignore or eliminate, if we want to remain true to the phenomena that psychologists deal with.'[191] The 'bedrock to psychology' is 'found in an elementary moral normativity'.[192] Correlatively, psychologists should 'make explicit and discuss the moral values they live by'.[193] For our purposes, the points of highlighting Brinkmann's challenges to psychology are manifold.

First, it should at least be noted the extent to which an expansive project such as Haidt's substantiates Brinkmann's assertions. This vast (and perhaps over-reaching) set of enterprises represents a trajectory where psychology can no longer resist or evade the normative, and where forms of intuitionism hint overtly and covertly at a frank moral realism. Two related developments are worth noting by way of example. A much-publicized major study of over sixty cultures, albeit by anthropologists, looked at the psychological valence of several forms of cooperative behaviour and found them regarded universally as positive across all those societies.[194] (The ensuing deduction, that all morality can be subsumed under principles of cooperation, is contestable.) In a different

---

188. Vaiva Adomaityte, 'Emotions and Ethics: A Conversation with Martha C. Nussbaum and Thomas Aquinas', *Dialogue and Universalism* 25.2 (2015), pp. 92–103 (92), doi: 10.5840/du201525242.

189. Brinkmann, *Psychology as a Moral Science*, pp. 18–19.

190. Brinkmann, *Psychology as a Moral Science*, p. 1.

191. Brinkmann, *Psychology as a Moral Science*, p. 2.

192. Brinkmann, *Psychology as a Moral Science*, p. 13.

193. Brinkmann, *Psychology as a Moral Science*, pp. 3–4.

194. Oliver Scott Curry, Daniel Austin Mullins, and Harvey Whitehouse, 'Is It Good to Cooperate? Testing the Theory of Morality-as-Cooperation in 60 Societies', *Current Anthropology* 60.1 (2019), pp. 47–69, online at: https://dx.doi.org/10.1086/701478, doi: 10.1086/701478.

register, leading positive psychologist Martin Seligman has edited a volume describing humanity as *homo prospectus* – in other words, the species marked out by its propensity to plan towards purposes.[195] This telic concept of humanity approaches the moral-philosophical thickness of various medieval accounts of human being and purpose.

Second: the acuity with which this literature is observing the moral implications of emotion – even when, in Brinkmann's terms, it has only psychologized morality – should finally put to rest any notions that emotions are not implicated in ethics, and ethics with emotion. The relation between them remains hotly contested, and indeed quite confusing. But the fact of their intricate relationship can no longer be denied.

Third, then, if moral psychology specifically (and if Brinkmann is correct, psychology in general) is fundamentally a moral science, it can no longer be regarded as a domain separate from those that have traditionally weighed morality. Thinkers such as Haidt know this well, and have attempted to engage with traditional moral philosophy. While they have been less adept at engaging with moral *theology*, by their own lights they are now participating also in its domain.

Finally, then, we have arrived at bringing moral theology's account to bear on the subject. It will remain to be seen, of course, in what manner it is of interest. It may only be of antiquarian interest, just as Galen or Harvey have no real bearing on the modern practice of medicine. Less thinly, there may be the kind of interest Haidt exemplifies – a respectful awareness of different thought-forms whereby others notice what they have missed; or attentive harvesting of various grassroots forms of wisdom ('folk psychologies'), for later confirmation by science. Even more substantively, if habits of thought and practice arising from Christian theological thinking have imprinted moral norms and so on upon (mainly) Western people in unique ways – say, in the 'weird' manner of recent anthropological claim[196] – then a richer account of theological history will be needed to interpret the archaeology of that thought.

Arguably of far more importance is whether the thick theistic claims of Christian thought enhance an account of human moral function. The point of divergence from psychological investigation, whether in its hard naturalist form or in its benignly sympathetic form, is that God is elemental to our environmental conditions, even though supernaturally; that God has also shaped those conditions, and our responses to them; that God's revelation, culminating in Christ, 'decodes' our condition in important ways; and that God's own Trinitarian

---

195. Martin E. P. Seligman, et al., *Homo Prospectus* (Oxford: Oxford University Press, 2016).

196. 'WEIRD' is a clever acronym for 'Western, Educated, Industrialized, Rich, and Democratic'. See Joseph Henrich, Steven J. Heine, and Ara Norenzayan, 'Beyond WEIRD: Towards a Broad-Based Behavioral Science', *The Behavioral and Brain Sciences* 33.2–3 (2010), pp. 111–210, doi: 10.1017/S0140525X10000725.

essence of love is constitutive of our own being. We are exposed as a kind of being that makes less sense, and whose function is compromised, when estranged from participation with God's own love. In all these respects, theological ethics and Christian perspectives on morals and emotions continue to operate in the domains psychology aspires to own.

Part 2

HEBREW AND CHRISTIAN BEGINNINGS IN AN ACCOUNT OF MORAL AFFECTIONS

The intention of this part is to illuminate some themes in biblical literature that are perhaps easily missed by moderns, but which served as the substrate for the tradition that followed. It will be of more than antiquarian interest, especially given Haidt's explicit dialogue with religious traditions including Christianity. It will highlight the way biblical authors addressed the problems under view, using two specific foci (selected from several possible candidates) – ancient Hebrew wisdom and Hellenistic Christian desire.

Chapter 4

THE PURSUIT OF WISDOM

A JOURNEY OF BIBLICAL PROPORTIONS

The purpose of this and the next short chapter is to offer a *prima facie* indication of the significance of moral emotions in Christian and Jewish Scripture. These comments are a prelude to the consideration of subsequent Christian thinkers in moral psychology (beginning in Chapter 6).

This chapter looks at how the rich and varied wisdom literature of Scripture schools desire towards various ends, and gives self-reflective recognition of desire at its moral best and worst. Less obviously but perhaps more important, this literature also functions at a subtle 'meta' level to indicate how desire is not merely a matter of individual expression. It is drawn forth from us, first towards aspects of the created order, then to become a pathway leading to definite, if invisible, further realities within God.

Biblical literature is variously categorized, but its wisdom literature is generally taken to include Job, Ecclesiastes, the Song of Solomon, Proverbs, and some Psalms. (Some intertestamental literature, such as the Wisdom of Solomon and Ecclesiasticus, also receives honourable mention in this context.) It is a wide-ranging literature with varying styles and emphases. But to hazard some defining features: it generally watches and comments upon the immanent social and natural order; has limited overt addresses from God; refers to the law of *Torah* allusively at best; and borrows liberally from extra-biblical sources, while also shaping the use of these. Wisdom themes are reprised in the teachings of Jesus[197] (who, to be fair, reprised ancient Hebrew teachings across all its genres) and some NT authors (most notably in the Epistle of James). As always, the literature on this material is vast, and so I will limit my attention to some aspects of the book of Proverbs to cameo its inchoate moral psychology. An introductory overview (I) will refract into discussions of desire in its relation to personhood (II) and morality (III) and the ways it can be altered (IV). We will then see its transcendental implications (V) and how it points to God (VI). The chapter ends with some conclusions (VII).

---

197. Cf. A. E. Harvey, *Strenuous Commands: The Ethic of Jesus* (London: SCM Press, 1990), pp. 39–67.

I. A manual of quotidian emotional and moral stances

Even a cursory reading of the Proverbs indicates a close interest in moral psychology. In its thematic opening statement, 'The fear of the LORD is the beginning of knowledge; fools despise wisdom and instruction' (1.7). The specifics of each referent – 'LORD', 'knowledge', 'wisdom', and 'instruction' – have not yet become clear, with the book's structure yet to unfold. But that the LORD is to be *feared* and that wisdom and instruction are not to be *despised* (or *scorned*), indicate strong emotional stances with moral imports.

These assertions in Prov. 1.7 function at a 'meta' level, to which we will return. An almost random sampling of the collected aphorisms beginning at Proverbs ch. 10, however, signals the interplay between morality and emotion in a range of quotidian encounters:

> Hatred stirs up strife,
>   but love covers all offenses. (10.12)
> Wrath is cruel, anger is overwhelming,
>   but who is able to stand before jealousy? (27.4)
> It is not good to eat much honey,
>   or to seek honour on top of honour.
> Like a city breached, without walls,
>   is one who lacks self-control. (25.27-28)

The verses in this sample highlight how we inhabit our emotions as evaluative truth. At the same time, each verse takes a further evaluative stance on various emotions, critiquing their outcomes.

The last verse quoted highlights the Proverbs' conventional interest to interrogate, challenge and restrain our emotionally laden evaluative stances; and at a pinch, we might further add in that connection this famous saying:

> There is a way that seems right to a person,
>   but its end is the way to death. (14.12)

While not referencing what we would regard in the first instance as an emotion, this saying observes an intellectual correlate: morally evaluative stances can occur within deeply convincing, yet fundamentally flawed, frames of reference. (My gloss of the original would be something like: 'A straight way appears before a person, but its end is death.') Arguably, it may not have occurred to ancient readers of this saying to regard it as a statement about cognition, as distinct from other statements concerning emotion. What we tend to divide is in this literature simply cut from the same human cloth.

Not all references to emotion have an overt moral content. Some sayings simply observe how emotional states or stances are inherent *per se* to the presence or absence of flourishing:

Hope deferred makes the heart sick,
  but a desire fulfilled is a tree of life. (13.12)
The heart knows its own bitterness,
  and no stranger shares its joy. (14.10)
Even in laughter the heart is sad,
  and the end of joy is grief. (14.13)
A tranquil mind gives life to the flesh,
  but passion[198] makes the bones rot. (14.30)
The sated appetite spurns honey,
  but to a ravenous appetite even the bitter is sweet. (27.3)

For late modern readers, even this short assay can be a little overwhelming. (It is worth noting, in passing, Claus Westermann's comment that 'If one does not reflect at length on a proverb, it remains inaccessible.'[199]) To hazard a bold claim: the late modern Western mind prefers linear sequences of carefully categorized thoughts, not an almost randomized anthology of allusive, metaphorical comments. So it won't really work for us further to multiply representative wisdom utterances. Analyses by Anne Stewart, Christine Roy Yoder, Sun Myung Lyu, Martin Laird, and Andrew Errington will take us further faster. I will use these thinkers' analyses to indicate how, in this literature:

- desire is fundamental to the Hebrew conception of the person (Stewart);
- desire does not sit outside the domain of moral concern (Roy, Stewart);
- desire is teachable, and proper forms of desire are communicable, albeit indirectly (Sun Myong Liu, Laird);
- desire is a window into invisible moral realities (Errington); and
- the proper object of desire is wisdom, which is somehow coterminous with the search for Yahweh himself (Errington).

II. Desire is integral to human personhood

Stewart notes that desire, for all its objects and kinds of desirers, 'has a broad semantic and conceptual range within the book' ranging from particular desires to 'the figuring of desirable objects' and 'the pursuit of that which is lacking.' It is also 'paradoxical, dangerous, destabilizing.'[200] It is 'assumed to be an innate part of the human' and '[i]n many respects, the book of Proverbs is a manual of desires,

---

198. Hebrew *qinah*; more usually translated 'envy', 'zeal' or 'jealousy'.
199. Claus Westermann, *Roots of Wisdom: The Oldest Proverbs of Israel and Other Peoples* (Louisville, KY: Westminster John Knox Press, 1995), p. 8.
200. Anne W. Stewart, *Poetic Ethics in Proverbs: Wisdom Literature and the Shaping of the Moral Self* (Cambridge: Cambridge University Press, 2016), p. 136.

for much of the book turns on identifying *what* humans desire, what they *should* desire, and *where* those desires may lead.'[201]

On this account, even 'the absence of strong desires is indicative of a perversion of character,'[202] such as in the case of the lazy person, who 'buries a hand in the dish, and is too tired to bring it back to the mouth' (26.15).

Although self-restraint against damaging emotions may seem *prima facie* to be a major concern of the book's anthology in chs. 10–31, the scene-setting chs. 1–9 are laden with emotional attitudes and postures, such as fearing and despising; greed, love, delight, hate, terror, distress, and anguish; and bodily appetites and desires.

III. Patterns of desire are part of the moral domain

All these emotional attitudes and postures are 'constitutive elements of character', observes Christine Roy Yoder.[203] She argues that 'the sages of Proverbs 1–9 engage the emotions as vital forms of perception and judgment, advocating certain patterns of emotions – which they deem may be taught – as characteristic of mature, flourishing human lives.'[204]

Stewart observes how the complexities of desire and its moral ambiguities are seen in the Proverbs' treatment, for example, of wealth, and women, and then via several typological characters: 'sinners', and 'the wicked' whose misguided desires are incorrigible; the unrestrainable impulsivity of 'the fool'; and the thinly undeveloped moral discernment of 'the simpleton'.[205] Conversely, 'the righteous', and 'the wise' are conceived as having desires that accord with moral order, such as longings for justice, understanding, knowledge, and even discipline or rebuke. As Yoder puts it, 'the wise are urged to embrace an emotional repertoire that promotes interdependence with God, wisdom, and others, while the fools' emotions alienate them from the same.'[206]

IV. Patterns of proper desire are indirectly communicable

Wisdom literature posits a mode of moral formation in which desire is more caught than taught. Stewart cites Sun Myung Lyu thus:

201. Stewart, *Poetic Ethics in Proverbs*, pp. 136–37.

202. Stewart, *Poetic Ethics in Proverbs*, p. 137.

203. Christine Roy Yoder, 'The Objects of Our Affection: Emotions and the Moral Life in Proverbs 1–9', in *Shaking Heaven and Earth: Essays in Honor of Walter Brueggemann and Charles B. Cousar* (eds Christine Roy Yoder et al.; Louisville, KY: Westminster John Knox Press, 2005), pp. 73–88 (74).

204. Yoder, 'The Objects of Our Affection', p. 75.

205. Stewart, *Poetic Ethics in Proverbs*, pp. 137–41. On these 'characters', see also Yoder, 'The Objects of Our Affection', pp. 76–83.

206. Yoder, 'The Objects of Our Affection', p. 75.

we can hope to induce desire *by showing what is desirable*. Moral instruction is in essence a process of persuasion and, to put it bluntly, a form of seduction. And seduction requires a lure, a prospect of palpable gain.[207]

The apotheosis of this patterning of desire is in the portrayal of Woman Wisdom, whose 'goal is to win the love of the simple'.[208] The overall effect of the book is to observe all the desires we may have, yet to pattern desire by 'undermin[ing] the desires it considers to be dangerous'.[209] Commenting on Gregory of Nyssa's similar approach, Martin Laird writes that:

> the pedagogical strategy of Proverbs does anything but attempt to extinguish desire. Rather Proverbs attempts to stir it up, inflame it by dangling before it beautiful, tantalizing images.[210]

V. Desire draws us towards a transcendent other

Laird continues that 'Proverbs seeks not to destroy or indulge soul's noetic-erotic capacity to be preoccupied with corporeal things, but to train this same desire to long for the incorporeal.'[211] By way of this observation, we may arrive at Andrew Errington's key insight into the book of Proverbs, which he terms the alterity or 'otherness' of wisdom. It is a subtle, 'meta' aspect of the work, indicating how desire may be drawn forth from us towards an order that (and eventually, the God who) transcends our immediate subjectivity.

Beginning with all the ways wisdom 'calls' in the book (1.20-21; 8.2-3; 9.4), Errington proceeds (via Gerhard von Rad) to 'an understanding of wisdom as somehow a predicate of the world, rather than just of the subject. Wisdom is in some sense an *other* to be loved.'[212]

But in what sense? In the first place, the Proverbs emphasize ways of 'walking' – acts in a world that is hospitable to some forms of action and not others.[213] 'In the

---

207. Sun Myung Lyu, *Righteousness in the Book of Proverbs* (Tübingen: Mohr Siebeck, 2012), p. 62; cited in Stewart, *Poetic Ethics in Proverbs*, p. 142 (emphasis Lyu's).

208. Stewart, *Poetic Ethics in Proverbs*, p. 143.

209. Stewart, *Poetic Ethics in Proverbs*, p. 146.

210. Martin Laird, 'Under Solomon's Tutelage: The Education of Desire in the Homilies on the Song of Songs', *Modern Theology* 18.4 (2002), pp. 507–25 (511), doi: 10.1111/1468-0025.00201.

211. Laird, 'Under Solomon's Tutelage', p. 511.

212. Andrew Errington, *Every Good Path: Wisdom and Practical Reason in Christian Ethics and the Book of Proverbs* (T&T Clark Enquiries in Theological Ethics series, London: Bloomsbury; T&T Clark, 2020), p. 105.

213. Errington, *Every Good Path*, p. 106; on creation's 'hospitality', pp. 118, 122, 219, and *passim*.

book of Proverbs, moral kinds are real [...] a determinate other, to be encountered, respected, and loved.'[214] 'Wisdom deserves to be *loved*.'[215]

We will go on to see that this sense of the love of various goods, and hence of moral kinds, bears strong resemblance to Augustine's logic of love.

VI. Desire's proper object, often named as wisdom, overlaps with Yahweh

Errington's main concern throughout his work is to elucidate what constitutes the practical reason of wisdom. Even so, his account pivots on the wise person's gaze of love, which is turn in predicated on how the being of God *somehow* emanates into the world.

For theologians, this emanation is hugely problematic (hence my weaselly 'somehow'). In the gargantuan literature on the book of Proverbs, the joint between God's uncreated wisdom and the wisdoms within creation is the subject of much discussion around Proverbs ch. 8. In this poem, wisdom stands alongside and above roadways, almost a marginalized ragamuffin, plaintively calling out (vv. 1-4). But she succeeds in putting forward a very seductive case for her worth (vv. 5-13; cf. Lyu, above), by which she inveigles her way into consciousness via her merits to rich merchants, effective counsellors, good kings, and wealthy inheritors (vv. 14-21).

Then, suddenly and totally unexpectedly, she unmasks as a co-creatrix with God (vv. 22-31), brought forth by God, and fundamentally aligned to God – which punchline to the poem amply explicates why creatures who walk within the grain of her works are blessed (vv. 32-36), and hence why some patterns of desire are proper, and others not. If she somehow undergirds creation, then creation is indeed hospitable to the kinds of acts we mark as morally good, and (ultimately, if not always proximally) to the kinds of people who love such things.

But for millennia, a storm-centre has attended what the theologian is to make of her semi-divine status (particularly in relation to what is revealed, much later, of the Second Person of the Trinity). I have no intention of visiting that storm-centre here. Errington dances around this literature adroitly, concluding that wisdom is both divine, and not; it is of God, yet creaturely. The uncreated God works the creation, and works within it. The Triune God's pinnacle work turns out to be the explosive, unanticipated wisdom of the Cross, wherein Jesus Christ makes accessible to us the depthless wisdom of God (1 Cor. 1.23-24).[216] Christ enacts a series of reversals in what we conventionally desire, unveiling what and who truly matter, so that we may grow to love them more.

---

214. Errington, *Every Good Path*, p. 112.
215. Errington, *Every Good Path*, p. 117.
216. Errington, *Every Good Path*, pp. 123–26.

VII. Provisional conclusions

What could all this possibly mean for the relation between human experiences of emotion and morality? To anticipate the thinkers to follow: namely, that the human propensity to love is inalienable to us; that there are loves (also known as desires, or passions, or affections or whatever) that are proper to human action, and others that make for immoral action; but that the capacity for such love (and loves) emanates finally from the Triune God of love, whose love overflows into structures and patterns and manifold elements of all that surrounds us. I believe that the quotidian emotion-therapies of the Proverbs (and of other wisdom literature), and its very alterity originating within God, maps fairly clearly onto the theological accounts we shall see unfolding in the chapters below. (I also believe that is what makes psychology a moral science that properly terminates in the transcendent God who is love.)

But these claims are perhaps to go too far too fast. It behoves us, next, to illustrate some of these ideas also reflected in the words and conceptions of the part-Hellenistic, part-Judaic New Testament.

Chapter 5

DESIRE AND CULPABILITY

A TRAGEDY OF BIBLICAL PROPORTIONS

The purpose of this short chapter, like the previous, is to offer a *prima facie* indication of the significance of moral emotions in Christian Scripture. These comments are intended as a prelude to the consideration of subsequent Christian thinkers in moral psychology (beginning in Chapter 6).

In it, we glimpse 'a tragedy of biblical proportions'. As in the wisdom literature, desire is inherent to humanity, often celebrated, and implicit in every moral evaluation. But tragically, those evaluations often turn out to be mistaken and morally culpable, because as also in the wisdom literature, desire has lost the deepest source of its goods.

I. A cameo of biblical desire

Several approaches to Hellenistic conceptions of desire as engaged within the New Testament (NT) could be undertaken. This chapter proceeds by the simple expedient of a brief lexical consideration of the Koine Greek term *epithumia* (ἐπιθυμία), and its uses in the New Testament (NT) and the Septuagint (LXX). It will rely for its warrant on an Appendix to the chapter (II). Readers less interested in that detail may be content with this section's short summary (I).

The term connotes 'strong desire', for which several other terms also exist (Appendix, §f and §g). But even merely in *epithumia*, we begin to see the complexity of feelingful human engagement with the moral domain.

Very often, NT *epithumia* is indicated as illicit or morally culpable through collocation with some other negative adjective or verb (see Appendix, §b–c). In this way, desire is rendered suspect by association. It is a word that attracts several negative qualifiers: in English, 'deceitful', 'lustful', 'worldly', 'corrupt', 'debauched', 'ungodly'. By volume alone of such references, it would be easy to assert that this literature is monolithically suspicious of desire itself, regarding it generally as morally suspect. Some later readings of the NT have done exactly that.

However, looking more closely (Appendix, §d–e), we find several moments where desire is morally unobjectionable, or better. Indeed in the LXX, *epithumia* is used across the moral spectrum (Appendix, §a), often positively. We also see several NT appearances of strong desire as a form of moral excellence. Disciples, prophets, and angels long to see divine truth; apostles long to see Christ, or to see their people, or for people to progress in faith; and young men rightly long to care for God's people.

Also, a most surprising twist becomes apparent in Lk. 22.25 when Jesus alludes to the LXX translation of Num. 11.4, using *epithumia* twice in a double-barrelled phrase – an emphatic conjoining of the noun and cognate verb – to tell of how ardently he longs to eat the Passover with his disciples. Not only can desires be very good; in Jesus we see the eclipse of obsessive and short-sighted craving with a righteous craving every bit as intense, and in context alluding to the fulfilment of his destiny or *telos*.[217]

Two texts in particular offer closer analyses of *epithumia*. In 1 Jn 2.16-17, 'all that is in the world – the desire of the flesh, the desire of the eyes, the pride in riches – comes not from the Father but from the world. And the world and [the desire for it] are passing away, but those who do the will of God live forever.'[218] It will turn out that this text is highly influential in Augustine's account of desire (Chapter 6), since its threefold use of *epithumia*, its parallelism with 'pride', and its characteristically Johannine use of 'world', are pregnant with meaning for a theological anthropology. It suffices here to notice the way world (as opposed to God) is construed as a particular kind of self-referenced desiring. This desiring originates in the immediacy of 'flesh', arguably also a quasi-technical term for the way we apprehend what surrounds us from the immediacy of personal need, and then using the limited immediacy of what is seen ('eyes'), as if that is all that matters. These perceptions are in turn woven into the self-promoting stance of pride (with the Greek tantalisingly referring to 'the pride of life'.) But all these stances are ephemeral, since not aligned God's own desires, denoted as 'God's will'.

If there is a kernel of truth to Kant's complaint against the emotions, it is seen in this biblical diagnosis of their self-absorbed subjectivity when we are at our worst. His countervailing valorization of a good will would seem to parallel this reference to God's good will, when the modern ear is used to parsing God's will as if it is effectively an impersonal and absolute power of fiat. But such a reading is anachronous if in NT usage God's 'will' is tantamount to what God desires, loves and finds pleasing. We will see how Augustine parsed 'will' as no more and no less than the enaction of love, and the same is likely true here in relation to the indivisibility (in God's simplicity) of God's person, love, and will. Hence the text serves both to interrogate desire, and to signal how it can terminate instead upon on God and on God's enduring desires (his 'will').

Similarly, Jas 1.14-16 gives a thumbnail sketch of the wily deceptions of *epithumia*. '[O]ne is tempted by one's own desire, being lured and enticed by it;

---

217. I am indebted to a former colleague, Rev'd Dr Richard Gibson, for this observation about the link between Num. 11.4 and Lk. 22.25.

218. The bracketed phrase denotes NRSV's alternative phrasing of the Greek.

then, when that desire has conceived, it gives birth to sin, and that sin, when it is fully grown, gives birth to death. Do not be deceived, my beloved.' Contrasting such deceit is the apprehension, in v. 17, that 'every perfect gift, is from above'. In other words, everything we appreciate as good, via the evaluative stances of desire, has its proper home and origin in 'the Father of lights' (v. 17). *Epithumia* in its deceived mode falls well short of that awareness.

The problem is reprised in Jas 4.2, when the verbal form of *epithumia* introduces the thought that 'You want something and do not have it; so you commit murder. And you covet something and cannot obtain it; so you engage in disputes and conflicts. You do not have, because you do not ask.' Premised on Jas 1.17, the object of asking is probably the Father of lights, who gives all good gifts. Proper connection to the home of all good would divert the chain of illicit desire. But in the gestalt where illicit desire holds sway, James' assessment accounts for the questions posed a verse earlier: 'Those conflicts and disputes among you, where do they come from? Do they not come from your cravings that are at war within you?' (4.1).

A project for another day might be to determine the extent to which James seeks, in summary form, to convey to his readers the insights of the wisdom tradition including the intertestamental books of *Wisdom* and *Sirach* (*Ecclesiasticus*). The burdens of this literature are on view in the third chapter of James' epistle, and even though *epithumia* does not make an appearance, the contest between two alternative forms of wisdom – one based on immediate desires and their resultant conflicts, and the other arising from God's enduring and proper desires – is most striking:

> Who is wise and understanding among you? Show by your good life that your works are done with gentleness born of wisdom. But if you have bitter envy and selfish ambition in your hearts, do not be boastful and false to the truth. Such 'wisdom' does not come down from above, but is earthly, unspiritual, devilish. For where there is envy and selfish ambition, there will also be disorder and wickedness of every kind. But the wisdom from above is first pure, then peaceable, gentle, willing to yield, full of mercy and good fruits, without a trace of partiality or hypocrisy. And a harvest of righteousness is sown in peace for those who make peace. (Jas 3.13-18[219])

It might be noted in passing that the passage immediately preceding, on the wildly untameable nature of human speech, is only resolved by this account of warring wisdoms. Only when divine wisdom is loved can there exist such a wellspring as to enable good speech even to become possible (cf. v. 11). But sadly, generations of Christians have suffered through sermonizing that simply *tells* hearers to speak better – even though the tongue explicitly cannot be tamed by mere willpower

---

219. I have added scare-quotes to the NRSV translation, to highlight the ironic, false 'wisdom' that is not 'from above'.

(v. 8). Such sermonizing has no cognizance of role desire plays in the overall arc of the chapter, or indeed in the conduct of life in general. (Theology denotes it as 'pelagian', a generalized continuation of the conceits of the sternly moralistic Pelagius, and his disciple Julian of Eclanum, whom we will meet in Chapter 6 via Augustine's polemics.)

All this terrain is straightforwardly moral-psychological. We see in these authors a conception of how desire can both motivate bad action, and also skew thought. At the same time, though, desire draws us towards the good. The predominance of morally negative contexts for desire has undoubtedly generated readings of Scripture, and entire Christian subcultures, where desire has been demonized and presumed to be represented only by its dark side. But that entailment has not always followed for astute readers of Scripture, given the moments where desire is valorized. In Chapter 6, we will examine Augustine's more nuanced account that morally evaluates states of desire even while describing them, as evidenced in biblical literatures. Augustine's synthesis is a more promising substrate for moral psychology, and potentially a better dialogue partner for modern moral psychology than those religious (and Kantian) accounts that are almost uniformly suspicious of desire.

In sum, a review of the Greek term *epithumia* and its uses highlights that the good or evil of desire can only be deduced from its moral context, not from the fact of desire as such. The moral nuancing of desire implicit in Greek Christian literature (including the LXX) immediately negates caricatures of Christian hostility to desire. To better understand a Christian moral psychology, we will need to turn to the integrative accounts of this data offered by the theologians to follow.

II. Appendix to Chapter 5: ἐπιθυμία in biblical thought

a. Various occurrences in LXX OT

Epithumia, either in singular or plural (ἡ ἐπιθυμία / αἱ ἐπιθυμίαι), describes:

- Jacob's longings for home, and Simeon and Rueben's desire to 'hamstring oxen', both illicit (Gen. 31.30, 49.6).
- 'The Tombs of Craving': Num. 11.34-35; cf. Ps. 78.23-31, esp. vv. 29-30 (LXX 77); and Ps. 106.14 (LXX 105). This episode becomes the archetypal example of desire expressed as hostility against God, and of desire considered as a disastrous form of craving. (Cf. 1 Cor. 10.6.)
- A blessing from God – 'eat all the meat you desire!' (Deut. 12.15, 20, 21).
- Solomon's desire to build whatever he wanted to build (2 Chron. 8.6).
- The boastful cravings of the wicked (Pss. 10.3, LXX 9.24; 112.10, LXX 111.10; and 140.8, LXX 139.9); but also the desires of the poor/afflicted (Ps. 10.17, LXX 9.38).
- The king's desires as given by God (Ps. 21.2; LXX 20.3).
- What God satisfies (Ps. 103.5; LXX 102).

- The person 'whose quiver is full' and 'whose desire is filled' (Ps. 127.5, LXX 126).
- The 'desire fulfilled', or 'a good desire' (LXX), that is a 'tree of life' (Prov. 13.12).

b. 'Guilty by association' in NT

Epithumia, either in singular or plural (ἡ ἐπιθυμία / αἱ ἐπιθυμίαι), are:

- what Jesus' opponents follow, like their father the devil (Jn 8.44);
- what God gives people over to ('the lusts of their hearts', Rom. 1.24);
- that aspect of mortal bodies that sin makes us to obey (Rom. 6.12);
- what is crucified with flesh (σάρξ) along with passions (πάθημα) (Gal. 5.24);
- what those pursuing riches fall into various of (1 Tim. 6.9);
- that which leads the weak (2 Tim. 3.6);
- what motivates people to gather false teachers (2 Tim. 4.3);
- the motivator for people in their ignorance (ἄγνοια) (1 Pet. 1.14);
- the vices of unconverted Gentiles (1 Pet. 4.3);
- what scoffers and malcontented false teachers follow (2 Pet. 3.3; Jude v.16);
- the whore of Babylon's longing (for fruit) (Rev. 18.14); and
- fleshly (σαρκικάι), warring against the soul (1 Pet. 2.11).

In addition:

- they are an aspect of what chokes the Word (Mk 4.19); and
- are produced when sin meets the tenth commandment (Rom. 7.7-8).
- Christ's followers no longer live for human desires, but for God's will (1 Pet. 4.2).

Also in verbal form:

- The adulterous-hearted man looks 'to desire her' (inf., Mt. 5.28).
- Paul has not desired other's money (Acts 20.33; usually translated as 'coveted', as also in Rom. 7.7 and 13.9).

c. Qualified as illicit by some adjective or verb

Epithumia, either in singular or plural (ἡ ἐπιθυμία / αἱ ἐπιθυμίαι), are:

- linked with genitive of flesh (σάρξ), (Eph. 2.3; Gal. 5.16; Rom. 13.14);
- paired with genitive deceit (ἀπάτη) so that 'deceitful desires' have corrupted 'the old person' (Eph. 4.22);
- evil (Col. 3.5);
- paired as genitive with πάθος ('ἐν πάθει ἐπιθυμίας') to describe pre-Christian approaches to sex (1 Thess. 4.5);
- youthful (νεωτερική), so needing to be fled (2 Tim. 2.22);
- worldly (κοσμική) (Tit. 2.12);

- enslaving (δουλεύω) (Tit. 3.3);
- paired with genitive φθορά and μιασμός, to be decadent and corrupt (2 Pet. 1.4, 2.10);
- debauched (ἀσέλγεια) and associated with σάρξ (2 Pet. 2.18); and
- paired with genitive ungodly (ἀσέβεια) (Jude v.18).

d. Strong desire as morally neutral

- The son's longing for the pods (Lk. 15.16).
- Lazarus' longing for scraps (Lk. 16.21).
- Spirit and flesh desiring in contrary directions (Gal. 5.17).
- People longing for death (Rev. 9.6).

e. Strong desire as morally very positive

- Prophets 'longed to see', and angels 'long to look' (Mt. 13.17; 1 Pet. 1.12).
- Disciples' longing to see the days of the Son of Man (Lk. 17.22).
- Jesus 'ardently longs' to eat Passover with the disciples ('ἐπιθυμίᾳ ἐπεθύμησα τοῦτο τὸ πάσχα φαγεῖν μεθ᾽ ὑμῶν', Lk. 22.25).
- Paul wishes to see the Thessalonians ἐν πολλῇ ἐπιθυμίᾳ (1 Thess. 2.17).
- Paul's desire to depart and be with Christ (Phil. 1.23).
- The desire to oversee is noble (1 Tim. 3.1).
- The author desires the Hebrews to show earnestness (Heb. 6.11).

f. Louw and Nida's[220] assessment of semantic domains for ἐπιθυμία

- §25.12: as noun and verb for strong and appropriate desire;
- §25.20: as noun and verb for illicit desire;
- with eighteen other entries on strong desire (nouns and adjectives): πλησμονή; ἐπιποθία; Θυμός; πλεονεξία; πλεονέκτης; ἁρπαγή; ἅρπαξ; αἰσχροκερδής/-ῶς; ἡδονή; κοιλία; σαρκὸς θέλημα; πάθος; πάθημα; ὁμοιοπαθής. verbs: ὀρέγομαι; ἐκκαίομαι (ἐν τῇ ὀρέξει); διψάω; πεινάω; ἐπιποθέω; ζηλόω; πυρόομαι; καταστηνιάω.

g. Examples of other words with a similar moral range:

Greek term	Morally problematic gloss:	Morally neutral gloss:
peirasmos	'Temptation': Mt 26.41; Mk 14.38; Lk. 4.13, 22.40, 22.46; 1 Cor. 10.13; 1 Tim. 6.9; Heb. 3.8.	'Trial': Mt. 6.13; Lk. 8.13; 11.4; 22.28; Acts 20.19; Gal. 4.14; Jas 1.2; 1.12; 1 Pet. 1.6; 4.12; 2 Pet. 2.9; Rev. 3.10.

220. J. P. Louw and Eugene A. Nida, *Greek-English Lexicon of the New Testament: Based on Semantic Domains* (New York: United Bible Societies, 2nd edn, 1989).

pathema	'Strong desire':	'Suffering':
	Rom. 7.5; Gal. 5.24.	Rom. 8.18; 2 Cor. 1.5ff; Phil. 3.10; Col. 1.24; 2 Tim. 3.11; Heb. 2.9f; 10.32; 1 Pet. 1.11; 4.13; 5.1; 5.9.
hedone	'Pleasure(s)':	'Pleasant':
	Lk. 8.14; Tit. 3.3; Jas 4.1; 4.3; 2 Pet. 2.13.	LXX Num. 11.8; Prov. 17.1; Wis. 7.2; 16.20.
pathos	'Strong desire':	'Deep interest':
	Rom. 1.26; Col. 3.5; 1 Thess. 4.5.	(other Hellenistic lit.)

Part 3

CHRISTIAN REFLECTIONS IN AN ACCOUNT OF AFFECTION

This part examines several theologians to offer something of a Christian moral psychology and its basis. They convey key directions in a tradition that is in conversation with itself across the millennia. The four mentioned in the chapter headings (Augustine, Aquinas, Coakley, and Chittister) will serve as banners under which to gather contributions from others. This endeavour suggests a thinkable, and eventually liveable, Christian account of moral psychology.

Chapter 6

AN AUGUSTINIAN SYNTHESIS

THE ORDERING OF DISORDER

We have seen that 'emotion' is a term largely conceived to describe some important feelings, but without inherent reference to morality (Chapter 1). From the perspective of philosophical ethics, we have also seen two approaches to morality and emotion that overtly split them asunder – Kant's, by marginalizing emotion from ethics; and Nietzsche's, by eliminating ethics from emotion (Chapter 2). Then followed (Chapter 3) some moral-psychological approaches to moral emotions, representing different strategies for making intelligible the moral emotions, but without (except for Brinkmann) offering much account of morality *per se*.

Our initial forays into a Christian response saw two biblical moods. A Christian account of desire within a pre-Christian Hebraic account of wisdom (Chapter 4) and within the NT's Hellenistic milieu (Chapter 5) instantiated some cognizance of the way what we would call emotional experiences can be threaded with implicitly moral evaluation. It remains, however, to show a more developed position along these lines. In the chapters following, we shall see two such positions, the first (Chapter 6) in the fourth-century Bishop of Hippo, Augustine, and the second (Chapter 7) in the twelfth-century Dominican, Thomas Aquinas. (More recent interlocutors follow in Chapters 8 and 9.)

Augustine's lively, discursive style of writing offers several summary cameos of his thought. This paragraph in the *City of God* (which occurs within a discussion of the passions, to which we will return) beautifully illustrates his general position on the relationship between ethics and emotion:

> We need not at present give a careful and copious exposition of the doctrine of Scripture, the sum of Christian knowledge, regarding these passions. It subjects the mind itself to God, that He may rule and aid it, and the passions, again, to the mind, to moderate and bridle them, and turn them to righteous uses. In our ethics, we do not so much inquire whether a pious soul is angry, as why he is angry; not whether he is sad, but what is the cause of his sadness; not whether he fears, but what he fears. For I am not aware that any right thinking person would find fault with anger at a wrongdoer which seeks his amendment, or with

sadness which intends relief to the suffering, or with fear lest one in danger be destroyed.[221]

Digging deeper, it will turn out that Augustine's account of the human person seeks to organize us around *love*, but using that term much more expansively than modern readers would expect. In this chapter, I will describe Augustine's logic of love, and its centrality to an account of ethics. The merit of attending to Augustine, I submit, will be in his capacity to integrate morality, emotion and sometimes action at a level that includes a telic dimension. That is, implicit to his account both of emotion and ethics, and of their interrelation, is also an account of human purpose. It is a theological account of humanity, since connected to God's own propensity to love (a theme that will be explored in more detail in Chapter 8). This theological account of human being claims, at least, to be more coherent and unified than the inductions arising from modern psychology's empiricism, and its attendant layers of evolutionary narration – and yet without eliding the human complexities that modern psychology observes. It follows that Augustine may be at least as able as modern thinkers to enable us everyday users of emotion to proceed through our complex and fragmented quotidian realities.

In this chapter, I will (I) overview the various senses of the logic of love, and (II) give a second overview of Augustine's theological and social context. A long section (III) then looks at how Augustine unpacks our affections at their best and worst. We go on to examine the tragedies he believes arises from their disorder (IV), with an excursus of sorts on his respect for the essential good of bodies and of desire (V). We see how he applies his heuristics of desire to the political and social domain (VI), looking then (VII) at how he regards the divine reordering of love to proceed. An analysis of various aspects of love (VIII) begins to give this portmanteau term more granularity. A summary in conclusion follows (IX).

I. Overview 1: The logic of love

Before proceeding to the details of Augustine's account, I will overview what I take to be the logic of love that arises from it. I use this phrase in two broad senses, each of which has, in turn, two complementary facets. I do not take what follows to be my own invention. Rather, it is my gloss on complementary themes within the history of Christian thought and practice.

The first broad sense arises from the relation between object and subject. Many and various objects reside before us in an overall moral field, and these have moral valence as human subjects respond to them in love. That is, a pluriform moral

---

221. Augustine, *The City of God Against the Pagans* (413–25; trans. R. W. Dyson; Cambridge: Cambridge University Press, *Cambridge Texts in the History of Political Thought* edn, 1998), p. 365 (IX.5). Dyson's translation of *City of God* is used throughout except where indicated.

field is replete with various goods, and love is a set of evaluative responses (such as desire, interest, care, concern, and attraction) to them. Hence love is the friend of moral knowledge.

Two facets of the logic of love, in its subject-object relation, assist moral knowledge. First: ontologically grounding our knowledge of what we perceive are the many telic and generic relationships before us. Things relate to each other in time and space, generically; and some things are ordered purposefully to other things, teleologically. We constantly parse these relationships according to conceptions of purpose that do not always arise obviously from empirical enquiry.[222] The intricate order of this field is the true substance of deliberative logic, and various goods intrinsic to this field elicit our love. Love responds to genera and *teloi* within the moral field (rather than springing *de novo* from humanity). Whether or not each good is existentially apprehended in love, each remains present as a good.

It is on this kind of basis that Christian theology can defend elements of moral intuitionism, and its related moral realism. Since love is a series of responses to a plethora of goods, it becomes appropriate to describe love as having its own logic. This is a logic that pertains to an already existing order, rather than being a logic of the lover's own making. The logic of love is, in this sense, a reference to love's basis in an order that precedes the lover's love of this order. We might summarize the objective and ontological basis of love by saying that *love has an ordinant logic.* It discerns and signals to us what matters more, and less.

But if moral order is ontologically prior to love, it follows that love is an existentially prior element in *deliberative* logic. Hence the second facet of the relationship between object and subject. Deliberative logic proceeds strongly in reference to what is loved, since love is among the first experiential moments of moral awareness.

Central to any deliberative moment or process are our various loves towards various goods before us. These loves are always present within us, even if covert, and are integral to our naming of various goods as good. In this sense, then, the logic of our deliberation is inescapably imbued with these loves. (It is on this kind of basis that Christian theology can reject, with Nietzsche, Kant's dichotomy of ethical deliberation from emotion. Thus, an Augustinian theological ethic takes deliberative logic to be subjective to a degree; it further asserts that *all* deliberative logic includes this subjective element, despite protestations, such as Kant's, to the contrary.) We might summarize this epistemological and subjective element of love by saying that *deliberative logic has its love(s)*, but noting now that the referent for 'logic' has changed. Whereas above the logic on view referred to an order within each moral field before us, now the logic on view pertains to our epistemic processes of deliberative discernment of this moral field. The process of

---

222. Readers familiar with Oliver O'Donovan will observe my indebtedness to him here and in what follows. See especially Oliver M. T. O'Donovan, *Resurrection and Moral Order: An Outline for Evangelical Ethics* (Leicester: Apollos, 1994).

this discovery is deeply coloured, tinged and touched by love – and it cannot be any other way, if love is indeed the response to the many goods of the moral field.

So much for the first broad sense of the logic of love, and its two facets. A loose kind of agreement, so far, might be parleyed with the psychologists mentioned in Chapter 3, for whom the natural order entails modes of congruence between reality and our moral-emotional responses to it. But the second broad sense of the logic of love arises, in the main, from the kind of knowledge theologians denote as 'revelation': those divine incursions into, and explanations of, human affairs that are unlikely to be deduced or anticipated, yet which bring intelligible sense to our condition. (The unlikeliness arises from epistemic blinkers that vary from person to person, group to group, and culture to culture; and also from aspects of God that can only be known as God unveils them.)

This second broad sense relies on a normative claim within revelation – that human love is not congruent to those goods that should rightly elicit our love; which is to say, human love is disordered. (Inherent to those norms are, in turn, assertions – revelations – about human purposes.) But the promise of the gospel includes a divine reordering, by the Spirit, of love. This second broad sense tells of *a logic, or grammar, of reordered love* in two complementary facets forming a theologic of grace and command.

Humans are somewhat helpless to reorder our own loves. But in a *logic of love poured in*, a work of divine reordering is adventitious. The Spirit's approach is, from our perspective, as variable and unpredictable as wind (cf. Jn 3.8). Even so, is possible to participate in this divine approach. Much as Nicodemus' only recourse was to listen and respond to Christ's unveiling of the salvation history that culminated in himself, so also may we attend to salvation history in its Scriptural record. To ponder, say, ancient theophanies, laws and prophecies, and then finally the person and work of Christ, highlights to us goods within the moral field that were previously veiled to us – hidden in plain sight by the misdirections of disordered love. The adventitious work of the Spirit is in concert with this revelation, to elicit love for goods towards which we were formerly indifferent (or worse).

This reordering is accessible to all because a constitutive element of divine reordering is an invitation (by command) for us to participate. This is a *logic of love commended*. The love that is commended to us includes the loving worship of God; the enjoyment of the neighbour and an embrace of their beauty; a thankful appreciation of the gifts of creation; and the curtailment or adjustment of loves (and behaviours) that are inimical to the proper love of persons and things. (A contemplative tradition in Christian practice – often building upon Augustine – will further elucidate our participation in terms of the purgation of false loves; then illumination concerning what really matters; and finally, forms of union with the good God.)

Both facets of this second broad sense are, obviously enough, the content of much traditional Christian theology and ethics. Their supernatural and theistic elements are precisely where those committed to a hard naturalism are dismissive. Perhaps more defensibly, modern moral psychology may simply not presume competence to counsel on this theological *ad extra*, since the sciences were never primarily about that. Whether this Christian schema for a moral psychology is satisfying will, perhaps, boil down to which body of thought offers the best account for our lives – and of course there may be instances of pleasing complementarity between them.

When a given logic of love is mentioned in what follows, context should make the relevant sense clear.

II. Overview 2: Augustine's context

A brief chronological perspective informing our discussion of Augustine will be useful since the intellectual developments of his long life are evident throughout his prodigious corpus.

Augustine's vocation shapes him, as the theoretician without responsibilities becomes the overseer with souls at stake. His discourse is shaped by his conflicts, with the late fourth-century threat from gnostic Manichean speculations giving way to the harsh moral imperatives of Julian and the Pelagians during Augustine's later years in the second and third decades of the fifth century. Scripture, increasingly regarded by him as normative, gradually supplants some habits of his philosophical heritage. After the self-confessed sexual obsession of his youth, the normal physical changes of ageing seem to cast different lights. His life spans epic geopolitical events, as the late Roman Empire moves inexorably from its Indian summer during Augustine's youth to the first of its death-throes in his old age. In the topic areas of interest to us, we can easily see a movement from preoccupation with the metaphysics of human essence, towards more experiential and pastoral emphases.

Peter Brown's biography[223] remains a work of major importance since it maps these changes in Augustine's thought. Our investigation will require the use of texts both early and late, and Brown's framework will largely be assumed.[224] Brown's revisions take into account over fifty major Augustinian documents (the Divjak letters and the Dolbeau sermons), all lost since the Middle Ages but rediscovered since Brown's first edition. These have caused Brown radically to revise his picture

223. Peter Brown, *Augustine of Hippo: A Biography* (London: Faber, 1967). An importantly updated edition is Peter Brown, *Augustine of Hippo: A Biography (A New Edition with an Epilogue)* (London: Faber, 2000). In the references to Brown that follow, the second pagination in brackets will refer to the new edition (except for those references where text unique to the new edition is on view).

224. Furthermore, to assist in placing the texts chronologically, Brown's dating will appear in brackets after the name of the text in its first citation. These are drawn from the chronological tables in Brown, *Augustine*, pp. 16, 74, 184, 282, 378 (pp. 3, 64, 178, 280, 380). But *circa* is always to be understood, given comments in Brown, *Augustine (new edn.)*, p. viii.

of a harsh older Augustine in decline. I will occasionally mention Brown's mature thought.

III. Unpacking the affections

It needs to be acknowledged that Augustine does not parse the operations of a person in the manner of modern moral psychology. Perhaps that should go without saying. But we shall see him use overarching concepts, especially love, that to the modern eye may seem to blur important distinctions such as, for example, in Valerie Tiberius's account, where a functionalist approach to the philosophy of mind discerns affective, conative and cognitive states or systems:

> Very roughly, affective mental states are feelings (e.g., emotions and moods), conative mental states are drives that propel us to action (e.g., goals and desires) and cognitive mental states are thoughts (e.g., beliefs, understanding and reasoning). Affective states tend to have associated bodily experiences and cognitive states tend to be ones over which we have more control, but these generalizations are not true of every state that counts as affective or cognitive. Moreover, affect, conation and cognition work together in many ways: how we feel can influence what we think and what our goals are, and what we plan to do can influence how we feel. [. . .] [I]t should be noted that we do not have exact definitions for these three kinds of states and the distinctions may not carve nature at its joints.[225]

Augustine does not have these terms-of-art at his disposal, and will tend especially to blend what the modern functionalist would denote as affective or conative; and sometimes the cognitive as well. This blending may tempt the psychologically astute modern reader to think Augustine's thought lacks precision – albeit, of course, that as Tiberius rightly notes, even these modern terms entail a judgment call. None is a straightforward empirical given, each having vague edges (in the philosophical sense of vagueness, where such a concept can refer substantively, yet with imprecision to the boundaries of its distinction).

a. The weight of the soul

As a starting point, we need to notice the striking way that love is for Augustine an essential constituent of being human. Love directs the soul, so that metaphorically speaking, the soul can be said to have 'weight'.

Augustine's statement regarding the importance of emotions, quoted at the start of the chapter, is clear enough. It parallels modern cognitive views (which,

---

225. Valerie Tiberius, *Moral Psychology: A Contemporary Introduction* (London: Taylor & Francis Group, 2014), p. 9.

we recall, understand emotions to be imbued with thoughts); and describes how Christian theology ('our ethics') is not against emotion *per se*. The statement occurs in a sprawling engagement with Stoics (and Platonists) within *City of God*, during which Augustine methodically distances himself from Stoicism as he understands it. Though significant in its own right, the statement builds towards something even more fundamental.

For Augustine, a broad consensus in ancient philosophy held that philosophy investigates the physical, the logical and the ethical (XI.25–28). If the universe comprises the physical, the logical and the ethical, then each person incarnates three personal correlates: being, knowledge and love. People exist, know and love; and these are the most properly basic attributes of humanity. 'In our present state, we believe that we possess these three things – being, knowledge and love – not on the testimony of others, but because we ourselves are aware of their presence, and because we discern them with our most truthful inner vision.'[226] Being, knowledge and love are properly basic to us, prior even to our awareness.

The point of interest here concerns Augustine's correlation of love with ethical existence. Ethics concerns a form of love. Humanity's deep care about right and wrong, and people's insistence upon various acts, signal a fundamental human capacity to love. Augustine does not mean that people necessarily love other people. Rather, each person simply has the capacity for delight, or love, directed towards various things. By love, Augustine has in mind a range of interested responses (including desire, care, concern, attraction, lust, etc.), and he will have much to say about the various things known and loved (or not loved). The primary point, though, is that ethics derives from this human given.

This claim might now seem to have reverted to a more sentimentalist or intuitionist account of morality. But that is not so: a cognitivist element is conferred when we learn that our subjective moments of love arise from something being known. Yet there is no knowing *without* love. *Our knowledge relationship to the world is irreducibly touched or imbued or tinged, with love.* That *deliberative logic has its love(s)* is true for all humanity, thinks Augustine.

His point anticipates something foundational to Brinkmann's argument (Chapter 3) wherein psychology needs to regard itself as fundamentally a moral science. Brinkmann appreciates the thought of mid-twentieth-century German Gestalt psychologist Wolfgang Köhler in this respect. 'At the bottom of all human activities are values, Köhler argued, the conviction that some things ought to be. It is part of our experience that we perceive these value qualities as immanent in objects and events.'[227] While the word 'values' here – *de rigeur* in modern moral discourse – is jejune in comparison to Augustine's love (see further Chapter 10), the point is similar: we are so constituted as to be drawn to what matters, even as existing and knowing are inalienable from the phenomenology of human life. (To be fair to Köhler and Brinkmann, their term of art has been forced by

---

226. Augustine, *City of God*, p. 488 (XI.28).
227. Brinkmann, *Psychology as a Moral Science*, p. 83.

interminable debate framed around facts versus values, a disjunctive conceit with which both profoundly disagree.)

Augustine's Greek heritage and Christian theology gives him even more to say: that this loving tends towards a proper *telos* not of our own choosing nor construction. Were humanity cattle, 'we should love the carnal and sensual life, and this would be our sufficient good'. Just as a stone is 'carried by its weight wherever it is carried,' so also 'the soul is carried by its love'.[228] (An odd image for moderns, the ancients meant by this weight 'a momentum by which each part of the universe sought out its place of rest, with the mute insistence of a homing pigeon seeking to regain its nest'.[229]) If each person's self was the proper gravity for this weight, then people would be blessed when their love terminated upon themselves, and all would be well. But such blessing is so often tried and found wanting that Augustine suspects the proper gravity of our love to have lain elsewhere all along. '[O]ur nature has God as the author of its being, [so] we must beyond doubt have Him as our teacher, that we may be truly wise; and Him also to bestow spiritual sweetness upon us, that we may be blessed indeed'.[230] This divine *telos* becomes the criterion for evaluating various loves (and here begins a key distinctive for a theological moral psychology, whatever its agreements with other accounts of psychology).

b. The soul as a rallying point

It is worth pausing to note an aspect of Augustine's understanding of the soul, which needs to be regarded as an emergently integrative condition (rather than as some ghost in a biological machine, Gilbert Ryle's caricature of Descartes' depiction of it).

Augustine's statement quoted at the start of the chapter[231] occurs in a strange context, worth bearing with for a moment. While attacking the worship of demons, he proceeds by sparring with the demonology of one Apuleius, a Platonist. The Apuleian demon functions as an *anthropological counterfactual*, indirectly showing what constitutes true humanity (which conception Augustine then uses in his attack of demon worship). In Apuleius' account, demons have a powerful ethereal body and a rational mind, but their mind is tossed upon a sea of passion, unbridled by virtue (cf. *City of God* VIII.14–17 and IX.3, 6). What constitutes the crucial difference between a demon and a human? The counterfactual point supplied by this demon is relatively straightforward. I give it here in two English quotations and in the Latin:

---

228. Augustine, *City of God*, p. 487 (XI.28).

229. Brown, *Augustine (new edn.)*, p. 512. Interestingly, Brown describes how this is the same 'weight' of 'glory' which God places into hearts (2 Cor. 4.7), making '*heavy people*, held on course, despite the high winds of the world, by the gathering momentum of a "gravity of love"'.

230. Augustine, *City of God*, p. 483 (XI.25).

231. See n 221, above.

Their minds, then, are tossed upon a sea, as Apuleius puts it; nor have they in any part of their souls the truth and virtue by which such turbulent and depraved passions might be repulsed.[232]

Their mind, as Apuleius says, is a sea tossed with tempest, having no rallying point of truth or virtue in their soul from which they can resist their turbulent and depraved emotions.[233]

[I]psius quoque mentis, ut iste appellauit, salu fluctuant, nec in ueritate atque uirtute, qua turbulentis et prauis affectionibus repugnatur, ex ulla animi parte consitunt.[234]

In contrast, humans *do* possess this rallying point. Human mind and soul *are* in league with the direction of *affectatio*.[235] The body is the locus of action for the soul's affections – but the unitive element between mind and body is the soul (elsewhere called 'the spouse' of the body.[236]) The storminess of (what we call) emotion, and the commitments of the mind, are recursive in their relation. This recursion takes place at the rallying point, the soul – which, we recall, has a weight of love. The soul brings together its mind and body, is directed in this by its loves, and action results.

In a masterful study,[237] William Babcock has shown that Augustine has a fundamentally integrated account of human being (which I believe is cameoed in Augustine's use of the demonic foil). Manichean accounts[238] presented errant

232. Augustine, *City of God*, p. 361 (IX.3).

233. Augustine, *The City of God* (413–25; trans. Marcus Dods; NPNF 1 series, Vol. II, including *On Christian Doctrine*; Grand Rapids, MI: Eerdmans, 1988), p. 167 (IX.3).

234. Augustine, *De Civitate Dei Contra Paganos* (ed. J. E. C. Welldon; 2 vols; London: SPCK, 1924), p. 373.

235. Dods' 'emotions' more likely picks up on the traditional English sense of 'turbulence' or 'commotion', rather than our modern value-neutral 'feeling'.

236. Augustine, *City of God* (XV.7).

237. William S. Babcock, 'Augustine and the Spirituality of Desire', *Augustinian Studies* 25 (1994), pp. 179–99, doi: 10.5840/augstudies1994259.

238. It is worth an extended note to clarify what is meant by 'Manichean', both in Augustine's initial discussion of it, and subsequently. Manicheism was an ancient gnostic sect originating with the third-century Persian Mani, or Manes, who taught that everything originated from one of two chief principles: light and darkness, or good and evil. Augustine's offhand comments in the *Confessions* remain a serviceable guide to its main claims. Evil, on the Manichean account, is a kind of 'substance, a shapeless, hideous mass, which might be solid [. . .] the Manichees called it earth, or fine and rarefied like air. This they imagine as a kind of evil mind filtering through the substance they call earth.' [Augustine, *Confessions* (401; trans. R. S. Pine-Coffin; Harmondsworth: Penguin, *Penguin Classics* edn, 1961), p. 104 (V.10); this translation also for quotes following.] Material existence comprises 'two masses of good and evil' (p. 106, V.11) that are antagonistic and infinite, 'the evil in a lesser and

human desires as a kind of occupation by an alien force, 'two souls within human beings, one good and a very particle of God, the other evil and an alien intrusion from the forces of darkness.'[239] Augustine's emphatic riposte was that for various reasons, we experience 'the soul's own pull against itself' as 'a disease from which it needs to be healed, not a foreign power from which it needs to be free.'[240] It may seem at first a too-subtle distinction between Augustine and the Manichees, or an irrelevant antiquarian dispute. However, his framing of our problem actually lays the groundwork for conceiving of us as an integrated whole, with hope for an integration of our desires towards the good. I cannot help but wonder, in passing, if modern naturalist accounts of human fragmentation, such as Haidt's conclusion (Chapter 3), echo ancient Manichaeism – but in the modern case, with evolutionarily ancient circuits performing the role of the alien intrusion, and with a concomitant resignation to endless moral fragmentation.

But that is perhaps to run ahead. For now, in sum, the soul unifies the weight of love and the actions of the body, and the soul is constrained by whatever is loved.

c. Stoic perversity

Another foil against whom Augustine develops his account are his contemporary Stoics who, as he sees them, sought to deny love as essential to the soul. (In this

the good in a greater degree' (p. 104, V.10). These materials also raged in conflict within each person, to the point that souls could themselves become materially and substantially corrupted (p. 135, VII.2). One antidote included a strict dietary regimen, since 'particles of the true and supreme God were supposed to be imprisoned in [. . .] fruit and could only be released by means of the stomach and teeth of one of the elect', who 'retch[ed] them up as he groaned in prayer' (p. 67, III.10).

In Augustine's subsequent writing, as in later theological usage, the term stands more generically for any radical dualism of good and evil, and for allied intellectual tendencies to decry aspects of material existence as inherently flawed, wrong, or bad, usually in an anthropological connection. Elsewhere, Augustine describes a 'manichean' anthropology: that 'man was formed by the prince of eternal darkness of a mixture of two natures which had ever existed – one good and the other evil.' [Augustine, *On Marriage and Concupiscence* (421; trans. Peter Holmes and Robert E. Wallis; NPNF 1 series, Vol. V, *Writings against the Pelagians*; Grand Rapids, MI: Eerdmans, 1987), 286 (II.9).]

Thus, descriptions of any bodily process as irremediably flawed or evil, and not open to any 'redemption' other than by eradication, would be regarded as 'manichean' in a theological anthropology. This broader derivative meaning will generally govern my usage. As with Pelagian and 'pelagian', the variation in case and the use of scare-quotes will refer respectively to the historic and the later generic usage (i.e., Manichean and 'manichean').

239. Babcock, 'Augustine and the Spirituality of Desire', p. 182.
240. Babcock, 'Augustine and the Spirituality of Desire', p. 192.

respect we might characterize them as antecedents to Kant.) Stoic views paralleled other ancient received wisdom, where a consensus held that 'the mind is master of all [emotional] disturbances, and, by withholding its consent from them and resisting them, exercises a reign of virtue.'[241] ('Disturb' functions here as a technical term, around which ancient discussions of passion or emotion were organized and conducted.[242]) An *apologia* for the Christian Scriptures follows straightforwardly. 'It subjects the mind itself to God, that He may rule and aid it, and the passions, again, to the mind, to moderate and bridle them, and turn them to righteous uses.'[243] The Scriptures do for the mind what the mind does for the body. This *apologia* only modifies the ancient consensus without upsetting it – until Augustine suddenly ambushes Stoicism on its attitude to compassion, which Augustine thinks Stoics exclude from the desideratum of a disturbance-free mind.

> The Stoics, indeed, are wont to reproach even compassion. But how much more honourable it would have been if the Stoic [. . .] had been disturbed by compassion for a fellow man [. . .] [W]hat is compassion but a kind of fellow feeling in our hearts for the misery of another which compels us to help him if we can? This impulse is the servant of right reason when compassion is displayed in such a way as to preserve righteousness, as when alms are distributed to the needy or forgiveness extended to the penitent. [. . .] [But] the Stoics are not ashamed to number [compassion] among the vices [. . .].[244]

For Augustine, the Stoic denies the soul's weight of love. By deploying strategies to eliminate disturbance, the Stoic curtails love, including what Augustine will later evaluate as proper love. (An amusing *ad hominem* describes a Stoic facing shipwreck. Though free from disturbance over the fate of fellow passengers, he remains highly disturbed. This Stoic could not, in fact, prevent his soul from loving *something*, his love in fact terminating upon his own most valuable self.) Augustine is opposed to this ancient denigration of disturbance, and elsewhere wrests disturbance away from philosophers into the realm of normalcy. One suspects he would trenchantly oppose Kant, and agree with Brinkmann: 'In our everyday lives we are much more certain of the correctness of the belief that we ought to try and save a drowning child, for example, than of any theory we can invoke to back that belief.'[245] Desire, joy, fear and grief are therefore not problematic but can be misdirected depending on what loves lie at their base:

> A righteous will, then, is a good love; and a perverted will is an evil love. Therefore, love striving to possess what it loves is desire; love possessing and

241. Augustine, *City of God*, p. 365 (IX.4).
242. Augustine comments upon the relevant lexical field at the start of *City of God*, IX.3.
243. Augustine, *City of God*, p. 365 (IX.5). For the full quotation, see n 221, above.
244. Augustine, *City of God*, pp. 365–66 (IX.5).
245. Brinkmann, *Psychology as a Moral Science*, p. 3.

enjoying what it loves is joy; love fleeing what it is adverse to is fear; and love undergoing such adversity when it occurs is grief. Accordingly, these feelings [pronominal: *ista*] are bad if the love is bad, and good if it is good.[246]

d. Will as love

We should also notice in this quotation his straightforward identification of love and will. Will is contingent upon what is loved and hated. Even a great ruler cannot be said to be free if 'they lay waste their own souls by their greater licence in wickedness'. A tyrant's subjects may be the more free, since 'the good man is free even if he is a slave, whereas the bad man is a slave even if he reigns: a slave, not to one man, but, what is worse, to as many masters as he has vices.'[247] This contention reflects both ancient wisdom and the teaching of Scripture (here, 2 Pet. 2.19, where 'people are slaves to whatever masters them'; cf. 1 Cor. 6.12.). As John Rist puts it:

> Augustine uses *voluntas* to signify a love that has been accepted or consented to, whether for good or ill. [. . .] If, then, we translate *voluntas* as 'will', we must be careful to identify 'will' as a term of art by which we indicate a conscious and determined application of love in some particular circumstance; we must not assume a faculty called the will which may or may not be 'free'. For Augustine, in the paradigm case, 'love' (*amor, caritas*) and 'will' (*voluntas*) are absolutely identical [. . .].[248]

'Augustine's *voluntas* thus signifies the whole person, the "I"'[249] – who cannot but also love. Other scholars parse Augustine's 'will' in along similar lines. It is 'the whole agent's total active relation to God and the world',[250] 'the integrating orientation of the very self [. . .] not distinguishable from reason and emotion because it is, as it were, the "subsistent relation" between every part of the integrated self, including reason and emotion.'[251]

'Will' is equally so in *Confessions*: 'I knew I had a will, as surely as I knew that there was life within me. When I chose to do something, or not to do it, I was quite

---

246. Augustine, *City of God*, p. 592 (XIV.7). In this quotation, 'good' and 'bad' rely upon a prior scriptural excursus, where the love of violence, money or 'the world' is contrasted to love for the Father.

247. Augustine, *City of God*, p. 147 (IV.3).

248. John M. Rist, *Augustine Deformed: Love, Sin and Freedom in the Western Moral Tradition* (Cambridge: Cambridge University Press, 2014), pp. 29–30.

249. Rist, *Augustine Deformed*, p. 31.

250. Charles T. Mathewes, 'Augustinian Anthropology', *Journal of Religious Ethics* 27.2 (1999), pp. 195–221 (207).

251. Gerald W. Schlabach, 'Augustine's Hermeneutic of Humility: An Alternative to Moral Imperialism and Moral Relativism', *Journal of Religious Ethics* 22 (1994), pp. 299–330 (305).

certain that it was my own self, and not some other person, who made this act of will.'[252] Of course Augustine knows well enough of the ambiguities, such as *akrasia*; indeed, trying to unravel this ambiguity is a large measure of his entire project. But that should not confuse, nor does he confuse, this straightforward starting point: 'will' simply describes that people are attracted to a good, choose it, and act. (I have adopted the slightly annoying convention of using quotation marks for 'will' when I use it in Augustine's sense of love's enaction. No quotation marks are used for the will in its modern connotations.)

Rist goes on to argue that this central insight in Augustine was misunderstood and distorted by centuries of philosophical speculation that effectively divorced love from will. It may even be that in this equation of love and 'will' Augustine has a substantive disagreement with modern functionalist moral psychology, if it overdraws distinctions between the conative, the affective and the cognitive.

e. Emotion, passion, affection

Augustine's disagreement with Stoicism demonstrates his thought about the integral nature of love within human being. But for moderns, not only is his discussion obscured by subsequent developments concerning the 'will' (and the will). We also learn more about Augustine's position by clarifying his use of terms that are translated as 'emotion', 'passion', and 'affection', in concert with his identification of love with 'will'. (This clarification partially vindicates Dixon's insights, noted in Chapter 1. To reprise Dixon's basic points: passion and affection were overthrown by the late modern term 'emotion', and it is mistaken only to speak of passion as moving us without reference also to how affections move us.[253]) Augustine counters Platonist rationalism by asserting that:

> [I]t is not only under the influence of the flesh that the soul experiences desire, fear, joy, and sorrow; it can also be disturbed by such emotions arising from within itself.[254]

> Unde etiam illis fatentibus non ex carne tantum adficitur anima, ut cupiat metuat, laetetur aegrescat, uerum etiam ex se ipsa his potest motibus agitari.[255]

Dyson's use of 'emotion' here for *motus* is hardly controversial. In traditional English usage, emotions are inner and outer stirrings or movements. Thus 'emotion' appropriately renders ancient disturbance; and Augustine uses *motus* and *perturbatio* synonymously in this connection. (Even if they were not

252. Augustine, *Confessions*, p. 136 (VII.3).
253. Dixon, 'Theology, Anti-Theology and Atheology', p. 303. On Augustine's use of these terms, see also the illuminating short study by Scrutton, 'Emotion in Augustine and Thomas', pp. 170–74.
254. Augustine, *City of God*, p. 590 (XIV.5).
255. Augustine, *De Civitate Dei Contra Paganos*, p. 90 (XIV.5).

synonymous for the philosophical schools, Augustine repeatedly brushes aside any distinctions.) The terms are value-neutral, but Augustine has more to say.

> What is important here is the quality of a person's will. For if the will is perverse, the emotions [*motus*] will be perverse; but if it is righteous, the emotions [pronoun] will not only be blameless but praiseworthy.[256]

Augustine begins to describe a *fundamental shift* in these motions – not an ontological change, but *a change in how they are regarded, depending upon the orientation of the 'will' (voluntas)*. He continues, 'The will is engaged in all of them; indeed, they are no more than acts of the will.' When moderns think Augustine only conceives of a coldly calculating will, we forget how *love* integrates human being: the soul that rallies mind and emotion is not neutral, but has a weight of love:

> For what is desire and joy but an act of the will in agreement with what we wish for? And what is fear and grief but an act of will in disagreement with what we do not wish for? When this agreement manifests itself as the pursuit of what we wish for, it is called desire; and when it manifests itself as enjoyment of what we wish for, it is joy. By the same token, when we disagree with something that we do not wish to happen, such an act of will is fear; but when we disagree with something which happens against our will, that act of will is grief.[257]

Augustine seeks to show that these motions cannot properly be understood apart from the ethical commitments, or better the loves, that govern them:

> And, universally, as man's will is attracted or repelled by the variety of things which are pursued or avoided, so it changes and turns into emotions [*adfectus*] of one kind or the other.[258]

> Et omnino pro uarietate rerum, quae adpetuntur adque fugiuntur, sicut adlicitur uel offenditur uoluntas hominis, ita in hos uel illos adfectus mutatur et uertitur.[259]

> And generally in respect of all that we seek or shun, as a man's will is attracted or repelled, so it is changed and turned into these different affections.[260]

Augustine is doing his utmost to signal a fundamental shift. *Something happens* when the 'will' incorporates these motions – they become our *affections*. Although Augustine is not particularly interested in the differences between various

---

256. Augustine, *City of God*, p. 590 (XIV.6).
257. Augustine, *City of God*, p. 590 (XIV.6).
258. Augustine, *City of God*, p. 590 (XIV.6).
259. Augustine, *De civ. Dei (ed. Welldon vol. II)* p. 90 (XIV.6).
260. Augustine, *City of God (tr. Dods)*, p. 266 (XIV.6).

motus, his distinction between *motus* and *adfectus* is highly important. Human disturbances become so completely fused within the loves of the soul as to become affections – instantiations of what is loved. These affections are then in turn the motions that help propel the 'will' – admixtures, somehow, of our primary love with the *motus* of our body. In the same way that being, thinking and loving comprise Augustine's essential basics of humanity, so also are these affections central to human being. Affections are 'ethico-emotional postures' in the most indivisible sense of that admittedly clumsy label.

Like moderns, Augustine struggles at the edge of language. But unlike moderns, he realizes that to denote these ethico-emotional postures as mere emotions (*motus*) is a significant loss. In using 'emotion' both for *motus* and *adfectus*, Dyson's late modern translation has missed a crucial turn, and Dixon's thesis shows why Dods' older translation is straightforward by comparison.[261] While it is not the case that Augustine makes a simple distinction between (good) affections and (bad) passions, it does seem to be the case that Augustine uses the language of

---

261. Indeed, there is further interesting affirmation of Dixon's idea. William James' epochal statement for modern 'emotion', published in 1884, is unlikely to have made much impact during the compilation of *A Latin Dictionary* (1896), where for entries under *adfectatio, adfectus, commotus, motus, passio, perturbatio* (and cognates), 'emotion' appears only once, under *motus*, and in the traditional sense we have already described [s.v. Charlton T. Lewis and C. Short, *A Latin Dictionary: Founded on the Andrew's Edition of Freund's Latin Dictionary* (Oxford: Clarendon, 1896), pp. 65–67, 383, 1168–69, 312, 359–60].

However less than thirty years later, Welldon's note on *De civ. Dei* IX.4 explains how *adfectiones uel adfectus* are 'words indistinguishable in meaning, so that [Augustine] uses *adfectiones* alone immediately afterwards.' That is reasonable, of course; but he continues that '[i]f it is necessary to translate both, some words like [. . .] "affects" may perhaps be coined as an equivalent of *adfectus*; but "emotions or motions" would probably be near enough.' [Augustine, *De civ. Dei (ed. Welldon vol. I)*, p. 374 n 2.]

Certainly, at IX.4 Augustine is himself content to loosely group *adfectiones uel adfectus* along with Greek *pathē* and Latin *perturbationes* and *passiones* under all 'those motions of the soul' (his *animi motibus*). This might seem completely to destroy our point made in reference to XIV.6, until it is remembered that in IX.4 Augustine is setting up the 'ancient consensus' we have already seen, from whose Stoic version he so radically differs. Thus, because this is the nature of Augustine's argument at IX.4, his use of *adfectiones uel adfectus* there neither confirms nor denies the point we are making about his use of it at XIV.6, at which point the argument has progressed far beyond the loose grouping of IX.4.

The main point is simply that the shift towards a late modern use of 'emotion' seems evident in Welldon's easy substitution. His 'probably [. . .] near enough' does *not* seem to derive from Augustine's reference to *animi motibus*; we are suggesting that it is 'probably near enough' because of the early twentieth century *loss* of what constitutes an 'affection' (which are now, for Welldon, merely 'affects').

affection (and passion) in a moral sense. The point is not to harangue Dyson over English lexical stock that is no fault of his, but simply that modern translations can confound us. Consider another example:

> Will, caution, gladness, then, are common to both good and evil men; and – to make the same point in different words – good and evil men alike feel desire, fear, and joy. But the good feel these emotions in a good way, and the bad feel them in a bad way, just as the will of men may be righteous or perverse.[262]

> Proinde uolent, cauent gaudent et boni et mali; adque ut eadem aliis uerbis enuntiemus, cupiunt timent laetantur et boni et mali; sed illi bene, isti male, sicut hominibus seu recta seu peruersa uoluntas est.[263]

Although desire and 'will', fear and caution, joy and gladness reside in all, the pivotal clause is the distributive *sed illi bene, isti male*, quite precisely conveying how these are directed towards comparatively different ends, depending on whether one is righteous or perverse. We might debate with Augustine over what constitutes righteousness or perversity, but the basic claim is framed with striking clarity: desire and 'will', fear and caution are fundamentally ethical.

However, the translator has thought it necessary to introduce 'emotions' and the threefold 'feel' for modern readers. Presumably, these psychological labels are intended as middle terms to make the thought intelligible. But the reverse might occur if moderns were to ask, against Augustine, 'How can an *emotion* be *felt* in a way either "good" or "bad"?' Once this question is put, Augustine's point is overthrown, and an opportunity lost for Augustine to subvert our own value-free conception of emotion through his own understanding that these same experiences are ethically bound, and that our loves are integral to them. Dods' version seems better (although the substitution of 'good' and 'bad' for 'righteous' and 'perverse' is perhaps a diminution):

> So that good and bad men alike will, are cautious, and contented; or, to say the same thing in other words, good and bad men alike desire, fear, rejoice, but the former in a good, the latter in a bad fashion, according as the will is right or wrong.[264]

A rigid semantic field is not being claimed for *adfectiones* in Augustine. A 'turbulent and disordered affection' (*turbulentis et prauis affectionibus*[265]) is synonymous with a passion. Sustaining the point that both are more than *motus* or emotion requires no rigid semantic distinction between affection as good, and passion as evil; Dixon's distinction along these lines applies conceptually in Augustine, but

---

262. Augustine, *City of God*, p. 596 (XIV.9).
263. Augustine, *De civ. Dei (ed. Welldon vol. II)*, p. 95 (XIV.9).
264. Augustine, *City of God (tr. Dods)*, p. 268 (XIV.8).
265. Augustine, *De civ. Dei (ed. Welldon vol. I)*, p. 373 (IX.3).

not semantically. The main point is that passion and affection are much more than *motus* because they pertain to *ethically related* disturbance.

Having seen Augustine's analytic basis for understanding the affections and their relation to knowledge and behaviour, we now turn to his account of the derangement of these affections. Passion and disordered affection reflect a disordering of love.

IV. The tragedy of disorder

The disordering of love consists in forms of voracity and 'selective sight', where plenitude becomes perceived as scarcity, and with some goods loved to the exclusion of others. I want in this long section to show how Augustine names the hegemonic claims of voracious, fixated love as 'concupiscence', using a variety of modes of rhetoric. We see him doing so in his *Confessions* and *City of God*, and in a different way through two anti-Pelagian treatises. These almost sermonic pieces show the implications for morality of disordered love, and the epic tragedy of how humanity nonetheless remains oriented to love, despite several modes of brokenness.

He shows how disordered love generates both pride and despair. Humanity's helpless bondage is finally revealed in the need of Christ's death for sin, but hope for reintegration arises once right responses to God and to the abundant moral field are secured by the pneumatological reorientation of love. His account engages both Manichean and Pelagian opponents, against whose opposing accounts of evil (as, respectively, *primordium* and dysfunction) Augustine forges his account of evil as the privation of good. We see his account unfold first within the *Confessions* and then in other works.

a. A melancholy plenty: The Confessions

People respond in love to myriad created goods, with varying degrees of intensity. Such love is disordered when some goods are loved to the exclusion of others – most notably God, who is the greatest good, with forms of disorder cascading down into absences of love for other significant goods. Absences and lacks such as these premise Augustine's account of evil.

The narrative structure of the *Confessions* states the problem poignantly. The background canvas is alive with earthy blessings: fertile ground, good food, sexual enjoyment. Layered onto this are a network of social goods: a loving family, good schooling, fine rhetoric, the bustle of a city, friends, and spouses. The impression is not that these revolve around Augustine in a life of ostentatious privilege. Rather, all the little human figures in the story move about on a massive, richly woven tapestry of riches, benefits, excellences, and goods. Yet a deep melancholy prevails, since no character can properly appropriate these goods. Certainly, they try. Augustine and his acquaintances seize so voraciously upon various of these goods, and so much to the exclusion of other excellences, that life is experienced by each character as a problem of scarcity.

An infant is 'pale with envy' at his sibling on the breast. He 'object[s] to a rival' finding life in this nourishment, 'when the milk flows in such abundance from its source'.[266] To object at the inclusion of infants, or to dismiss this behaviour as a natural drive, misses the point. Like us, Augustine tolerates such behaviours, knowing that children grow out of them. He also knows that he writes of this infant, and of his own infancy and childhood, from the perspective of adult voracity. But he can detect no point of turning, no dividing line, when people cross into voracity. It colours every human and all relationships.

He also sees clearly where his infant self was wronged by others in this. The straightforward benefits of learning were eclipsed by grammar schoolteachers who laughed while beating him. When the good of learning is used by these same teachers to deride play as an evil, they exhibit selective sight: not only is the good of education used to denigrate the good of play – these grown men fail to notice their own versions of play (called 'business'!). This selective sight is hypocritical. 'Was the master who beat me himself very different from me? If he were worsted by a colleague in some petty argument, he would be convulsed with anger and envy, much more so than I was when a playmate beat me at a game of ball.'[267] Even the educational process is marred by selective sight. The gods' ethical corruption is sidestepped in Greek literature studies. 'A man who has learnt the traditional rules of pronunciation, or teaches them to others, gives greater scandal if he breaks them by dropping the aitch from "human being" than if he [. . .] hates another human'.[268]

The boy Augustine cheats to win yet hates to be cheated and is angered when found out.[269] In this succinct collocation, externally viewed irrationality seems internally rational under voracity and selective sight. This observation forms the subject of his extended reflection on the theft of pears. '[O]f what I stole I already had plenty, and much better at that, and I had no wish to enjoy [them.] [. . .] We took away an enormous quantity of pears, not to eat them ourselves, but simply to throw them to the pigs.'[270] The scarcity of plenty, instantiated by enjoyment of theft and in grasping the forbidden, admits of another (selectively seen) love:

> This was friendship of a most unfriendly sort, bewitching my mind in an inexplicable way. For the sake of a laugh, a little sport, I was glad to do harm and anxious to damage another; and that without thought of profit for myself or

266. Augustine, *Confessions*, p. 28 (I.7).
267. Augustine, *Confessions*, p. 31 (I.9).
268. Augustine, *Confessions*, pp. 38, 39 (I.18).
269. Augustine, *Confessions*, p. 40 (I.19).
270. Augustine, *Confessions*, p. 47 (II.4).

retaliation for injuries received! And all because we are ashamed to hold back when others say 'Come on! Let's do it!'[271]

Friendship itself is not impugned; rather, the tragedy of this selective seeing is that friendship could have been had – was already had – without the theft. It cannot be overstated how emphatically Augustine defends every good in itself. They are not made suspect by voracity and selective sight. The pears 'had beauty, because they were created by you, the good God.'[272] Augustine had being, sensation, pleasure, memory, verbal skill, friends, and the innate ability for effective self-preservation. 'Should I not be grateful that so small a creature possessed such wonderful qualities? But they were all gifts from God [. . .] His gifts are good and the sum of them all is my own self.'[273] Augustine continues in thanks to God and in penitence for his ignorance of God at that time. Thus opens Book V: 'Accept my confessions, O Lord,'[274] and the more obtuse (modern?) reader realizes with a jolt that almost every section of every book has followed the same pattern. Augustine has continually erred, within this rich tapestry of plenty, by failing to see its plenitude and by responding with voracity to its perceived scarcity. The confession that closes almost every section thanks God for his bounteous modes of action at each time, offering repentance for never having seen it. These literal confessions form the grand substance of the work.

Renewal of perception after his conversion enables Augustine to see these isolated patches of so-called scarcity as the constituent elements of an entire moral field. The central paragraph of II.6[275] puts the point forcefully. A plethora of goods each have their rightful appeal: beauty, power, sexual love, scientific enquiry, simplicity, justice, inactivity, generosity, acquisitiveness, safety, and even grief. When held aloft to God, each finds in him their greater fulfilment and fuller exemplar. (Thus, to turn away from God as Augustine always did is an 'unchaste love.') Rather than some Platonic marginalizing of these goods against the invisible excellence of God, the reverse occurs: by deeply knowing the good Creator of these goods, the entire moral field can be accessed with a powerful sense of its completeness and abundance. Voracity is no longer always required. The way is open to a new kind of love: contentment. The logic parallels that of Christ, where to seek first God's kingdom makes 'all these things [to] be given to you as well' (Mt. 6.33; Lk. 12.31).

On this conception of the moral field, evil is 'the removal of good until finally no good remains.'[276] This deceptively simple conception is the outcome of Augustine's agonizing personal struggle with Manichean dualism, whose easy

271. Augustine, *Confessions*, p. 52 (II.9).
272. Augustine, *Confessions*, p. 49 (II.6).
273. Augustine, *Confessions*, p. 20 (I.20).
274. Augustine, *Confessions*, p. 91 (V.1).
275. Augustine, *Confessions*, pp. 49–50.
276. Augustine, *Confessions*, p. 63 (III.7).

account of evil held certain substances in the world to be intrinsically foul. Thus, in VII.12, an important statement on evil represents a breakthrough for Augustine. In his post-Manichean understanding, for something to be corrupt its goodness has simply drained away to the point where the object under scrutiny is finally deprived of existence itself (rather than leaving a residuum of evil substance). Gen. 1.31 ('indeed, it was very good') now makes deep sense for him: existence itself is always good, and this goodness is greater by the degree to which divine order is retained.

However, this kind of philosophical statement is no longer Augustine's method of choice, and he is bemused at the younger Augustine's *Beauty and Proportion*, a lost work that celebrated beauty in relation to an overall order. The *Confessions* has moved far beyond a neoplatonic fundamental kinship of all fine things (borrowing Nussbaum's phrase),[277] to the melancholy of disorder. The disorder is not intrinsic to the good creation but is a failure of misdirected human love. As Taylor puts it,

> This perversity can be described as a drive to make ourselves the centre of our world, to relate everything to ourselves, to dominate and possess the things which surround us. This is both cause and consequence of a kind of slavery, a condition in which we are in turn dominated, captured by our own obsessions and fascination with the sensible.[278]

Such was the theft of the pears: 'a greedy love', 'my own love of mischief [. . .]. The evil in me was foul, but I loved it. I loved my own perdition and my own faults, not the things for which I committed the wrong'.[279] In this Augustinian 'zone in which we live, of half-understanding and contrary desires, the will is as much the independent variable, determining what we can know, as it is the dependent one, shaped by what we see. The causality is circular and not linear.'[280]

b. A lost peace: City of God

The tragedy of disorder, written in *Confessions* from within one life, is writ large for human society in *City of God* where it takes sinister social forms. Again,

---

277. Martha C. Nussbaum, 'Augustine and Dante on the Ascent of Love', in *The Augustinian Tradition* (ed. Gareth B. Matthews; Berkeley, CA; London: University of California Press, 1999), pp. 61–90 (64).

278. Taylor, *Sources of the Self*, pp. 138–39.

279. Augustine, *Confessions*, p. 47 (II.4). Cf. ibid. 48 (II.5): 'The life we live on earth has its own attractions [. . .] because it has a certain beauty of its own in harmony with all the rest of this world's beauty. Friendship [. . .] is a delightful bond, uniting many souls in one. All these things and their like can be occasions of sin because, good though they are, they are of the lowest order of good, and if we are too much tempted by them we abandon those higher and better things, your truth, your law, and you yourself, O Lord our God.'

280. Taylor, *Sources of the Self*, p. 138.

evil is voracity, selective sight, and a turn towards nothingness;[281] and the social consequences are melancholic (XIX.5-8). Friendships are uncertain and prone to treachery. Families experience conflict. The judiciary indulges in torture. Communication with a pet is easier than crossing cultures: 'a man would more readily hold a conversation with his dog than with another man who is a foreigner.'[282] The best peace is a pretence, and warfare a necessity. So severe is this disorder that the ontology of a good universe, peopled with those who love all its varied goods, almost seems submerged. Instead, a series of vices and woes seem to rule as the final statement of reality. '[I]n the midst of the error and calamity with which human society is so full', even the consolations of friendship become 'perfidy, malice and wickedness'; '[t]he earth is full of this great mass of evils.'[283]

He amplifies the tragedy by juxtaposing a thick form of peace with the thin form that Roman society settles for and even celebrates. Instead of the calamity of 'this great mass of evils', there could have been peace in its thick form – 'that state of security where peace is most full and most certain.'[284] But among the calamity, there only remains a thin rump of it, a counterfactual: the emaciated residuum of the ordered tapestry of many goods. 'Here, in this world, we are said to be happy when we have such little peace as a good life can accord.' [285]

Such thin peace is eclipsed by the City of God's final peace (XIX.13), where balance and rightly ordered love bring concord and harmony between people. '[S]uch peace as there can be in mortal affairs' is had when *virtue* 'makes right use of the blessings of peace.'[286] That is, virtue is only virtuous when it is informed by and so directed towards the thick final peace. (This conclusion overturns another ancient debate, XIX.4. Virtue does not cause some inner peace of the rational soul to flourish. Ancient eudaimonism is a sham, since earthly life is so filled with woe. The very existence of the four classical virtues points to the ambiguity, vice, and decrepitude of life in the flesh. Classical eudaimonism 'begins to creak and crack before our eyes'[287] when Augustine argues that in the face of such woe, disturbance is entirely appropriate.)

281. Augustine, *City of God*, pp. 498–540 (XII) *passim*, especially 509 (XII.8); cf. also 461 (XI.9), 471 (XI.17), 477 (XI.22).

282. Augustine, *City of God*, p. 928 (XIX.7).

283. Augustine, *City of God*, pp. 929–30 (XIX.8).

284. Augustine, *City of God*, p. 932 (XIX.10).

285. Augustine, *City of God*, p. 932 (XIX.10).

286. Augustine, *City of God*, p. 932 (XIX.10).

287. Nicholas Wolterstorff, 'Suffering Love', in *Philosophy and the Christian Faith* (ed. Thomas V. Morris; Notre Dame, IN: University of Notre Dame Press, 1988), pp. 196–237 (205); cf. 232 n 9. This challenge to ancient eudaimonism represents a shift from Augustine's earlier philosophical arguments. *The Morals of the Catholic Church* offered a 'Christianized' account of the four classical virtues, with each subsumed under the 'greatest commandment' to love God, as a facet of it. This approach established a 'bridgehead' onto the eudaemonist grounds of classical philosophy, and prim object-lessons could follow. Prudence was 'love

The hard task is to live among the calamity while allowing that final peace to inform, shape and guide virtue. Such travellers recognize that peace as the soul's proper gravity, reshaping the soul's loves. Thus, they 'maintain their identity not by withdrawal, but by something far more difficult: by maintaining a firm and balanced perspective on the whole range of loves of which men are capable in their present state'.[288] This balance is not like the Aristotelian doctrine of the mean, but instead conceives of real enjoyment coming from an appreciation of the source of all loves. (Hence Augustine's ambivalence to pleasant sensory experiences: 'He made them all very good, but it is He who is my Good, not they'.[289]) Moreover, the balance understands the moral ordering of the present to be unveiled in part by the divine revelation of final peace.

c. A concupiscible helplessness: On the Spirit and the Letter

But such balance seems supremely difficult in the anti-Pelagian literature, where extreme human helplessness is brought to the fore. Without affective renaissance, free and unfettered commission of sin is a foregone conclusion:

> A man's free-will, indeed, avails for nothing except to sin, if he knows not the way of truth; and even after his duty and his proper aim shall begin to become known to him, unless he also takes delight in and feel a love for it, he neither does his duty, nor sets about it, nor lives rightly. Now, in order that such a course may engage our affections, God's 'love is shed abroad in our hearts', not through the free-will which arises from ourselves, but 'through the Holy Ghost, which is given to us'.[290]

Glib constructions of the will, and underestimates of disordered love, compel Augustine in the Pelagian controversy. A bad 'will' is like a ship's company stricken with plague (rather than the ship's captain going mad). Only the love of God as mediated by the Holy Spirit can overcome this affective deficiency.

Augustine understands this human need for psychological healing to explain St. Paul's ambivalence towards law. For Paul, divine law is supremely good, but it remains a subjective disaster for people who have not undergone pneumatological

---

distinguishing with sagacity between what hinders it and what helps it', and fortitude was 'love readily bearing all things'. But by *City of God*, XIX.4, prudence and fortitude are like canny, streetwise veterans who audit and enforce respectively, to prevent headlong rushes into evil.

288. Brown, *Augustine*, p. 325 (325).

289. Augustine, *Confessions*, p. 239 (X.34); cf. X.31–33. An aside in *City of God*, XI.25 also seeks to clarify this right enjoyment.

290. Augustine, *On the Spirit and the Letter* (412; trans. Peter Holmes and Robert E. Wallis; Writings against the Pelagians series, NPNF 1, Vol. V; Grand Rapids, MI: Eerdmans, 1987), pp. 84–85 (§5).

reorientation of the affections. This accounts for Pauline aphorisms such as 2 Cor. 3.6b, 'the letter kills, but the Spirit gives life' (and Rom. 7.7-11, which Augustine takes to be a fuller expression of the same thought[291]). Augustine appreciates Paul's use of the tenth commandment (against coveting) to highlight the affective disorder that the Holy Spirit must reorder:

> The apostle, indeed, purposely selected this general precept, in which he embraced everything, as if this were the voice of the law, prohibiting us from all sin, when he says, 'Thou shalt not covet;' for there is no sin committed except by evil concupiscence; so that the law which prohibits this is a good and praiseworthy law. But, when the Holy Ghost withholds His help, which inspires us with a good desire instead of this evil desire (in other words, diffuses love in our hearts), that law, however good in itself, only augments the evil desire by forbidding it.[292]

The conundrum of the pears remains. *Concupiscentia* appears in Augustine's writing to drive home the extremity of disordered love and the subject's helplessness to change. The term *concupiscentia* was little used classically but became a Christian technical term often denoting biblical *epithumia* (Chapter 5). Augustine used it broadly and interchangeably with *libido* (which is used classically). Strong sexual passion is a typical symptom, but concupiscence is not identical with sexual feeling, as when it is used of the soul's deep desire for wisdom. Concupiscence for wisdom is unambiguously good, but concupiscence is generally a sickness and a wound. It is not sin itself since it results from but is not identical with original sin.[293]

d. A christological hard point: On Nature and Grace

On Nature and Grace lifts Augustine's claim of human disorder beyond experience and phenomenology towards a theological domain. The treatise has the interesting structure of a three-cornered fight. The stern moralist Pelagius attacks justifications of moral irresponsibility that appeal to human nature. His attack is, as a theologian might say, quite 'pelagian': that since God created human nature as good, an evil nature cannot arise from it. Therefore, that which ought to be done can be done.

Unlike in his earlier and more philosophical works, Augustine's terms of reference in *On Nature and Grace* are conspicuously christological. Augustine agrees that moral irresponsibility cannot be excused by human nature. Even so,

---

291. Augustine, *On the Spirit and the Letter*, p. 85 (§6).

292. Augustine, *On the Spirit and the Letter*, p. 85 (§6).

293. Margaret R. Miles, *Augustine on the Body* (American Academy of Religion Series Number series, Vol. 31; Missoula: Scholars Press, 1979), p. 67; Gerald I. Bonner, 'Libido and Concupiscentia in St Augustine', in *Studia Patristica: Papers Presented to the Third International Conference on Patristic Studies (Oxford 1959)* (ed. Frank Leslie Cross, Vol. VI; Berlin: Akademie-Verlag, 1962), pp. 303–14, especially p. 305 and p. 308.

Pelagius' solution is christologically defective. In the first of two pivotal rebuttals, Augustine finds Pelagius' solution to ignore 'the righteousness that comes from God,' instead 'to establish their own', as in Rom. 10.2-3. Augustine takes the following verse (v. 4, that 'Christ is the end [*telos*] of the law') to mean that lawful obedience proceeds only from the grace of Christ. The second pivotal point against Pelagius concerns Christ's death. The absurdity of Christ's death 'for nothing' (Gal. 2.21) drives the rebuttal forward. Christ died to become sinful humanity's 'physician', thus 'human nature cannot by any means be justified and redeemed from God's most righteous wrath – in a word, from punishment – except by faith and the sacrament of the blood of Christ.'[294] In other words, the dire extremity of human disorder could be resolved by no other method than Christ's atonement. It, therefore, functions as an epistemic hard point to which any version of human nature and 'will' must interlock. 'Our whole discussion with [Pelagians] turns upon this, that we frustrate not the grace of God which is in Jesus Christ our Lord by a perverted assertion of nature.'[295]

On Nature and Grace must perforce investigate not only human nature, but also the manner of engagement between agencies divine and human, and in this treatise, pride (*superbia*), rather than *concupiscentia*, emerges as humanity's central problem.[296] The conundrum of one Psalmist becomes apposite:

> I said in my prosperity, 'I shall never be moved.'
> By your favour, O LORD, you had established me as a strong mountain;
> you hid your face; I was dismayed. (Ps. 30.6-7)

The whole Psalm is surprising, and pivots on the lines quoted. It seems shockingly non-sequential until we understand that the Psalmist's overconfidence, and the Lord's disapproval, began when the Psalmist forgot the source of his prosperity. For Augustine, this failure sums up the Pelagian account of divine agency in humanity. After God heals 'sick' humans, 'pride only has to be guarded against in things that are rightly done' and people must not 'attribute to their own power the

---

294. Augustine, *On Nature and Grace*, p. 122 (§2). Augustine offers no specific theory of the atonement here, but a comment elsewhere is clearly substitutionary, perhaps propitiatory: 'You had not yet forgiven me any of these sins in Christ nor, on his cross, had he dissolved the enmity which my sins had earned me in your sight.' (Augustine, *Confessions*, p. 102, V.9.) Cf. 'he was able to redeem us from sin by His own death, because He died, but He died for no sin of His own' (Augustine, *City of God*, p. 426, X.24).

295. Augustine, *On Nature and Grace*, p. 150 (§81).

296. For Augustine on *superbia* also see Miles, *Augustine on the Body*, p. 69, where she argues for a development in Augustine's understanding. Earlier literature accounted *concupiscentia* as the root of human sin, but in Augustine's mature account *superbia* displaces *concupiscentia* as sin's root cause. Also see Augustine, *City of God*, pp. 608–11 (XIV.13–14); and Augustine, *On the Spirit and the Letter*, pp. 131–35 (§§31–36).

gifts of God'.[297] So on Phil. 2.12-13 ('work out your own salvation with fear and trembling; for it is God who is at work in you, enabling you both to will and to work for his good pleasure'):

> Why, then, must it be with fear and trembling, and not rather with security, since God is working; except it be because there so quickly steals over our human soul, by reason of our will (without which we can do nothing well), the inclination to esteem simply as our own accomplishment whatever good we do; and so each one says in his prosperity: 'I shall never be moved?' (Ps. 30.6). Therefore, He who in His good pleasure had added strength to our beauty, turns away his face [. . .].[298]

Recalling our discussion above of 'will' as an expression of love: the affirmation of 'will' embedded in this warning makes clear that 'will' simply describes human power to act. Its operation is not the offence of *superbia*. The failure in *superbia* is more subtle: it is the failure to understand how *even human 'willing' is actually a form of response.*

Conversely (and perhaps paradoxically), when people fall into sin, they 'perish rather from the recklessness of despair, and not only neglect the remedy of repentance, but become the slaves of lusts'.[299] In this case, they misunderstand 'will' in an equal and opposite direction, failing to grasp that there *is* a capacity for response, a 'will'. This illusion brings a 'recklessness of despair', where the capacity of proper response is not lost, but somehow becomes hidden. Disordered love again rules through the 'will', but to self-destruction. (Here is an undeniable common ground with Nietzsche, deep in the heart of this anti-Pelagian treatise. He also saw the will surging namelessly beneath the oppressed *ressentiment* of the 'slaves'.)

Therefore, in addition to the problem of *concupiscentia*, both *superbia* and despair are equally sad disorders of human love. In the rising heat of anti-Pelagian battle, Augustine again hopes for *a right love*, and ordered affections. But that Christ must die for sin confirms the extremity of the problem. The epistemic hard point confirms that Augustine's account of human nature is no mere projection of his unhappy past.

Likewise, however, the incarnation and resurrection of Christ offers irresistible hope for the sufficiency of the solution that is mediated by the Spirit of God:

> Now all things are easy for love to effect, to which (and which alone) 'Christ's burden is light' [Mt. 11.30] – or rather, it is itself alone the burden which is light. 'And his commandments are not grievous' [1 Jn 5.3]; so that whoever finds them grievous must regard the inspired statement about their 'not being grievous' as

---

297. Augustine, *On Nature and Grace*, p. 131 (§31).
298. Augustine, *On Nature and Grace*, p. 132 (§31).
299. Augustine, *On Nature and Grace*, p. 135 (§40).

having been capable only of this meaning, that there may be a state of heart to which they are not burdensome, and he must pray for that disposition which he at present wants, so as to be able to fulfil all that is commanded him.[300]

Christ's death for sin, and the pneumatological reorientation of love, secure a rightful operation of the 'will' in response to God and his good universe. Augustine makes room for the rightful actions that Pelagius seeks to defend, but without room for *superbia* and with no cause for 'the recklessness of despair'.

V. On bodies

So far, we are seeing that in Augustine's moral psychology, desires cannot be abstracted from 'will' and hence from morality. But desires are felt in the body. A standard trope has become that Augustine inaugurated a hatred of the body, in turn perceived to arise from his commentary on sex. While we cannot pause for too long on this matter, it is important at least to clarify that this trope is essentially false.

The entire corpus states and restates the general principle that 'corruption of the body [. . .] was not the cause of the first sin, but [was] its punishment; nor was it corruptible flesh that made the soul sinful, but the sinful soul that made the flesh corruptible.'[301] That vices can range from the overtly bodily (like drunkenness) to those that seem less physical (like envy or hatred), implicates the soul rather than merely the body. (This anti-Manichean stance does become tricky in the later Pelagian dispute, when Augustine describes a fundamental 'change' in human nature.)

Augustine's view of the body-soul relation is never hard and fast. After a lightning tour of philosophical disputes in metaphysical anthropology, Augustine refuses to arbitrate and seems tired of such enquiry. 'This dispute is not easy to settle; or, if the proof is plain, the statement requires time. This is an expenditure of time and strength which we need not incur.'[302] Despite this shrug, he secures a high place for the body, and informs language of Greek dualism with the biblical account of a creature well-made as *imago dei*. The significant result here is that 'the chief good of man is not the chief good of the body; but what is the chief good either of both soul and body, or of the soul only, that is man's chief good.'[303] This statement is not the prevarication it may first seem. Augustine is asserting equivalence between the chief good of soul and of body. In Augustine, soul is

---

300. Augustine, *On Nature and Grace*, p. 151 (§83).

301. Augustine, *City of God*, p. 585 (XIV.3).

302. Augustine, *On the Morals of the Catholic Church* (388; trans. Richard Stothert; Writings against the Manichaeans and the Donatists series, NPNF 1, Vol. IV; Grand Rapids, MI: Eerdmans, 1989), p. 43 (§4).

303. Augustine, *On the Morals of the Catholic Church*, p. 43 (§4).

never far from body. Without the soul, the body would be as if anaesthetized. Soul is 'an entity whose activities underlie the being and behavior of the body in such a way as to make the difference between merely physical activity, and the conscious, animated, purposive behaviour characteristic of living human beings.'[304] His clear endorsement of bodily existence becomes more pronounced in *City of God*:

> There is no need, then, in the matter of our sins and vices, to do injustice to our Creator by accusing the nature of flesh, which, of its own kind and in its due place, is good. But it is not good for anyone to forsake the good Creator and to live according to a created good: whether according to the flesh, or the soul, or the whole man who, because he consists of both soul and flesh, can be signified by either 'soul' alone or 'flesh' alone.[305]

A christology of incarnation and atonement guarantees bodily goodness. In Christ, humanity has received 'a most merciful cleansing of mind, body and spirit alike.'[306]

> [T]he good and true Mediator showed that it is sin which is evil, and not the substance or nature of the flesh. He showed that a body of flesh and a human soul could be assumed and retained without sin, and laid aside at death, and changed into something better by resurrection.[307]

The incarnate Christ is seen to have experienced rightly ordered affection, and the disturbances he felt were his appropriate human responses 'to the infirmity of this present life.'[308] 'For human emotion was not feigned in him Who truly had the body of a man and the mind of a man. [. . .] Truly, He accepted these emotions into His human mind for the sake of His own assured purpose, and when he so willed.'[309] Again, Augustine's point is not based rigidly in semantics (although the subservient role of *motus* can again be detected in this discussion). The point is rather that God in Christ *instantiates* rightly ordered emotion. (This insight is further developed in Paul Gondreau's work, Chapter 8.)

The idea that body and soul can be mixed 'was deeply troubling both to classical (Stoic and Neoplatonic) and to dualist (Gnostic-Manichean) thought', describing 'an experience of contamination of the higher by the lower elements.'[310] Yet by *City of God* XV.7, Augustine can describe the body as 'spouse' of the soul. For Miles, Augustine has seen to the heart of Pauline uses of body (Greek *soma*) and

---

304. Gareth Matthews; cited in Miles, *Augustine on the Body*, pp. 14–15.
305. Augustine, *City of God*, pp. 588–89 (XIV.5).
306. Augustine, *City of God*, p. 432 (X.27).
307. Augustine, *City of God*, p. 426 (X.24).
308. Augustine, *City of God*, p. 366 (IX.5).
309. Augustine, *City of God*, p. 599 (XIV.9).
310. Miles, *Augustine on the Body*, p. 2.

flesh (Greek *sarx*).[311] Likewise, 'the Pauline description of the radical disjunction between *sarx* and *pneuma* [. . .] formulated for [Augustine] the central problem of human being, a "moral conflict within the human soul, not an encounter between opposing substances."'[312] That is, Augustine understands with St. Paul that the offence of 'flesh' is emphatically *not* that it is bodily. Flesh is body understood without reference to Spirit – which is to say, without reference to God. It is the body of disordered love.

Against this backdrop, it is not really the case that Augustine is somehow obsessed with and hostile to sexuality (as cherry-picked digests of quotation can be made to make him seem). The first reference to sexual lust in *City of God* only occurs in XIV.15 as one among many lusts typical of disordered affection. When Augustine thinks of sex, he immediately thinks of these other lusts.[313] This is the same territory as *Confessions*: the common denominator is, again, voracity. Beings who only perceive the scarcity of a fragmented moral field can be expected to react in this extreme manner. The desperation that people display from infancy for every other good is seamless with the desperation of some for sex. This seamlessness strikes him; and in his musings about the original fault in humanity, human conception after an orgasmic moment of intense desperation inaugurates, so he thinks, a continuum of voracity that appears in all people even from infancy. It is a just-so story that he pushed too far. But the more prevailing attitude in his corpus is that the soul is the spouse of the body; and 'what pertains more closely to a body than its sex?'[314] Not only is sexual concupiscence no major preoccupation for Augustine; we rather find that his high view of the body extends to a high view of sexual intercourse. The vision of sexual intercourse in paradise (XIV.26) instantiates the peace of XIV.10, describing a thankful, joyful, and honest love that the pair always experience – and with no hint that it is not deeply, and bodily, pleasurable. This kind of sex is highly regarded by Augustine, and pleasure itself, either sexual or otherwise, is never an offence.[315]

In this respect, the point of marriage is to bring a peaceful order where those goods can be enjoyed. Marriage is one shelter (and celibacy the other) where peace begins to be found. In 'the restraint of the marriage alliance, contracted for the

---

311. Miles, *Augustine on the Body*, p. 132, n 11 (following J. A. T. Robinson).

312. Miles, *Augustine on the Body*, pp. 24–25 (quoting W. A. Schumacher).

313. Cf. Augustine, *Marriage and Concupiscence*, p. 272 (I.20), where sexual lust is just a species of the more generic 'lusts' of 1 Jn 2.15–17.

314. Augustine, *City of God*, p. 195 (V.7).

315. This high view of sex is reiterated elsewhere, for example, Augustine, *On the Good of Marriage* (401; trans. C. L. Cornish; On the Holy Trinity; Doctrinal Treatises; Moral Treatises series, NPNF 1, Vol. III; Grand Rapids, MI: Eerdmans, 1988), p. 407 (§18), where 'carnal delight' 'cannot be lust' when 'used' rightly; and Augustine, *Marriage and Concupiscence*, p. 291 (II.22), where 'pleasure can be [. . .] honourable'.

purpose of having children',[316] children can be a welcome fruit. Disordered desire is stilled, ceasing to range over all humankind, so that one other person becomes the grateful and constant locus of desire, rather than the pitiful love triangles so vividly portrayed in Augustine's own past.

Thus, the generic categorization of sexual concupiscence alongside more general lusts is not fanciful, and the travails it can bring are no less severe than those brought by any other lust. This is the backdrop against which Augustine longs with Paul for redemption of the body (Rom. 7.24) in the kingdom of heaven, 'where there shall be not only no guilt for sin, but no concupiscence to excite it'.[317]

'The nature of the original fault had, for Augustine, nothing essentially to do with the creation of the body'[318] because 'Augustine had come to a firmly-rooted idea of the essential goodness of created things'.[319] In the arena of sexuality, Paul Ramsey's study shows this conviction actually to be the *distinguishing* feature of Augustine.[320] Brown also defends Augustine unequivocally in this respect. Despite Augustine's idiosyncrasies, 'the pace of his thought on sexuality was set by firm if courteous disagreement with other Christians and upholders of radical ascetic ideals, most notably with Jerome.' Against such contemporaries, Augustine's is 'a call to moderation'.[321] Brown's powerful comments on the anti-Pelagian works describe a realization that this harsh literature was actually triggered by Augustine's earlier venture into uncharted territory:

> He had come to envision, in a manner far more consequential than many of his Christian contemporaries, Adam and Eve as fully sexual beings, capable of [. . .] a glorious intercourse, unriven by conflicting desires, without the shadow of sin upon it. [. . .] [T]wo fully physical bodies follow[ing] the stirrings of their souls, 'all in a wondrous pitch of perfect peace'.[322]

For married and other sexually involved people now, any regrets are to be had against *this* vision. Indeed, Brown is hotly polemical towards the 'egregious cultural narcissism' that blames Augustine for all manner of Western sexual discontents,[323]

---

316. Augustine, *Confessions*, p. 72 (IV.2).

317. Augustine, *On the Spirit and the Letter*, p. 279 (I.38).

318. Miles, *Augustine on the Body*, p. 67.

319. Brown, *Augustine*, p. 325.

320. Cf. Augustine, *City of God*, pp. 628–30 (XIV.26) for his account of sexual intercourse in paradise; and cf. Paul Ramsey, 'Human Sexuality in the History of Redemption', *Journal of Religious Ethics* 16.1 (1988), pp. 56–86 (62).

321. Brown, *Augustine (new edn.)*, p. 500.

322. Brown, *Augustine (new edn.)*, p. 501, citing one of the recently discovered letters (Divjak 6*).

323. Brown, *Augustine (new edn.)*, p. 502.

even branding one scholarly treatment in this vein 'a travesty'.[324] Augustine's main concerns actually lay elsewhere than sex: in our lusts for mastery.[325]

VI. A social judgment on the will to power

For Augustine, love recognizes a preciousness intrinsically *there* (thanks to God), rather than creating demand through voracity. Such an account offers a basis for justice and a common life,[326] and in so doing, critiques what would become in Nietzsche the valorization of a will to power that glorifies emotion and action at the expense of ethics.

As we have seen, Augustine accepts that people have 'will', and its various powers. He even anticipates Nietzsche's diagnosis of our will to power by seeing how love expressed as 'will' constitutes much of who we are and what we do. But we have also seen Augustine diagnose as a problem the way love and 'will' conflate to become hungry and then hegemonic. Manifold voracious obsessions are our tragic plight.[327] The epic melancholic refrain in *City of God* is of a humanity persistently missing what could be, because of relentless and hegemonic strivings of power.

The two cities correlate respectively with humility and pride, and the earthly city 'when it seeks mastery, is itself mastered by the lust for mastery even though all the nations serve it'.[328] 'This "lust for mastery" disturbs and consumes the human race with great ills'.[329] The minor-key melodies that follow are too numerous to list, but special attention might be paid to Books III and IV, where Augustine repeatedly observes all the goods that were destroyed in the bloody, lordly establishment of *Pax Romana*.[330] Likewise, the melancholic first half of Book XIX treats the quest for peace by various forms of mastery, but these are regarded as a pale shadow of true peace.

When Bonner enumerates Augustine's many references to various lusts, he also finds the predominant concupiscence to be the domination of others by the exercise of power. Sex was always a secondary topic of discussion – as we have already seen, the first clear reference to sex in *City of God* is only at XIV.15 (and in the later Pelagian disputes, generally only when forced upon him). Bonner suggests that the later Christian emphasis on sexual concupiscence, though having

---

324. Brown, *Augustine (new edn.)*, p. 518, n 69.

325. I credit my doctoral supervisor, the Rev'd Professor Michael Banner, with first illuminating to me this 'centre of gravity' in Augustine's treatment of concupiscence.

326. Cf. Augustine, *City of God*, p. XIX.21.

327. Cf. Augustine, *City of God*, pp. 613–14 (XIV.15, final paragraph).

328. Augustine, *City of God*, p. 3 (I, preface).

329. Augustine, *City of God*, p. 111 (III.14).

330. See especially I.31, 33; III.10, 13–14; and a summary statement at IV.3. Similar reflections are found at V.17, 19, 22, but this time to consider God's supervening sovereignty.

a clear basis in Augustine, developed once the apologetic intention of *City of God* was eclipsed in the post-Constantinian empire. It was in the interests of empire to supplant, as it were, Augustine's attack on the lust for power, through adroit use of his writings on sexual morality.[331]

VII. Twin logics of love reordered

It remains to be seen how Augustine understands love to become reordered. This section outlines a logic of 'love poured in', with God's embrace reordering human loves. This pouring in is not ours to control; yet, participation is accessible in a logic of love commended, stretching our horizons and mitigating our voracious selective sight. Augustine's project reflects Christ's treasures of the heart (Mt. 12.34; Lk. 13.34).

For Augustine, 'otherness' (in Charles Mathewes's phrase) is already at the base of the self;[332] more specifically, 'at the core of the self is an other, God.'[333] As Augustine puts it, by God's 'incorporeal embrace alone' the soul is 'filled up and impregnated with true virtues.'[334] Yet in agreement with Christ, each person is invited (by command) actively to participate in the reorientation of love, through the two great commandments (Mt. 22.37). The connection between ethics and worship is constituted in an attention to love. It connotes both worship of God and enjoyment of neighbour, while ruling out a set of postures and behaviours towards these other persons. These commandments are a form of participation in what is already immanent, and in God's own agency, and is reminiscent of the cooperative dual-agency on view, for example, in Mt. 7.7, Rom. 8.13, or Phil. 2.13. Indeed, that last verse listed inspires Augustine to conclude that the 'great work' of a repentant life 'no doubt' 'belongs to human agency to accomplish, yet it is also a divine gift.'[335]

The nature of this assistance is *not* mere instruction 'in the knowledge of what he ought to avoid and to desire in his actions'. On this Pelagian account, free 'will' is simply tutored to give a 'just and pious course of life' that 'deserves to attain to the blessedness of eternal life.'[336] Augustine certainly respects the tutoring power of divine teaching, but he also insists that the Spirit works within us, beyond our reach. The next two subsections examine each facet of this twin logic.

331. Bonner, 'Libido and Concupiscentia', pp. 312–14.

332. Mathewes, 'Augustinian Anthropology', p. 214.

333. Mathewes, 'Augustinian Anthropology', p. 216.

334. Augustine, *City of God*, 395 (X.3). Similar declarations are found *passim*, e.g., 399 (X.6); 419 (X.17).

335. Augustine, *On the Spirit and the Letter*, p. 84 (§2).

336. Augustine, *On the Spirit and the Letter*, p. 84 (§4).

a. The logic of love poured in

> [W]e are assisted by divine aid towards the achievement of righteousness, –
> not merely because God has given us a law full of good and holy precepts, but
> because our very will, without which we cannot do any good thing, is assisted
> and elevated by the importation of the Spirit of grace [. . .].[337]

Although freedom of 'will' and divine teaching are goods, Pelagians have not
grasped that affections truly *cannot* be commanded. The work of the Spirit is
radically to do with affective reorientation:

> [By the Spirit] there is formed in [a person's] mind a delight in, and a love of,
> that supreme and unchangeable good which is God, even now while he is still
> 'walking by faith' and not yet 'by sight;' in order that [. . .] he may conceive an
> ardent desire to cleave to his Maker, and may burn to enter upon the participation
> in that true light, that it may go well with him from Him to whom he owes his
> existence.[338]

By alluding to 2 Cor. 5.7 (which distinguishes the operation of faith from the
operation of sight), Augustine acknowledges that delight and desire are not at first
without ambiguity and trial, sure though their object may be.[339] Augustine finally
depends upon Rom. 5.5, where the love of God is 'poured into our hearts' by the
Spirit, taking this gift as the key element in divine reordering of human beings. The
Spirit pours a love for God into the human heart. The verse and his reading of it is
fundamental to Augustine's account of the how God changes the 'will', appearing
in this usage throughout his writings.[340] An inconvenient exegetical point may
challenge Augustine's reading of the verse, undercutting his theology of love's
reordering.[341] However a meditation on Ps. 36 in *On the Spirit and the Letter* is one
of many texts that avert the problem. Augustine celebrates God as the prevenient,
proactive lover and preserver of humanity, and this love is the locus and glory
of God's grace. A string of metaphors, including feasting at God's banquet and

---

337. Augustine, *On the Spirit and the Letter*, p. 91 (§20).

338. Augustine, *On the Spirit and the Letter*, p. 84 (§5).

339. Cf. Augustine, *Spirit and Letter*, p. 112 (§64).

340. For example, *Commentary on Psalms*, 87.1; *On Nature and Grace*, §67, §84;
Homilies on 1 John, VI.8–10; VII.6; VIII.12.

341. For example, C. E. B. Cranfield, *A Critical and Exegetical Commentary on the Epistle
to the Romans (I-VIII)* (Vol. 1; 2 vols; Edinburgh: T&T Clark, 1975), p. 262 and n 2. When
the genitive construction in 'the love of God' is taken as grammatically 'objective', human
love towards God is made the referent, as in Augustine's reading. But Cranfield finds this
reading hard to defend, since the main point is to give assurance of hope despite tribulation,
premised on God's love for humans, and irrespective of our subjective awareness of it.
Therefore, the majority reading is of a 'subjective' genitive, with God's own love towards
people on view.

drinking at his fountain, picture people in response. These metaphors of God's extravagant love poured in are the conceptual substrate for Augustine's reading of Rom. 5.5. The verse functions as a slogan for what can be easily derived from elsewhere in the Bible, where the Spirit originates human love towards both God and humans.[342]

b. The logic of love commended

Augustine's hope of the Spirit reordering turbulent affections towards the love of God, releasing people from voracity and selective sight, opens up a tricky pastoral gap for those who have not yet experienced this reordering. It all seems a bit chancy.

Augustine begins to close this gap by speaking of a 'flight' to God: a movement of dependence and humility, spoken in prayer.[343] Augustine does not wish this flight to be misunderstood in particularly difficult or inaccessible categories. The *Confessions* show it worked out in one man's life, and although there is mystery there (the unconverted Augustine's unawareness that God was at work), the architectonics of the work suggest that whoever takes and reads the *Confessions* can easily do as Augustine did, praying as he prays. Likewise, Brown refers to a Dolbeau sermon delivered in Carthage near the time of Augustine's arrival. Vividly drawing upon the experience of the stadium, he reminds the (apparently young male) listeners of what comes over them there. Simply by watching their friends, and attending to the action, a deep love for the sportsmen and the sport grows. Though mysterious, this participation with another is quite accessible.[344]

Hence despite the logic of love poured in, there is no embarrassment to commend love; and love can be commended in this way on the understanding that the mysterious changes are themselves divinely gifted. By enjoining his hearers to engage in love for God and for others, Augustine understands people simply to be finding the correct response to the reality already before them.

The homilies on John's first epistle work and rework this principle in a variety of ways, since the epistle commends love so 'ardently'.[345] 'It is by charity that other things come to be rightly loved; then how must itself be loved!'[346] If our life in the

---

342. For example, Rom. 15.30; Gal. 5.22; Col. 1.8; or 2 Tim. 1.7. Interestingly, on Rom. 15.30 Cranfield can argue here *against* a subjective genitive (the Spirit's love towards humanity), and for a genitive of origin. C. E. B. Cranfield, *A Critical and Exegetical Commentary on the Epistle to the Romans (IX–XVI)* (Vol. 2; 2 vols; Edinburgh: T&T Clark, 1979), p. 776 and n 2.

343. Augustine, *On the Spirit and the Letter*, pp. 105–06 (§51).

344. Brown, *Augustine (new edn.)*, pp. 448–49.

345. Augustine, *Homilies on the First Epistle of John* (416; trans. H. Browne; Homilies on the Gospel of John; Homilies on the First Epistle of John; Soliloquies series, NPNF 1, Vol. VII; Grand Rapids, MI: Eerdmans, 1986), p. 513 (VIII.14).

346. Augustine, *Homilies on 1 John*, p. 501 (VII.1).

world is like a desert wandering, then love 'is the fountain which God has been pleased to place here' to sustain our sojourn.[347]

O'Donovan finds 1 Jn 4.8 ('Whoever does not love does not know God, for God is love') prolifically quoted throughout Augustine's corpus,[348] and the homily majors upon it. 'God is love'; therefore, love 'is God'. The linguistics may be flawed,[349] but Augustine knows the difference between an abstract noun and a personal Trinitarian God,[350] while at the same time making a profound claim about the indivisible simplicity of God and God's attributes. The equivalence graphically expresses God's most striking affection. Thus 'to act against love is to act against God'[351] – and by extension, against the proper ordering of his world.

The outcomes that follow are too numerous to list or examine here. Polemic against loveless religious counterfeits gives way to a conception of rightful, loving worship. The biblical witness of Christ's crucifixion (and incarnation) confirms God's loving nature; thus, to be cavalier about love is to scorn not only God's essence, but its foremost historical expression. Pride extinguishes love, humility strengthens it, and certain communal behaviours emerge. Voracious false loves are to be resisted, but the intrinsic goodness of creation is reaffirmed.

An intriguing metaphor, picturing the neck of a skin sack being stretched,[352] equates to what we would call the stretching of our horizons. When people apply themselves to John's exhortations, the ordered moral field – the integrity of which is grounded in the God who is love – begins to open before them. Old loves change, and new loves grow. An analysis by O'Donovan further teases out the responses of love to the horizons of the moral field.[353]

VIII. Aspects of love

I have shown Augustine's twin logics of the divine reordering of love. However, I have not yet developed the other sense of the logic of love, where *love has an ordinant logic* and *deliberative logic has its love(s)*. To do so, I use Oliver O'Donovan's early analytic presentation of Augustinian love as a series of 'aspects'. These aspects constitute the love towards which God reorders people. When love is divinely reordered, the lover loves according to each of these aspects.

---

347. Augustine, *Homilies on 1 John*, p. 501 (VII.1).

348. Oliver M. T. O'Donovan, *The Problem of Self-Love in St Augustine* (New Haven, CT: Yale University Press, 1980), p. 11.

349. Some argue here for the applicability of 'Colwell's rule' in the Greek, which governs articular subjects and anarthrous predicates in the nominative case; although the matter is contested.

350. Augustine, *Homilies on 1 John*, p. 503 (VII.6).

351. Augustine, *Homilies on 1 John*, p. 503 (VII.5).

352. Augustine, *Homilies on 1 John*, p. 485 (IV.6).

353. O'Donovan, *The Problem of Self-Love in St Augustine*, pp. 18–35.

Augustine uses three important words (*dilectio, caritas, amor*) sometimes synonymously, and sometimes not. Thus simplistic lexicographical approaches that 'label certain motifs by the Latin or Greek words which [modern thinkers] think encapsulate them' are of no assistance for understanding Augustine's love.[354] *Dilectio* and *amor* are used indifferently, often for stylistic variation; Augustine notices good and bad senses for them in Scripture.[355] *Caritas* translates the *agapē* of 1 Jn 4.8, and never denotes the inordinate desire for worldly things, while *cupiditas* generally always does.[356] Rather, to notice Augustine's aspects of love is to discriminate among love's various responses to the complex order of the moral field, since 'the loving subject stands in a complex and variable relation to the reality which his love confronts.'[357]

Two such aspects follow the classical tradition. In *cosmic love*, the subject is drawn by her *telos* to the love of God. In *positive love*, the subject self-directs towards some end she has chosen for her happiness. The later Augustine considers his earlier sole reliance upon these two aspects of love as a misstep, not least because it generated the ill-advised *uti-frui* distinction, in which persons can all too easily be used merely as means to the good end of loving God.

So, two further aspects represent 'intermediate possibilities which became increasingly important to Augustine as he continued his search for an "ordered" love where the subject was neither victim nor master.'[358] In *rational love*, the subject recognizes, in appreciation and approval, a teleology and order which she has not herself imposed.[359] (The adjective 'rational' becomes unhelpful in our context. But I think O'Donovan has in mind the kind of love I felt in my garden when I stared in awestruck wonder at new buds, just doing their own thing as other buds like them had done for millennia, without any reference to my little human plans and purposes.) Love of lesser goods becomes appropriate, as long they do not displace God. The language of 'use' takes on a new connotation. Loving someone for God now includes seeking their welfare for their sake; loving for God is a way of correctly appraising them, without seeking to dethrone God.

Alongside is *benevolent love*, where 'the subject, having recognized the objective order of things, may freely affirm it, thus giving the weight of his agency to support an order which he did not devise.'[360] It is possible only between creature and creature; it is concerned with an order independent of the subject; and the lover and the beloved are separate. This love is for people's own sake – not as a counterpoint to God's sake, but in denial of any personal advantage to the lover. In

354. O'Donovan, *The Problem of Self-Love in St Augustine*, p. 10.

355. O'Donovan cites *City of God*, XIV.7 and *Homilies on 1 John*, VIII.5.

356. O'Donovan, *The Problem of Self-Love in St Augustine*, pp. 10–11.

357. O'Donovan, *The Problem of Self-Love in St Augustine*, pp. 12–13.

358. O'Donovan, *The Problem of Self-Love in St Augustine*, p. 18.

359. O'Donovan, *The Problem of Self-Love in St Augustine*, pp. 18, 31.

360. O'Donovan, *The Problem of Self-Love in St Augustine*, p. 18.

benevolent love, we acknowledge that others have a destiny given by God, whether or not our own agency is called upon to assist fulfilment of that destiny.[361]

The mature Augustine constantly moves between these four aspects of love:

> The choice of means to ends, the admiration of the neighbor's goodness, the pursuit of the neighbour's true welfare, all these are the subjective aspects of a single movement of the soul which reflects the one dominant cosmic movement, the return of the created being to its source and supreme good.[362]

This approach does justice to Christ's two-fold love-command; and 'virtue is the conformity of love to the structure of reality.'[363] Regard for the other, whether divine or human, certainly accrues benefit to the self – but simply and only in virtue of the self's proper engagement with a good reality.

Augustine upholds the logic of love, then, in a highly nuanced form. That *love has an ordinant logic* and *deliberative logic has its love(s)* can be further understood in terms of these aspects that O'Donovan has described. Augustine said that 'the soul is carried by its loves'.[364] Looking to the source of Augustine's whole project, we recall Christ's 'where your treasure is, there your heart will be also' (Mt. 6.21, Lk. 13.34).[365] The language is different, but Augustine's thought plausibly interprets it if treasure is any object of the affections, and heart the seat of 'will'. ('[I]n man's heart are his spiritual hands'.[366])

We are in a position, now, to comprehend Augustine's most popular aphorism, 'Love and do what you will',[367] which has become a well-worn summary of his ethic and is often used to sanction tradition-naïve agendas of ethical improvisation.[368] Augustine intended the aphorism to describe how action between people must be ordered by love, understood in its aspects. But the aphorism is seriously misused if used apart from Augustine's logic of love, a logic where the command of God plays a key role in the reordering of love, since the love of many specific goods is commended to us by God's command.

IX. Conclusion

Augustine approaches ethics and emotion by way of a logic of love. Love is fundamental to our knowledge and behaviour, but love is disordered by voracity

---

361. O'Donovan, *The Problem of Self-Love in St Augustine*, p. 34.

362. O'Donovan, *The Problem of Self-Love in St Augustine*, pp. 35–36.

363. O'Donovan, *Resurrection and Moral Order*, p. 47.

364. Augustine, *City of God*, p. 487 (XI.28).

365. Cf. also Mt. 13.44–46 and 19.21, where a change of 'treasure' drives radically new action.

366. Augustine, *On Nature and Grace*, p. 151 (§83).

367. Augustine, *Homilies on 1 John* (VII.8, on 1 Jn 4.4–12).

368. Cf. O'Donovan, *Resurrection and Moral Order*, p. 47.

and selective sight. However, this conception of disorder does not constitute a hatred of the body or of bodily life – indeed, love for human others is integral to Augustine's account of love for God. Reordered love is a divine gift, formed in part by our 'willing' participation in the divinely ordered moral field. Reordered love diffracts into a series of aspects that give granularity to our descriptions of the objects of love.

Aquinas attempted to complete Augustine's grand vision in the finest possible detail, and Augustine's analysis became amplified into Aquinas' well-developed psychology. In Chapter 7, I will examine Aquinas' refinement of Augustine.

Chapter 7

AQUINAS' REFINEMENT

THE FULLY CHRISTIAN ORGANISM

In the previous chapter, we saw Augustine's logic of love. The purpose of this chapter is to examine the thirteenth-century Dominican genius, Thomas Aquinas, and his deep interest in this logic. He utilizes it to understand the interplay between emotion and ethics in a highly integrated and nuanced way. But let us sidle up to his nuance by first considering another modern construction of emotions, which is thick with moral implications.

I. Another modern account

Among modern theories of emotion, an excellent contribution is offered by Andrew Ortony, Gerald Clore and Allan Collins.[369] Their typology of emotion is shown in Figure 3. In a thoroughly positive review of their work, emotion researcher Aaron Ben-Ze'ev appreciates that it does not fall into reductionisms typically found in the field, since it takes in account how '(a) emotions are highly sensitive to contextual and personal factors; (b) there is no essence which is a necessary and sufficient condition for all emotions; and (c) typical emotional attitudes do no [sic] consist in merely one simple emotion.'[370]

We can see in Figure 3 how this sophisticated modern description notices morally suspect emotions (such as resentment, and gloating); the way interiority roves between general descriptions and reactions to sensory particulars, and various tussles between attraction and repulsion. There is also a ubiquity of desire reflected in it. But arguably its most significant moment occurs in the headline, where emotions are 'valenced reaction[s] to' various modes of perception and action. Ben Ze'ev thinks that the authors' cognitive lens belies their demonstrably

---

369. Andrew Ortony, Gerald Clore, and Allan Collins, *The Cognitive Structure of Emotions* (Cambridge: Cambridge University Press, 1988).

370. Aaron Ben-Ze'ev, 'Describing the Emotions: A Review of *The Cognitive Structure of Emotions* by Ortony, Clore & Collins', *Philosophical Psychology* 3.2–3 (1990), pp. 305–17 (305), doi: 10.1080/09515089008573006.

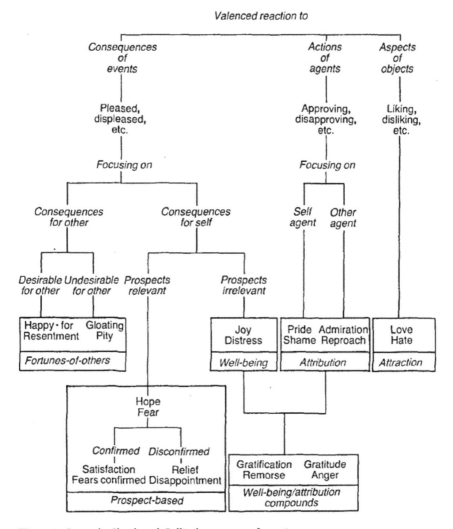

Figure 3 Ortony's, Clore's and Collins's structure of emotion types.

prior commitment to the fundamentally *evaluative* nature of emotion. 'Accordingly, a more suitable title of [their] book may be "The Evaluative Structure of Emotions".'[371]

Evaluations are norms, and norms are evaluations. Evaluation, elemental to our emotional functioning, is a prime candidate for what makes psychology fundamentally a moral science. In other words, the complex interplay between the goods that surround us, our moment-by-moment semi-conscious evaluations

---

371. Ben-Ze'ev, 'Describing', p. 306.

of them, our instantaneous and continual responses of passion and affection, and our decisions to act towards them or to inhabit joyful repose – large tracts of this all-embracing ecology are what we name morality or ethics, and are indivisible from much, perhaps all, of psychology. I mention Ortony's, Clore's, and Collins's schema because it reminds me of what Thomas Aquinas also achieved. It will not be productive to compare or contrast the two schemas beyond what I have said here. But if Ortony's, Clore's, and Collins's approach in any way appeals to us, then it is safe to say that Thomas' will also.

II. Overview I (for the uninitiated): Navigating Thomas

Thomas' works are many, but I will confine my attention to the *Summa Theologica* and then mainly to its *Prima Secundae Partis* (the First Part of its Second Part, '1a2æ').

There is some impertinence to this chapter, given the depth of scholarship on Thomas,[372] particularly among Roman Catholic Thomists. Thomas has not been a part of my own tradition or early theological learning, and his legacy is well and truly owned by others. Tracey Rowland's non-exhaustive summary identifies at least twenty-one different schools or moods of Thomism. My attempt here likely falls into her miscellany of 'freelance' Thomisms![373] As a freelancer, I am conscious

372. Of the vast literature on Aquinas in general, recent studies of direct relevance to this chapter are worthy of note: Diana Fritz Cates, *Aquinas on the Emotions: A Religious-Ethical Inquiry* (*Moral Traditions* series, Washington, DC: Georgetown University Press, 2009); Nicholas E. Lombardo, O. P., *The Logic of Desire: Aquinas on Emotion* (Washington, DC: The Catholic University of America Press, 2011), and his illuminating shorter study, Nicholas E. Lombardo, O. P., 'Emotion and Desire in the *Summa Theologiae*', in *Aquinas's Summa Theologiae: A Critical Guide* (ed. Jeffrey Hause; *Cambridge Critical Guides* series, Cambridge: Cambridge University Press, 2018), pp. 111–30; Robert C. Miner, *Thomas Aquinas on the Passions: A Study of Summa Theologiae, 1a2ae 22–48* (Cambridge: Cambridge University Press, 2011), and his excellent short piece, Robert C. Miner, '*Affectus* and *Passio* in the *Summa Theologiae* of Thomas Aquinas', in *Before Emotion* (ed. Juanita Feros Ruys et al.; New York: Routledge, 2019), pp. 121–30; and Mark D. Jordan, *Teaching Bodies: Moral Formation in the Summa of Thomas Aquinas* (New York: Fordham University Press, 2017) – a magisterial treatment in general, but see especially Part III, and also his shorter treatment: Mark D. Jordan, 'Aquinas's Construction of a Moral Account of the Passions', *Freiburger Zeitschrift für Philosophie und Theologie* 33.1–2 (1986), pp. 71–97. Earlier studies widely referenced include Marcel Sarot, 'God, Emotion, and Corporeality: A Thomist Perspective', *The Thomist* 58.1 (1994), pp. 61–92, doi: 10.1353/tho.1994.0043; and Shawn D. Floyd, 'Aquinas on Emotion: A Response to Some Recent Interpretations', *History of Philosophy Quarterly* 15.2 (1998), pp. 161–75.

373. Tracey Rowland, *Catholic Theology* (*Doing Theology* series, London: Bloomsbury, 2017), pp. 43–44.

that I know very little about how the major commentators stand in relation to one another. Even so, I hope this chapter will assist those for whom, like myself, Thomas' work has been new and surprising. With that in mind, a few introductory comments for the uninitiated may assist, but readers more at home in Aquinas might like to skip ahead to the next section.

There are various conventions in the scholarship on Aquinas, such as a penchant to flip between 'Thomas' and 'Aquinas' in naming him. Thomas also wrote a *Summa contra Gentiles*, which will not be used in this chapter, and *Summa* here will always mean the *Summa Theologica*. Anyone new to this work may find it intimidating at first. But its ordered granularity is fairly straightforward. Formally broken into three main Parts (effectively four in practice, with the huge second Part subdivided into two), each Part has dozens of 'articles'. An article answers a question posed by Thomas. He leads off each article with several 'objections' he imagines raised by his contemporaries – usually attempts to negate or confirm the substance of the question. Thomas will generally argue that these are wrong, with his positive or negative answer to the question found in a summary statement, 'I answer that' (the *sed contra*) – a kind of clarion call to hammer home his main point – followed by a more fulsome paragraph arguing his claim (the *corpus*). Several answers then follow to mop up the initial objections.

It is therefore possible, if a cheat, to read the question then skip to the *sed contra* and *corpus* to get his argument in broad brushstrokes, at least. His objections and their answers can be more alien to us, often relying on the use of shared Aristotelean reasoning within his milieu, and so not always easy for modern uninitiates. That way of thinking can also appear within the *sed contra* and *corpus*; but his lines of argument there are relatively more accessible. Using the cheat, a hyperlinked version[374] is an invaluable way to get a sense of the whole. It is almost as if Thomas wrote the work with this modern format in mind.

Unless otherwise noted, the edition used throughout will be the translation by the English Dominican Fathers.[375] My decision to use this older translation is

374. Good examples are the English and Latin version at https://aquinas.cc; or the English version at https://www.newadvent.org/summa or https://ccel.org/ccel/aquinas/summa. These sites (accessed 15 September 2021) use edited versions of the Dominican Fathers' translation, for which see footnote following.

375. Thomas Aquinas, *Summa Theologica* (trans. Fathers of the English Dominican Province; London: Benzinger Brothers, 1937). References to the *Summa* will follow in the main text, and will abbreviate the Parts as 1a, 1a2æ, 2a2æ and 3a (with 'supp.' for the supplement to the Third Part), followed by a number for the relevant question, then 'a' for each article. Article subdivisions will be 'obj' for objections, 'sc' for the *sed contra*, 'c' for the *corpus*, and 'ad' for each answer (and 'prol.' for the occasional prologue near the start of each Part): e.g., 1a2æ.109.a7.obj3. Where smaller divisions are not noted the reference should be regarded as *passim* to the article or question. For readability, references to Augustine occur both in footnotes and in main text, but references to the *Summa* only in the main text, also for readability. No pagination is given (in accord with general practise).

partly due to its availability in the public domain, but mainly because it does not conflate passion with emotion, unlike some modern translations. The absence of gender-inclusive language is an unfortunate outcome.

III. Overview II: Thomas' (and this chapter's) project

Alasdair MacIntyre's quick summary interpretation of Thomas' project is a useful orientation to it:

> In [Thomas Aquinas's account of virtue], inadequacies are remedied by using the Bible and Augustine to transcend the limitations not only of Aristotle but also of Plato [. . .] and by using Aristotle as well as Augustine to articulate some of the detail of the moral life in a way that goes beyond anything furnished by Augustine.[376]

We will eventually arrive at how Thomas understands virtue. Before that (and essential to it), I will assert that much in Thomas' syntax of human being in the *Summa* remains serviceable, insofar as it offers a more granular account of our responses arising from (Augustinian) love. These include: our longings and lusts as pursuits of some perceived good; our angers as attempts to preserve or defend them; and our sadnesses as lamenting their loss. Aquinas shows that within the portmanteau of love, certain structures can be discerned. Love refracts into a series of emotional responses, and these responses reflect a complex array of goods within moral order. There is a recursive relationship between these responses and moral reasoning. Augustine had already said as much concerning the logic of love. But Aquinas tells more of the array of goods, the responses to them, and the relationship between these responses and moral reasoning.

These insights into the phenomenology of human emotions, and their moral correlates, are interesting enough. Many of the insights probably derive from several previous compendia of canny observations, all of which indicate that modern moral psychology is not novel in its endeavours. But Thomas' work offers something potentially far more exciting for anyone willing to work with it – namely, a substantive account of how and why, as Brinkmann intuits (Chapter 3), psychology can be regarded as fundamentally a moral science. For if at the base of us are goods to be loved (and an other, the God who is love), then our movements of 'appetition' as Thomas calls them are also fundamentally good, even when feelings are distressing and some actions turn out to be bad. Thomas' account of human being, including our full range of emotions, is wholesome, we might say, in many senses of that word. The wholesome-human-whole homes-in on and is completed within God, who loves perfectly.

---

376. Alasdair MacIntyre, *Three Rival Versions of Moral Enquiry* (London: Duckworth, 1990), pp. 140–41.

(We will touch upon the vexed notion of God's supposed impassibility in Chapter 8. Suffice for now to note that if passion is taken as synonymous with emotion, impassibility implies that God is 'emotionless'. Thomas makes no such implication. Passion is for him a term denoting something occurring within bodies as they seek a goal. God has no such bodily need, therefore no passion, but God is replete with what we may call divinely holy *affections* that prove to be the source, destination, and fulfilment of all such things in us.[377])

Even so, Aquinas' writing is such that this exciting outcome is not easily apparent at first. We may not warm to his interest in Aristotle, to his oddly mechanistic ordering of articles and their various objections, or to his scholastic tone. But my own journey in reading him is well-captured by Thomas Gilby:

> [Thomas writes] in his customary rather dead-pan manner; some may have the impression, from a hasty scanning of these pages, that it purveys somewhat sober stuff, doubtless improving, yet civic and Aristotelean and not very generous. Where the leap, the abandon, the fire in face of divinity? They will have missed the climax of each Question, which breaks out of the gates of the City of Reason, not in a desperate sortie, but at full strength and equipment, a theology with all of its philosophy intact.[378]

Not only so; likening the *Summa* to an opera, Nicholas Lombardo reckons that one 'presciently modern' theme swells and rises, reappearing throughout in several guises.

> For a while, we would wonder what it was and why it kept coming back, and why it seemed to play such a pivotal role. Then it would hit us. The theme was *appetitus*: desire. [. . .] Aquinas does not mention desire in his overview of the Summa's plot, but desire is its unspoken engine. It makes the story's movement possible.[379]

Thomas' account is a crucial waypoint in the theological story of morality and emotion (our terms, assuredly not his). To summarize Thomas' expansion of Augustine's logic of love: we are each an array of parts and powers, and our will operates as an amalgam of intellect and appetite. (On the face of it, then, he amplifies Augustine's concept of 'will' as the enacted instantiation of love.) Human will reaches for humanity's proper end. It involves intellectual assessments about that end and is affected by emotional responses to more immediate circumstances.

---

377. For detailed analysis and argumentation on this matter, see Miner, '*Affectus* and *Passio*' ('[D]ivine being and the *affectus* of love are inseparable. God is love', p. 170); and Scrutton, 'Emotion in Augustine and Thomas'.

378. In Thomas Aquinas, *Summa Theologica: Purpose and Happiness (Vol. 16, 1a2æ.1–5)* (London: Blackfriars; Eyre & Spottiswoode, 1969), p. xiv.

379. Lombardo, 'Emotion and Desire', pp. 111–12.

These emotional responses reflect the complexity of the moral field and can be ordinate or inordinate, depending upon their fittingness to humanity's true end. Therefore, *virtue* necessarily becomes a central element in moral life, since each virtue is a special amalgam of thought, habit and ordered passion, with all virtues helping people towards their true end. Virtue, in turn, requires the power of the Spirit, working through Christ's teaching and as God's kind gift, to produce that kind of moral organism who is properly ordered to humanity's true end. Equipped with this conception we are better equipped to examine the recursive relationship of emotion to moral reasoning. This reasoning can be misled in various ways by emotion – and can itself maliciously mislead emotion. Polish scholar Vaiva Adomaityte arrives at a similar conclusion:

> Aquinas speaks of the human person as consisting of a body-soul composite with its various faculties working in an intimate relationship with each other. The passions, though essentially movements of a sensitive appetite, still collaborate with reason, apprehension, and will. The passions in Aquinas' thought are also relevant to morality: only if they are discussed as a philosophical construct in itself they fall short of ethical assessment. If, however, we take passion in reality, it takes up a moral character of good or bad, just as the species of human action.[380]

Before launching into the detail of Aquinas' account, let us pause to overview some recurrent themes and conceptions. These can be lost within the granularity of Thomas' format. In his account of human parts and powers in their relations, Thomas seamlessly orchestrates various aspects of being human into what I will call a *syntagma* (a word that ontologizes a syntax) of human being, so that human willing is located at the intersection (roughly) of intellect and appetite. Actions then become intelligible when the *syntagma* operates towards its *telos*, and conversely, human action is unintelligible without this *telos*. In other words, he develops a holistic account (for want of a less-hackneyed adjective) of human moral and emotional being. In it, *appetition* steers people towards ends.

Aquinas' mention of rationality would seem, to a modern person, to preclude emotion. That is not the case once we understand his distinction between passion and affection, and then his distinctive form of rationality. For example, happiness is humanity's rational end, but this affection is not regarded by Thomas as a passion (leading some moderns to think it is not an emotion either). Nor will he generically label various other experiences (such as love, enjoyment, and delight) as emotions. In his taxonomy, *passions* involve those *bodily* appetites that move us towards something concrete. But other appetites that move us he does not call passions, even though they are recognizable to us as emotions. In Aquinas, then, it is common for us to be moved by affections in a manner that is understood as rational. That the movement is not strictly passionate does not entail that the rational is devoid of affection – or in Augustinian language, of love. I will unpack

---

380. Adomaityte, 'Emotions and Ethics', p. 102.

all that as I am able,[381] but suffice here to note how the possibility of misreading Thomas is ever upon us, if we project our own terms onto his.

The concept of proper ends for humanity gives Thomas a criterion of judgment for *ordinate* passions that move the soul to its proper end. All passions can be morally evaluated by the moral visions they serve. Virtue governs appetition (the genus, and locus, of passion) so that right ends may be chosen, thus producing ordinate passion. The formation of virtue, towards lives populated by a variety of interesting virtues, begins naturally and continues with elements both of love commended and love poured in (Chapter 6). Passion is directed by the work of the Spirit (an example of love poured in), and new loves are commended in Christ's evangelical teaching. Hence an integrated moral organism is formed, who responds rightly to God's good order, and for whom virtues are existentially primary. The logic of MacIntyre's comment[382] will become clear: Thomas' categories of thought, though Aristotelian, are more primarily grounded in Christian theology.

Thomas' emphasis upon the immediacy to us of sensory particulars shows how we can move from this immediacy to a lively understanding of the interconnections between emotion and moral reasoning. Central to his account of these interconnections is an agenda for personal ethics within the teleological givens of the Christian gospel, which are taken not to be a sectarian conceit, but as the best framing of every human person's being.

The sections to follow will overview the *Summa*'s intent (IV); outline the *syntagma* (V); consider human *telos* or purpose (VI); examine Thomas' nuanced concept of passion (VII); suggest that Thomas offers deep reasons for the intrinsically moral nature of psychology (VIII); show how Thomas powerfully reiterates and deploys Augustine's insight that love lies at the base of all the operations of soul (IX); examine his view of how virtue works to shape passion (X); and (XI) of how God gives and commands love, to shape virtue. I will end with a summary of how Thomas helps us (XII). It is a long chapter, and still only a cursory introduction to Aquinas' thought. But his genius makes it worth the effort.

---

381. Robert Miner has unpacked this same complexity in a manner that I find most helpful, but I will not attempt to interleave his account within my own. He frames as a 'simple teaching' in Thomas that the affections reside in the intellectual appetite, and the passions in the sensitive appetite. But he then goes on to show that this 'simple teaching' is not the whole story in Thomas, who strenuously avoids the implication that passions are worse than affections. To the contrary, the whole human soul moving in response towards God and God's goods needs passion joined with affection in the operation of the will. A will operating from a dispassionate intellectual affection only is regarded by Thomas as defective. Miner, '*Affectus* and *Passio*', pp. 125–29.

382. See above, n 376.

IV. Anthropology and the Summa's *ethical intent*

The First Part of the *Summa* outlines the theistic universe in which humanity is located. The massively central Second Part (divided, in turn, into two sub-parts) answers general and then specific questions about humanity, with particular reference to what we regard as morality proper. The Third Part is a theological meditation upon the place and work of Christ for humanity. A vast literature exists on the architectonics of the work, but taking Mark Jordan as our guide:

> The first [Part] treats God's essence and the distinction of persons in the Trinity, God as exemplar, and the creatures that proceed from God. The second part considers 'the motion of the rational creature towards God'. It is further divided into two sections. The first of them presents moral matter generally or 'universally': the end of human life, the elements of properly human action, and the intrinsic or extrinsic principles of human acts. The second section surveys moral questions compendiously under the headings of the main virtues before integrating them into ways of life. [The Third Part] presents Christ as the way by which the rational creature can reach God.[383]

For our purposes, Lombardo's summary from the perspective of desire is illuminating:

> In the First Part, Aquinas tells how God brought the world into being through his will, or intellectual appetite, and how God guides created things towards their proper end by the appetites he implants within them. In the Second Part, Aquinas outlines how we bring our desires to fruition, or fail to, through our free actions, and discusses the role of emotion, virtue, and grace in bringing us to human and spiritual maturity. Finally, in the Third Part, he tells how, through the harmonious exercise of Christ's divine and human appetites, Christ's humanity became a bridge between heaven and earth, for our humanities.[384]

The pivotal prologue to the Second Part clearly signals Aquinas's shift to the question of who, and what, is humanity:

> Since [. . .] man is said to be made in God's image, in so far as the image implies 'an intelligent being endowed with free-will and self-movement': now that we have treated of the exemplar, i.e. God, and of those things which came forth from the power of God in accordance with His will; it remains for us to treat of His image, i.e. man, inasmuch as he too is the principle of his actions, as having free-will and control of his actions. (1a2æ.1.prol.)

---

383. Jordan, *Teaching Bodies*, p. 10.
384. Lombardo, 'Emotion and Desire', p. 112.

Hence the Second Part can be construed as outlining the correct human responses to divine order. In this outline, passion (particularly understood) furnishes the soul with impetus for its movement forward in action. Given the complexity of the soul and of external reality, passion is many-faceted, and virtue is necessary to shape it. But in turn, virtue must itself be shaped by the love that is both poured in and commended.

Jordan describes the First Part of the Second Part (*Prima Secundae*, 1a2æ) as 'something like a fundamental philosophical anthropology designed to undergird a moral treatment of human life in particular.'[385] The particulars appear in the *Summa*'s second half, and so are perhaps Thomas' main point. But his philosophical anthropology enables us to consider the operation of passions and affections in ethics, and to begin to see their relationship to virtue and to moral reasoning.

This primarily ethical intention of the *Summa* has been widely noticed. Jean Porter finds 'that an account of action is the common thread' running through its Second Part.[386] This account of action is not just any kind of account, as Alasdair MacIntyre notes, seeing the *Summa* 'forc[ing] us back upon the question of what kind of persons we will have to be or become [. . .] in order to read it aright.'[387] Servais Pinckaers describes its main concern to be the formation of a 'Christian moral organism'.[388]

Despite a first impression of complexity, the argument actually builds upon itself quite clearly. What we regard as emotions are constantly under scrutiny, being central to humanity's response to the divine order in which people are situated. Thus, emotions are woven throughout the *Summa*, since for Aquinas, they are woven through the deepest structures of being human.

V. A syntagma *of being human*

Any taxonomy of the soul into various parts and powers usually attracts the term 'faculty psychology', as if a person is a collected set of highly demarcated departments that oversee various functions. (In one popular source, Thomas is lightly discarded in these terms – along with all other medieval theologians![389])

To enable a fresh approach, I will employ the term *syntagma* (which denotes any systematic body, system, or group) to describe the totality of the various parts and powers of the soul and their complex interrelationship. It is this interrelationship, or syntax, of parts and powers that constitutes the human person who operates in

---

385. Jordan, 'Aquinas's Construction of a Moral Account of the Passions', p. 86.

386. Jean Porter, *The Recovery of Virtue* (London: SPCK, 1990), p. 70.

387. MacIntyre, *Three Rival Versions of Moral Enquiry*, p. 133; cf. 129–30.

388. Servais Pinckaers, *The Sources of Christian Ethics* (trans. Mary Thomas Noble; Edinburgh: T&T Clark, 1995), p. 178.

389. 'Faculty psychology', online at: https://en.wikipedia.org/wiki/Faculty_psychology (accessed 7 September 2021).

the world. To describe the being so constituted as a *syntagma* is to highlight the syntax without prejudice as to whether Thomas is guilty of departmentalization. But he is really not, since 'all the soul's powers are rooted in the one essence of the soul' (1a2æ.77.a1.c).

> [T]he soul is not a part of the human being in the way a roof or wall is part of a building. Rather, the soul organizes or configures the body, giving it not only its shape, but the operations characteristic of its species. Seen this way, 'body' and 'soul' are not complete substances in their own right. They are conjoined so as to create one complete substance – the human being.[390]

I will labour the use of this deliberately awkward word ('syntagma') to highlight how Thomas can conceive of a being who is not merely a body, nor a random collection of mental modules, nor a crude amalgam of an immaterial soul with a material body. We are, in his conception, an interwoven whole, with our various parts and powers and feelings and thoughts integrated (hylomorphically) to be a soul that is, in turn, embedded in materiality, communities, cosmos, and God. In our experience of the *syntagma* there is disorder in it, to be sure, but that need not be final. The *syntagma* exists to find restful joy – in God, in one another in God, and in our participation as creatures with creation.

a. Humans as desirous knowers

Aquinas considers humanity to be by nature a 'knower' of the divinely ordered universe:

> Since everything is knowable according as it is actual, God, Who is pure act without any admixture of potentiality, is in Himself supremely knowable. [. . .] For there resides in every man a natural desire to know the cause of any effect which he sees; and thence arises wonder in men. But if the intellect of the rational creature could not reach so far as to the first cause of things, the natural desire would remain void. (1a.12.a1)

The bedrock of the *syntagma* is that human knowers are drawn relentlessly to the supremely knowable. We are reminded of Augustine's assertion that each human is constituted by being, knowledge, and love. As with Augustine, it follows for Aquinas that in our awareness, the good is contingent upon the true. This is obvious to him for an ontological and an epistemological reason:

> First, because the true is more closely related to being than is good. For the true regards being itself simply and immediately; while the nature of good follows being in so far as being is in some way perfect; for thus it is desirable. Secondly, it is evident from the fact that knowledge naturally precedes appetite. Hence, since

---

390. Floyd, 'Aquinas on Emotion', p. 163.

the true regards knowledge, but the good regards the appetite, the true must be prior in idea to the good. (1a.16.a4)

That 'the true regards being itself simply and immediately' is, of course, a little contentious for moderns. It is beyond our scope to defend the claim other perhaps than to suggest that it is easier to defend in a good divine order than elsewhere. The main point of interest is that 'thus it is desirable' – Aquinas' way of saying, with Augustine, that we love what we sense and know. 'As the good denotes that towards which the appetite tends, so the true denotes that towards which the intellect tends' (1a.16.a1.c). We are first knowers of, and then responders to, the order of reality; and hence there follows (what we call) ethics. And thus we also discover the distinction in Aquinas' *syntagma*, between appetite and intellect.

b. A diagram of the syntagma

At this point it might be useful to pause and offer a diagram (Figure 4), to assist us better to grasp the developing *syntagma*. For completeness, additional material on the 'vegetative' power is included, but that is of less interest to us than the powers of sense and intellect.

Figure 4 should be read hierarchically since Aquinas follows Aristotle's hierarchical view of functionality. At base, natural, vegetative traits (e.g., nutrition and growth) are shared with all living things. But only animals and humans have forms of cognition, and forms of appetition. Animals and humans have a cognitive power called *sensation*, and an appetitive power called *sensuality*, or sensitive appetite. We share with animals the way these powers attend to particulars before us.

Specific to humanity are the rational powers: a cognitive power called *intellect*, and an appetitive power called *will*. It is not that animals are somehow not rational. Rather, human rationality attends to universals, beyond particulars. As Eleonore Stump puts it:

> The intellective appetite produces desires on the basis of all the information coming into the mind. This appetite is what Aquinas understands as the will; and it is responsive to all the deliverances of the intellect (including those deliverances based on the intellect's connection to the senses), rather than to the deliverance of the senses alone.[391]

Therefore, in ways both like and unlike animals, the soul, broadly, is both cognitive and appetitive. Moving from bottom to top of the diagram shows how in Aquinas' understanding, the soul's attention moves further and further beyond the self. (The 'locomotive' power should somehow straddle the topmost part of the powers

---

391. Eleonore Stump, 'The Non-Aristotelian Character of Aquinas's Ethics', in *Faith, Rationality, and the Passions* (ed. Sarah Coakley; Malden, MA: Wiley-Blackwell, 2012), pp. 91–106 (101).

		COGNITIVE *concerned with the true*	APPETITIVE *concerned with the good*	
RATIONAL powers specifically human.		INTELLECT / REASON	WILL → *directed to UNIVERSALS* *and to a 'common notion of the* *good' (1a.82.5)*	
SENSIBLE powers Shared only with other animals	(higher animals also have a *locomotive power*).	SENSATION	SENSUALITY/ SENSITIVE APPETITE → *directed to PARTICULARS*	
			Irascible *Attacks* *the harmful,* *and* *hindrances to* *the suitable*	**Concupiscible** *Acquires* *the suitable,* *flees from the* *harmful*
VEGETATIVE powers Shared with all living things.		GENERATIVE – *the power whereby the body continues its existence*		
		AUGMENTATIVE – *the power whereby the body acquires its due quantity*		
		NUTRITIVE – *the power whereby the body is preserved in its existence and in its* *due quantity*		

Figure 4 Visual representation of human 'soul' as a *syntagma* of powers.

of sense since higher animals *go to get* objects of sense). Moving from left to right shows how this attention moves from contemplation to action – from perception and reflection to deliberation and action, we might say. (The exception to the left-right movement is the irascible and concupiscible, which are in recursive relation and to which I will return later.)

The diagram shows that when Aquinas calls intellect a 'cognitive power in the soul' (1a.12.a4.c), the words are not synonyms: cognition is the genus of which intellect is a species, and we are also being cognitive when we sense things, not only when we think things.

But for those specifically human powers, the will chooses from among goals proposed by the intellect, after the intellect considers ends and means. Aquinas sometimes refers to the 'intellect', and sometimes to 'reason'; but I suggest that these are not really to be distinguished, except insofar as reason is the *process* by which people 'advance from one thing understood to another' (1a.79.8), so as to bring understanding.

(I should note that the diagram is not exhaustive of Thomas' view. For example, an 'apprehensive' power might be imagined three-dimensionally, as if lying across all the boxes of the grid. It will not help us to attempt to show it. Sarot: 'the apprehensive power apprehends its object, while the appetitive power seeks it. This implies that the objects of apprehension and appetite are "one subject but taken under two aspects. It is apprehended as a being that is sensed or understood. It is desired as something desirable or good."'[392] Since it is our estimation of *good* that directly concerns us, I have sidestepped Thomas' conception of the apprehensive power.)

We have seen debates around whether desire, passion, feeling, and certain forms of motive and intention, should be regarded as emotion. Aquinas covers all such concepts as appetition – an Aristotelian principle of tendency as applied to the human person.[393] When in 1a.80 (esp. a2) Aquinas classifies appetitive powers by a distinction between higher, intellectual appetite (the will), and lower, sensitive appetite (sensuality), we find he can account for the tug of the external world in all its pluriformity. Both powers tend outside of the self – but the intellectual appetite tends towards universals (e.g., that which is good), and the sensitive appetite tends towards particulars (specifically, the objects of sense). In this, 'the higher appetite moves the lower', and so at the outset Aquinas contends that appetite can actually be shaped and governed by the intellect. And yet, a little more cryptically, when considering 'motive' powers, Aquinas can also say that 'the higher appetite moves by means of the lower' because 'a universal opinion does not move except by means of a particular opinion'. So, the relationship between these two, though hierarchical, is also dialectical – or perhaps better, recursive: desires of sense are somehow shaped by prior intellectual decisions, and yet these decisions can also be shaped by that to which the senses are exposed.

c. The 'concupiscible' and its guardian, the 'irascible'

Sensuality is further subdivided into the 'concupiscible' and 'irascible' (1a.81.2). Respectively, one pursues the desirable and the other repels the undesirable.

392. Sarot, 'God, Emotion, Corporeality', p. 71, citing 1a.80.1.ad2.
393. Anthony Kenny, *Aquinas on Mind* (London: Routledge, 1993), pp. 59–61.

Anthony Kenny rejects this further 'anatomizing' as largely a 'forced assimilation' of conceptions by previous thinkers.[394] Although it is true and well known that previous anthropological descriptions are woven into the *Summa*,[395] Thomas' retention of this distinction is surely among the most defensible, noticing as it does both the violent and hungry feelings that strongly impact human decision and action. He introduces it as groundwork for a claim of significant interest – that people emote and act in order to protect or accrue or displace whatever they construe to be goods or evils. (That much is obvious, except when it is not.)

But interestingly, the will itself does not itself contain the irascible-concupiscible distinction, for the will governs generalized conceptions of the good. It is the sensitive appetite that construes the good in different aspects. With the single-mindedness of a referee, then, the will decides for or against sense:

> Now the sensitive appetite does not consider the common notion of good, because neither do the senses apprehend the universal. And therefore the parts of the sensitive appetite are differentiated by the different notions of particular good: for the concupiscible regards as proper to it the notion of good, as something pleasant to the senses and suitable to nature: whereas the irascible regards the notion of good as something that wards off and repels what is hurtful. But the will regards good according to the common notion of good, and therefore in the will, which is the intellectual appetite, there is no differentiation of appetitive powers [. . .]. (1a.82.5.c)

That there is no significance in the left-right placement of irascible and concupiscible in Figure 4 is because Aquinas sees them to be equal and interconnected – or at least, that the grounding of irascence in concupiscence is insignificant. (As Mark Jordan puts it, '[t]he irascible is [. . .] teleologically subordinate to the concupiscible, from which it begins and in which it ends.'[396])

394. Kenny, *Aquinas on Mind*, p. 63.

395. See e.g. Lombardo, 'Emotion and Desire', p. 119 and n 23; or Thomas Aquinas, *Summa Theologica: The Emotions (Vol. 19, 1a2æ.22–30)* (trans. Eric D'Arcy; London: Blackfriars; Eyre & Spottiswoode, 1967), p. xxv, where the source for the irascible-concupiscible distinction is identified as William of Moerbeke's Latin translation of Aristotle's *De Anima*, with *irascibilis* rendering Greek *thumikē* and *concupiscibilis* for Greek *epithumikē*. For more information on Thomas' sources, Lombardo refers his readers to Paul Gondreau, *The Passions of Christ's Soul in the Theology of St. Thomas Aquinas* (*Beiträge zur Geschichte der Philosophie und Theologie des Mittelalters* series, Münster: Aschendorff, 2002), pp. 101–35, 211–18. This work, like Lombardo's, also helpfully elucidates Thomas' general theory of the passions, in service of showing how Christ inhabited this aspect of his humanity. We will examine it further in Chapter 8.

396. Jordan, 'Aquinas's Construction of a Moral Account of the Passions', p. 89. Note that Sarot disagrees with Jordan on this and other assessments (Sarot, 'God, Emotion, Corporeality', p. 70 n 28 and 73 n 39).

[T]he irascible is, as it were, the champion and defender of the concupiscible when it rises up against what hinders the acquisition of the suitable things which the concupiscible desires, or against what inflicts harm, from which the concupiscible flies. And for this reason all the passions of the irascible appetite rise from the passions of the concupiscible appetite and terminate in them; for instance, anger rises from sadness, and having wrought vengeance, terminates in joy. (1a.81.2.c)

Aquinas contends that the irascible and the concupiscible obey reason (1a.81. a3). Given the principle that 'the higher appetite moves the lower appetite', this obedience is understood to mean that the intellect has a kingly rather than a despotic rule over these appetites. It has a right to rule, even though that rule is resisted (with Aquinas pointing here to the phenomenon of dividedness, that 'other law at work' in Rom. 7.23).

Universal principles held in the intellect are processed by reason. These principles are applied (via the 'will', in that Augustinian sense of enacted love) to particular circumstances, and in this way, the appetites receive direction. The account explains why the appetites of animals are immediately responsive to the inputs of sense, while that is not always so in humans. As yet, intellect and reason are not called into question; Aquinas later discusses their malfunctioning. But already we can see that this malfunctioning would not seem to involve an infection of reason by sense. It will be more a misleading of reason by sense.

Aquinas thus imagines the human person as a single 'unicity of substantial form', to which he can refer in entirety by its distinctively human aspect of rationality[397] – and a rationality that is *particularly understood as appetitive, in its own respect.*

VI. *The human* telos *and its means*

So far, we have seen Thomas observe human being as a complex interplay of thought and appetite directed towards various ends. For anyone who has thought about ethics since Aristotle, that is hardly novel. Furthermore, human action is constituted in appetition towards ends; for anyone sympathetic to any kind of moral intuitionism, nor is that insight novel. The directions taken by the *syntagma*, illustrated in the movement from left to right in the diagram, simply clarify our movements from perception and contemplation to action.

But the next steps in Thomas' reasoning, while straightforward enough within his milieu, have become supremely confusing within ours. They concern how human action is unintelligible without a *telos*, but intelligible when the *syntagma* operates towards a *telos*. Furthermore, normative action is intelligible once we discern what the *syntagma* is *for*, and towards what ends it might *rightly* be directed.

397. Norman Kretzmann and Eleonore Stump, 'Aquinas', in *Routledge Encyclopedia of Philosophy* (ed. Edward Craig, Vol. 1; 10 vols; London: Routledge, 1998), pp. 326–50 (335).

The function of the irascible and the concupiscible within the *syntagma* flag the significance of emotion for human functioning, but an account of *telos* is required before Aquinas can expand upon the place of emotion. Aquinas's account of that to which humans are directed is necessary to, and will govern, his account of the relationship between emotion and ethics.

Thomas represents the zenith, perhaps, of a way to see human habitation of the world as benchmarked against our final purpose. Oliver O'Donovan's discussion of our problems with *telos* remains highly illuminating,[398] giving insight into why a teleological account such Thomas' has come to seems to us quaint, stipulative, or wrong. O'Donovan outlines several twists and turns in the history of Western thought after Thomas, but one line of O'Donovan's thought may suffice for our purposes:

> The belief in final causes, it has been maintained since Francis Bacon, was the great impediment to the search for a scientific understanding of the relationships among natural phenomena. Only when thought could escape the inhibiting influence of a teleological philosophy could it examine the universe in a way that was open to the contingency of relations, not presupposing that it would find a unifying purposiveness but prepared to find exactly what it did find. [. . .] [S]cientific thought proceeds by self-conscious abstraction, in which the more obvious determinants of kind and end are forgotten in order that the object of investigation may be hypothetically included in other, less obvious classes [. . .]. [S]uch an abstraction is a perfectly legitimate stratagem of thought. [. . .] But the question is whether the refusal of 'final causes' which led to the discovery of new generic relationships was actually necessary to it. Granted the historical sequence, that voluntarist discomfort with Aristotelian teleology at the end of the Middle Ages bred the new experimental cast of mind, does that mean that natural teleology is false, or merely that abstraction from it was a helpful ascesis for the scientific mind?[399]

Scientific empiricism was never in the business of contemplating purposes, and then inadvertently generated the cultural conceit that there are no such purposes. Modern moral psychology can therefore, at best, only warily posit some observable immanent purposes (such as in the account of *homo prospectus*[400]), perhaps also with some coy inferences that people seem to need something 'spiritual'. At worst, it will elide or deny substantive conceptions of human purpose, in the manner of the psychologizations Brinkmann opposes (Chapter 3). In contrast, Thomas' full-throated elucidation of humanity's purpose within the divine is at least bracing. At most, it may be literally revelatory.

398. O'Donovan, *Resurrection and Moral Order*, pp. 46–72.
399. O'Donovan, *Resurrection and Moral Order*, pp. 63, 66–67.
400. Seligman, et al., *Homo Prospectus*.

As his account of a human *telos* unfolds, the most immediate problem for modern readers becomes precisely the salience of that Aristotelian teleology, since set aside. He often buttresses his account with simple Aristotelian examples of natural teleology, since the will is teleological, but these examples will seem outmoded to modern minds and may therefore seem to discredit his wider account of a human *telos*. Kretzmann and Stump succinctly describe how for Thomas the will parallels natural teleology:

> [The will is] the most subtle terrestrial instantiation of an utterly universal aspect of creation. Not only every sort of soul but absolutely every form, Aquinas maintains, has some sort of inclination essentially associated with it [. . .]. Inclination is the genus of appetite, and appetite is the genus of will.[401]

So fire, 'by its form, is inclined to rise, and to generate its like' (1a.81.1.c). The irascible and concupiscible aspects of the appetitive power are also reflected in fire, which 'has a natural inclination, not only to rise from a lower position, which is unsuitable to it, towards a higher position which is suitable, but also to resist whatever destroys or hinders its action' (1a.81.2.c).

When moderns imagine a dismissal of Aquinas's anthropology can follow – as if over-imagination about the physics of fire makes teleology implausible for a human *syntagma* – the point is seriously missed. Aristotle and Aquinas were guilty (perhaps) of a much less serious error, by seeing in fire a teleological behaviour more applicable to living things. Aquinas' *syntagma* seeks to codify the obvious observation – phenomenological, but surely indubitable – that humans are teleologically oriented beings. Whether or not fire should be seen in this way is moot. Human will is 'the most subtle terrestrial instantiation' of something teleological. Thus, neither does it follow from the rejection of Aristotelian teleology by modern science that human thought and behaviour is not profoundly appetitive and oriented towards ends.

In MacIntyre's description of Aristotelian and Thomist moral logic, '[t]o progress in both moral enquiry and the moral life is [. . .] to progress in understanding *all* the various aspects of that life, rules, precepts, virtues, passions, actions as parts of a single whole.'[402] Aquinas uses humanity's true end as the principle bringing unicity to this single whole: 'The end is the rule of whatever is ordained to the end' (1a2æ .1.prol.).

At first, his treatment of humanity's end closely parallels Aristotle's. But as he proceeds it becomes apparent that for Aquinas, the best account of morality's single whole is Christian, not Aristotelian.

> That in which a man rests as in his last end, is master of his affections, since he takes therefrom his entire rule of life. Hence of gluttons it is written (Phil. 3.19):

401. Kretzmann and Stump, 'Aquinas', p. 338.
402. MacIntyre, *Three Rival Versions of Moral Enquiry*, p. 139.

'Whose god is their belly': viz. because they place their last end in the pleasures of the belly. Now according to Mt. 6.24, 'No man can serve two masters,' such, namely, as are not ordained to one another. Therefore it is impossible for one man to have several last ends not ordained to one another. (1a2æ.1.a5.sc)

Of course, the belly is an improper end by which to discern order, and the *Summa*'s Second Part seeks to ascertain humanity's true *telos*. Thomas' long build-up to the discovery of humanity's true *telos* almost reads like a detective novel.

He begins the search with the eudemonistic premise that to find whatever brings true and lasting happiness will be to discover humanity's true end. But happiness (1a2æ.1–5) does not consist in bodily goods, of which a variety are considered (1a2æ.2). Neither is delight the essence of happiness, and pleasure certainly is not. Happiness is not primarily found in any operation of the senses, and neither is it shared with animals (1a2æ.3.a3). This process of elimination is familiar terrain to readers of Aristotle's *Nichomachean Ethics*, and for thirteenth-century Parisian Aristotelians, the treatment of happiness so far is uncontroversial. (In some respects too, it also bears striking parallels to Haidt's process of elimination.)

Having eliminated the usual suspects (bodily goods, delight, and pleasure), Aquinas turns to consider how might come about that final happiness which lulls and quenches bodily appetites and desires. Such complete happiness can only be mediated by the soul rather than by the body. Therefore, it must occur in response to something found by the soul, among universals, rather than among sensual particulars (1a2æ.2.a8).

At this point Thomas is reminded of Scriptures such as Jer. 9.23-24 ('Let those who boast, boast [. . .] that they understand and know me, that I am the LORD' – 1a2æ.3.a6–a7); Ps. 103.5 ('Bless the LORD, O my soul [. . .] who satisfies you with good as long as you live' – 1a2æ.2.a8); Ps. 73.25 ('Whom have I in heaven but you? And there is nothing on earth that I desire other than you' – 1a2æ.4.a7), and the other references to personal *telos* that abound in Scripture.[403] These Scriptures discern among universals a source of happiness that eclipses bodily desires and satisfies the soul.

It is 'by His infinite goodness' that God 'can perfectly satisfy man's will.' God is happy within God's essence, but humanity's happiness consists in participation with God (1a2æ.3.a1, esp. ad1). It is in this way that happiness can be considered both as uncreated and created, as both belonging to the soul and outside the soul (1a2æ.2.a7). This participation is mediated by 'the vision of the Divine Essence' that is also described as a 'union' (1a2æ.3.a8). Happiness fulfils hope when the intellect completes knowledge by vision and comprehension, and when the will delightfully reposes in its beloved object (1a2æ.4.a3). Ethics and virtue are, therefore, teleologically contingent: biblical 'cleanness' and 'holiness' are for

---

403. See for example: Ps. 17.15; Isa. 66.14; Mt. 5.8; Jn 17.3; 1 Cor. 9.24; Heb. 12.14; 2 Tim. 4.7–8; 1 Jn 3.2; and Rev. 14.13.

Aquinas the 'rectitude of the will' when duly ordered to the last end (cf. 1a2æ.69. a3.c, end). In addition,

> the will of him who sees the Essence of God, of necessity, loves, whatever he loves, in subordination to God; just as the will of him who sees not God's Essence, of necessity, loves whatever he loves, under the common notion of good which he knows. (1a2æ.4.a4)

In other words, perhaps, we can know and love many goods and some concept of the good, but until our horizons are expanded into knowing something of who God is essentially, we cannot know what goods are being omitted from our love.

While bodily perfection is not integral to final happiness (1a2æ.4.a5), Aquinas is adamant that the soul's perfection is necessarily connected to the body (but not via some sort of physical bodily perfection). Aquinas thinks 'one man can be happier than another', since 'the more a man enjoys this Good the happier he is', which 'happens through his being better disposed or ordered to the enjoyment of Him' (1a2æ.5.a2.c). It will follow for him that bodily disposition to virtue conduces to happiness (1a2æ.4.a6, with Jn 13.17 used in support, where Christ promises a blessing to disciples if they do his teaching).

VII. Passion and emotion

A human *syntagma*, then, journeys to its proper end. How does that account for human moral emotion? An inexorable chain of subjects follows in the *Summa*, concerning first the nature of acts and decisions; then, the passions; next, what habits are, and how vices happen, or how instead virtues are built under the tutelage first of laws and then finally the gospel. These are all 'those things by means of which man may advance towards [the] end, or stray from the path' (1a2æ.1.prol.).

Human moral emotion relates, we intuit, to his discussion of the passions. But a small waypoint is needed to disambiguate what he means by those, and how they do and do not relate to emotions. Surprisingly for moderns, Aquinas' discussion of the passions is not a discussion of the emotions.

For Aquinas, passion is a species of our broader genus, emotion, and he does not directly name this broader genus. We have already seen an important example. Most people would call happiness an emotion. In Aquinas, it is humanity's true end. Yet, it would never occur to him to call it a *passion*. There is no more movement to be had when someone is finally happy, since the subject has arrived, and passion for Aquinas always connotes *change or movement*. Equally, enjoyment is a function of the appetitive power, but it represents a kind of final fruition that 'should calm the appetite with a certain sweetness and delight' (1a2æ.11.a3.c; cf. a3 *passim*). 'To enjoy is to adhere lovingly to something for its own sake.' This aphorism from Augustine is twice quoted, first (a1) to impress upon us how human appetition can find a final home in the good order of reality, and then surprisingly (a4.sc), to show that this end can be enjoyed even when not yet possessed, but in anticipation and prospect, as it were. (Cf. 'one is said to possess the end already, when one hopes to possess it', 1a2æ.69.a1.c.) But passion is a different kind of mover for the soul than is happiness, delight, and enjoyment – experiences that we (but not Thomas) would call emotional.

(I may have slightly overdrawn Aquinas' line between bodily passions and other emotions. Eleonore Stump prefers to speak of the former as 'basic passions', and the latter as passions 'in an analogous or extended sense'. The basic passions are 'material', given their connection to the body; those within the intellective appetite she regards as more 'formal'.[404] '[A] passion in its extended or analogous senses [. . .] can have cognitive content; and so, depending on the account of emotion given [such as that emotions have cognitive content], a passion in this extended sense might well be the same as an emotion.'[405])

Passion is also passion insofar as it is not 'simple'. By this is meant that there remains a potential for action. 'Passion is a kind of movement' (1a2æ.23.a2.c), and 'sorrow is more properly a passion than joy' (1a2æ.22.a1.c) since in sorrow, the potential movement to regain what was lost is greater than the potential for movement in joy, where what is desired is already received, or nearly so. Moreover, it follows that in such states there is no conflict of goods. Conversely, situations are not simple when more than one good is sought after; hence, passion is heightened in response to complex situations involving several goods.

An illustration may help. A person gazing at a splendid work of art feels a deep satisfaction that reflects, Aquinas might say, the activity of the soul's appetition. Yet, he would not regard the experience as passionate – except if the feeling concerned potentialities, such as an unrequited possibility of ownership, whether through purchase or theft. (If we complexify with another good – such as a love for the owner, if I am contemplating theft; or a love for my sick spouse, on whom my limited funds should better be spent – then passion is heightened.) If the artwork was a painting of a beautiful scene, the longing or craving to hike there might be passionate. But awed wonderment at the beauty of the place would not, since there can be enjoyment without possession.

> Now passion pertains to defect, because it belongs to a thing according as it is in potentiality. Wherefore in those things that approach to the Supreme Perfection, i.e. to God, there is but little potentiality and passion: while in other things, consequently, there is more. (1a2æ.22.2.ad1)

'Defect' here may also invite our misunderstanding. A passion is not itself defective. The defect concerns the degree to which a thing has potentiality: passion is strong in reference to such things. But for more perfect things – that is, things that display less potentiality – the less intensely passionate is the soul's appetition of it. Thus, non-simplicity concerns the degree to which the soul is

404. Stump, 'Non-Aristotelian Ethics', pp. 101–02.
405. Stump, 'Non-Aristotelian Ethics', p. 104 n 7.

in movement towards some good, and the number of goods, though possibly conflicting, towards which it attends. The less simple the emotion, the more passionate it is; and so the degree of simplicity represents a non-moral axis for analysing passion. (There is a moral axis to this analysis: the less in accord with the soul's true end a passion is, the more inordinate, and so evil, it is. I will discuss this axis later.) Aquinas' notion of simplicity may remind us of modern metaphors that rely upon non-simplicity. Distressed people are 'conflicted', 'divided', or 'not integrated'. What is meant by these is largely what Aquinas means: sometimes, that a desired good is absent while at other times, mutually exclusive goods are desired. Yet experiences of well-being, such as love and joy, do not readily attract such metaphors of division.

In 1a2æ.23.a1, Aquinas returns to the irascible-concupiscible distinction, which he previously flagged as integral to human functioning, but whose function can now be delineated with clarity. Aquinas uses the distinction to find the differing flavours of certain passions. He names joy, sorrow, love, and hatred as passions that have a certain straightforwardness – they evaluate an object. On the other hand, daring, fear and hope concern the path towards (or away from) an object. That is, some passions are more concerned with problems of action. Aquinas concludes the article with an abrupt summary:

> [T]here are altogether eleven passions differing specifically; six in the concupiscible faculty [love and hatred, desire and aversion, joy, and sadness], and five in the irascible [hope and despair, fear and daring, anger which has no contrary]; and under these all the passions of the soul are contained.

Sarot's summary is worth quoting at length:

> He includes six basic passions within the concupiscible appetite and five within the irascible appetite. There are three basic passions of the concupiscible appetite which have the good as their object: love (*amor*, the psychical union of the lover with the beloved), desire (*desiderium*, the movement of the lover towards the beloved) and joy (*gaudium*, the rest in the beloved when it has been obtained). Correspondingly, there are three concupiscible passions with the bad as their object: hate (*odium*), aversion (*fuga*) and sadness (*tristitia*). There are three basic irascible passions relating to evil: fear (*timor*, when the object is an impending evil, so difficult to avoid that it exceeds one's capacity), courage (*audacia*, when the object is an impending evil, difficult to avoid but not exceeding one's capacity) and anger (*ira*, when the object is present, difficult to avoid but not exceeding one's capacity). There are only two basic irascible passions regarding the good. The reason for this is that when the good is possessed, it does not cause any difficulty. And when there is no difficulty, there is no irascible passion. Thus the two irascible passions are: despair (*desperatio*, if one judges that the good is so difficult to obtain that it exceeds one's capacity) and hope (*spes*, if the good is difficult to obtain, but is judged not to exceed one's capacity). These are the basic passions according to Aquinas. He acknowledges that in reality there are many

more passions than these eleven, and he accounts for them by referring to the greater or lesser intensity of passions [. . .].[406]

This conclusion is further reworked in 1a2æ.25, and although the mechanics of the reworking might seem forced to us, the resulting 'four principal passions' – joy, sadness, hope and fear – retain a certain elegant force. The appeal for Aquinas is in their symmetry and finality – that all other passions finally resolve into one of these, with the first pair pertaining to objects-as-ends, and the second pair to paths-towards-objects. We should also pause to note the sensitive portrayal of anger within this schema:

> The passion of anger is peculiar in this, that it cannot have a contrary [. . .]. For anger is caused by a difficult evil already present: and when such an evil is present, the appetite must needs either succumb, so that it does not go beyond the limits of 'sadness', which is a concupiscible passion; or else it has a movement of attack on the hurtful evil, which movement is that of 'anger'. But it cannot have a movement of withdrawal: because the evil is supposed to be already present or past. (1a2æ.23.a3.c)

Again, here is an interesting anticipation of therapeutically oriented typologies that understand anger sometimes to be a masking emotion. On this view, therapist and client are tasked to uncover underlying sadness, helplessness, or hopelessness. If no such sadness is discerned, client and counsellor might switch to another view of the anger – that it is a basic and irreducible defence by the client, in view of his or her own (God-given) preciousness. (Moreover, Aquinas' reference to 'evil' in the quoted passage flags a debate to be had with any therapy that claims intelligibility for anger without reference to some conception of evil. That is, his analysis of anger implies a dispute with any therapy which claims to proceed in disavowal of moral knowledge. Such a therapy must either declare anger to be trivial; or if it respects anger, its account of anger will be incoherent, deceitful, or both.) In her study of anger in the *Summa*, Vaiva Adomaityte frames its moral relevance most astutely. Anger, in Thomas,

> [. . .] works in close collaboration with reason, as reason here serves as a light that uncovers an injury [and] its object is to apply something good to something bad. Anger points us to the understanding that we were hurt on a very personal level. Anger is the 'fire in our bellies' when we experience situations of indignation. Oppressed nations are angry; women were and still are angry, people enslaved by evil institutions are angry. And this anger is a blessed anger because it uncovers that something is wrong, that we might be experiencing injustice. Thus anger, as a moment of recognition of moral value, is an emotion worth thinking of in ethical terms. However, while making a conceptual space to think of the

---

406. Sarot, 'God, Emotion, Corporeality', p. 74.

meaning of anger, we should also keep in mind the transitional character of this emotion. Anger can be indicative but it is not a final stop in any complex moral/social situation.[407]

By any estimate, Aquinas' insight into the nature of anger is striking, and at this point the view that the soul has its irascible and concupiscible projects is actually quite illuminating. Quite simply, anger is presented as an accompaniment to the soul's attempt to dispose of a sad object. Anger would seem to melt away into sadness when all avenues for such attempts are proven blocked. His later refinement will argue that anger is 'a concurrence of several passions, because the movement of anger does not arise save on account of some pain inflicted, and unless there be desire and hope of revenge' (1a2æ.46.a1.c). Also, reason is integral to anger (1a2æ.46.a4).

Even if this account of anger is not exhaustive, most people could remember enough corroborative examples to make it comprehensive. There is a significance for ethics: angry action can be evaluated by further consideration of the sad object it seeks to avoid, and more specifically, by the justice it seeks to achieve (cf. 1a2æ .46.a2.sc). That is, what sadness attends the anger's object? What wider moral commitments render the existing situation unjust? (Better here perhaps might be the term 'unfair', which can include those claims to missing goods as perceived by a single subject, to the exclusion of some other valid claim.)

Aquinas' technical use of 'passion', and his delineation of it from other emotions (our term) is at one level of antiquarian interest only. He is at liberty to use his words in his way, and we to use ours in ours. However, serious results ensue when significant modern commentators on moral emotion miss the point. Consider the pioneering modern rehabilitator of the dignity of the emotions, Robert C. Solomon, when he refers to:

> the curious observation that the highest virtues, such as love, hope, and faith, were not classified as emotions as such, but were rather elevated to a higher status and often (e.g., by Thomas Aquinas) equated with reason. The old master-slave metaphor [of reason over passion] remained alive and well, and as some emotions were seen as sins, the highest virtues could hardly be counted among the mere emotions.[408]

Let us put aside, for the moment, that Thomas expressly does not merely name 'some emotions [. . .] as sins', since passions are morally neutral apart from the moral visions each serves (see next section). For now, let us notice how Solomon's summary execution makes Thomas Aquinas into a thirteenth-century Immanuel Kant. But Solomon's criticism in the final sentence only works absent of Thomas' more general conception of appetition. As Lombardo puts it:

---

407. Adomaityte, 'Emotions and Ethics', p. 103.
408. Solomon, 'The Philosophy of Emotions', p. 6.

> Natural appetite leads to physical movement; sensory appetite leads to passion, a kind of psychological movement; and intellectual appetite leads to intellectual affection, another kind of psychological movement.[409]

Aquinas is not required to think of emotion as we do. Rather than depositing all experiences within the same bucket, Aquinas is interested to understand them as inordinate passion, as ordinate passion, and as something unmixed and simple, and as directed to concrete particulars, or to unseen universals. Thus, his highest virtues indeed had emotional aspects. Solomon knows of a 'tight [medieval] linkage between the study of emotion and ethics'[410] and is not unsubtle concerning differences between passion and emotion. But when he thinks Aquinas excludes love, joy and happiness from *emotion*, Aquinas does not; he excludes them from *passion*. They certainly remain highly affectionate, as does God. ('[F]or Aquinas, the claim that God is love is not poetry; it is a technical claim about God's identity. God is identical with a movement of the intellectual appetite: the intellectual affection of love.'[411])

Similarly, the usually impressive Robert C. Roberts misreads the *Summa* here. Roberts rightly wants to insist that emotions are rational, and that rationality is central to them. An erroneous entailment then takes exception 'to locat[ing] the emotions, as [Aquinas] does, in the "sensory appetite"', even though 'Aquinas' rationality-account of the morality of emotions is the right kind of account'.[412] Aquinas would agree with the burden of Roberts's concerns; but Roberts's thinking is subverted by his prior agreement with a translation of *passiones animae* as 'emotions'. At a number of key points, Roberts's argument against Aquinas turns upon Roberts claiming as emotion what Aquinas denies to be passion proper (such as love, joy, or happiness), as if Thomas did not regard these as feelingful.

Stump argues against several other scholars who regard Thomas, whether approvingly or disapprovingly, as merely an Aristotelian who gives reason the whip-hand over emotion.[413] When important modern thinkers make this error, it will follow that Thomas, and his elegant, cosmically woven *syntagma*, are tossed aside, so that moderns then try to reinvent his wheel. In the name of the conceit that Thomas was merely another player in the narrative that subjugated feeling to cognition – a narrative that apparently, only clever moderns have sought to overcome – we miss the opportunity to find how that very problem was substantively addressed, in the thirteenth century. We also, therefore, miss the opportunity to see how the moral nature of psychology has already been given to us.

---

409. Lombardo, 'Emotion and Desire', p. 113. This framing may reflect what Miner calls the 'simple teaching' of the *Summa*, which needs to be further nuanced (Miner, '*Affectus* and *Passio*', pp. 125–29). As we will see below, Lombardo goes on to do so.

410. Solomon, 'The Philosophy of Emotions', p. 6.

411. Lombardo, 'Emotion and Desire', p. 114.

412. Robert C. Roberts, 'Thomas Aquinas on the Morality of the Emotions', *History of Philosophy Quarterly* 9.3 (1992), pp. 287–305 (288).

413. Stump, 'Non-Aristotelian Ethics', p. 92.

VIII. What makes psychology intrinsically moral

As mentioned above, 'those things by means of which man may advance towards [the] end, or stray from the path' (1a2æ.1.prol.) include the nature of acts and decisions; the passions; and our vices, habits and virtues formed under law and gospel. I have found it personally and spiritually formative to follow Thomas' reasoning on these matters (and later, on their culmination in Christ). A gloss such as this chapter can do little justice to it. But with the help of Nicholas Lombardo's outstanding exposition of this intricate material,[414] we will review how Thomas offers reasons for a psychology that is also a fundamentally moral science.

Aquinas' evaluation of appetite is 'implicitly positive', and 'goodness implies desirability. If something is good – and anything that exists is necessarily good – then it is also appetible, or desirable'. That estimate extends even to 'God's appetite, since God wills everything that exists'. Conversely, 'evil consists in the frustration of appetite': 'it thwarts appetite and leads to disintegration.'

That conception of both the good and our longing for it should astonish moderns severally. It lies at the ontological base of all normative conceptions and amalgamates norms with desires prior even to the quantum level, as it were, as emanating from the divine. (We will visit this concept of divine desire in the next chapter.) Aquinas' account implies a fundamental truth in moral intuitionism, whatever the hue. This conception of desire also honours our yearnings, contrary to those sub-Christian deteriorations that demonize desire (and also contrary to secularist caricatures of Christian anthropology, albeit that these are likely based in sad and commonly found deteriorations). It asks us to try to see, understand and imagine how evil actually represents the *failure*, somehow, of appetition.

Passions of the soul and intellectual affections 'are intrinsically ordered to human flourishing', and 'appetites are ordered to what is perfective and completing'.[415] The complexity for us, though, is that our resultant *movements* are not always so. This subtle distinction opens the way for various moral evaluations of emotion. Aquinas wrestles with this matter in reference to the passions in 1a2æ.24.a1, where the erroneous objections point to the non-rational, animal nature of the passions to argue that they should attract neither blame nor praise. (These medieval objectors anticipate a modern emotional purism, where 'I can't help what I feel!'.) In reply Aquinas cites Augustine, where passions 'are evil if our love is evil, good if our love is good' (*City of God* XIV.7). 'Even the lower appetitive powers are called rational, in so far as "they partake of reason in some sort"' (1a2æ.24.a1.ad2). The claim is a little startling, suggesting that *every* desire is open to moral evaluation. Yet, Aquinas steadfastly rejects the view that passions are evil of themselves (1a2æ.24. a2). Passions *serve broader moral visions and are to be evaluated accordingly*. In 1a2æ.24.a4, this kind of view is repeated in a different way. There, pity and envy are offered as examples of good and evil passions respectively, precisely because the

---

414. Quotes following are all from Lombardo, 'Emotion and Desire', p. 115.
415. Lombardo, 'Emotion and Desire', p. 117.

words themselves signify this wider moral field: pity is an emotion that concerns the good of another, whereas envy despises it. Aquinas remains consistent here, having explained that on their own such passions are morally neutral, but take on moral shades once their object is in view. In their non-simplicity then, passions can also be inordinate, corrupting the soul by the degree to which they represent the soul favouring some good over another, greater good. (This is something like what in Augustine I called 'selective sight'.) By contrast, *ordinate* passions help the soul to be moved towards its proper end.

The (erroneous) objections of 1a2æ.24.a3 claim that the goodness of an act decreases in proportion to the passion that accompanies it. Aquinas deftly reverses this proto-Kantianism by arguing for a holistic view – that where reason, passion and action are in concert, the rightness of the act is enhanced – which prefigures his view of what constitutes virtue. '[S]ince the desires of good actions are good, and of evil actions, evil; much more are the pleasures of good actions good, and those of evil actions evil' (1a2æ.34.a1.c).

> This orientation toward the good permeates the structure of appetitive movements. According to Aquinas, the first movement of every appetite is love, that is, a configuring of appetite toward a particular object that somehow corresponds to its telos. The first movement then sets off a chain of other appetitive movements. Some movements propel the subject toward the attainment of the loved object; other movements help it overcome or avoid obstacles to that attainment. Eventually, hopefully, the loved object is attained and the subject rests in its possession. In this way, appetitive movements are ordered to rest, which, paradoxically, is itself a kind of movement, insofar as the resting implies that the loved object is moving the appetite from potency to act.[416]

In Lombardo's apt summary, Aquinas invites us to an approach to both psychology and ethics in tandem. On the one hand, we are asked to discern the deepest treasure in play – whether covertly or overtly – as we engage in this and that thought, feeling and action. On the other hand, we are asked to imagine where arrival and repose may lie, in a life that need not be ceaselessly restive. Thomas gives us windows into what, and how, we love.

IX. Love: The substrate of ethics

After deducing the four principal passions, Aquinas proceeds to refine the passions – first the concupiscible (1a2æ.26-39: love and hatred; desire and aversion; pleasure and sadness), and then the irascible (1a2æ.40-48: hope and despair; fear and daring; and anger). An increasingly fine-grain is obvious in articles such as 'whether [sorrow] is assuaged by sleep and baths?', 'whether hope abounds in

---

416. Lombardo, 'Emotion and Desire', p. 117.

young men and drunkards?' and 'whether a person's defect is a reason for being more easily angry with him?' The significance of the passions for ethics is equally clear in articles such as 'whether doing good to another is a cause of pleasure?', 'whether love conduces to action?' and 'whether [fear] hinders action?'

The usual Aristotelian categories are pressed into service in 1a2æ26.a4.c to give the helpful conclusion that persons are to be loved as ends in themselves. To paraphrase Aquinas, a primary friendship-type love is as opposed to a secondary concupiscible-type love that has non-personal goods as its object. We experience both in relationships. 'Accordingly, man has love of concupiscence towards the good that he wishes to another, and love of friendship towards him to whom he wishes good. [. . .] [T]hat which is loved with the love of friendship is loved simply and for itself'.[417] To enjoy people in these ways inhabits us appropriately within the supervening divine moral order.

Other sweeping statements are made concerning love itself, lying at the base of all our responses. Citing Augustine, 'All the other emotions of the soul [*affectiones animi*] are caused by love' (1a2æ.27.a4.sc), Thomas goes on to amplify: 'There is no other passion of the soul (*passio animae*) that does not presuppose love of some kind' (1a2æ.27.a4.c), including even hatred (1a2æ.29.a2). '[E]very agent, whatever it be, does every action from love of some kind' (1a2æ.28.a6.c). This Augustinian bedrock is quoted repeatedly throughout 1a2æ.26–48. (It reprises the crucial 1a.20.1.c, on God's love, to be considered in Chapter 8.)

But 'love demands some apprehension of the good that is loved' (1a2æ.27. a2.c), meaning that knowledge is required before love can settle lovingly upon an object. Then, as already recounted, the passions react, responding to and requiring the prior moral commitments constituted by love. '[W]hen we love a thing, by desiring it, we apprehend it as belonging to our well-being' (1a2æ.28. a1.c); therefore '[e]vil is never loved except under the aspect of good' (1a2æ.27. a1.ad1). That is, love is always directed to a good, but the estimate of good can be blinkered from the wider field of view. Aquinas will later use this kind of approach to arbitrate between Stoics and Epicureans on the morality of pleasure (1a2æ.34. a2), and hate is also assessed along these lines:

[I]n the animal appetite, or in the intellectual appetite, love is a certain harmony of the appetite with that which is apprehended as suitable; while hatred is

---

417. Aquinas offers further account of both friendship and disharmony in a later discussion on love's propensity towards 'likeness' (1a2æ.27.a3). But his commitment to people as ends in themselves, and implicitly to personal relationships, is never clearer than when the simple facts of human relationships subvert his best efforts to analyse them. In answering 'whether the actions of others are a cause of pleasure to us?' (1a2æ.32.a5), Aquinas points to 'the fact that we obtain some good through the action of another.' Why is this? Because 'in this way, the actions of those who do some good to us, are pleasing to us' – for what reason? – 'since it is pleasant to be benefited by another.' This question-begging may raise an appreciative smile.

dissonance of the appetite from that which is apprehended as repugnant and hurtful. Now, just as whatever is suitable, as such, bears the aspect of good; so whatever is repugnant, as such, bears the aspect of evil. And therefore, just as good is the object of love, so evil is the object of hatred. (1a2æ.29.a1.c)

To react to something emotionally is intrinsically to express an opinion about good and evil. Love, hate and the like offer a window into one's moral commitments. Some occurrences of emotion offer an avenue for reflection about one's ethic that is not as easily accessible by other means.

It is obvious on this view that the locus of a person's pleasure becomes a key test of their moral commitments. Since 'the repose of the will and of every appetite in the good is pleasure', then 'that man is good and virtuous, who takes pleasure in the works of virtue; and that man evil, who takes pleasure in evil works' (1a2æ.34.a4.c). This aphorism is not the mere truism that, out of context, it may appear. Rather, pleasure moments a transcendental reflection that asks, 'Why *am* I shaped *this* way? What *makes* my pleasures pleasant? *What has brought me* to so valorize this or that?' The power of Aquinas at this point is precisely in the consistent refusal to decry pleasure, and other passions. That they are morally neutral, while I am not, means that they can be used for insights into what I believe, and even who 'I' am. We are put in mind of the same kind of transcendental questioning invited by the words of Christ in Mt. 6.21 ('where your treasure is, there your heart will be also'), and Mt. 12.33-35 (of good and bad trees and their fruit).

X. Virtue: Shaper of passion

Much more should be said on Thomas' handling of virtue than can be outlined here. However, it is important at least to notice that the development of virtue is, for Thomas, an integral aspect of the human *syntagma*'s navigation of emotion.

That 'no virtue is a passion' (1a2æ.41.a1.obj1; cf. 1a2æ.45.a1.obj1) may intrigue us. Given that in Aquinas virtue is a lynchpin in the account of moral life, and given the preceding steadfast refusal to condemn passion, it remains to be seen what the one has to say to the other. Virtues are, of course, a species of habit (1a2æ.49–54). Virtues are a series of both moral and non-moral operative habits in the soul. They are 'operative' dispositions because they pertain to act, not to being (1a2æ.55.a2.c). A virtue can only be established within a history of action (1a2æ.51.a2–a3).[418]

Thomas' discussion of virtue entails three claims that might surprise a modern reader. First, *acts* are logically prior to virtue, and acts are evaluated both by their

---

418. So far, so Aristotelian; but I wholeheartedly recommend Stump's argument that Aquinas' virtues are assuredly not Aristotelian, *tout court*. See Stump, 'Non-Aristotelian Ethics', pp. 91–96.

ends and their nature. Therefore, in the spectrum of virtue theories, Thomas is among those for whom acts are epistemically prior to agents. Also, since the rightness of acts is governed both by their ends and their nature, Thomas has no interest in those outdated modernist fights between the primacy of deontological versus consequentialist or utilitarian ethics.

Intellectual virtue assists this evaluation of an act. But concupiscence threatens to derail the soul's appropriation of these acts. Therefore, second, moral virtue is needed to govern appetition (the locus of passion) so that right ends may be chosen (cf. 1a2æ.58.a1.c). Actually, moral virtue and passion become *triumphantly consonant* (cf. 1a2æ.59.a2.sc) – that is, moral virtue produces ordinate passion, and rather than threatening to derail the virtuous life, passion can now actually assist in its formation! (Admittedly, the *syntagma* becomes a little confusing when we discover that while all moral virtues pertain to the appetitive part of the soul, not all pertain to the passions of the *sensitive* appetite, since there is also the *intellectual* appetite. Justice and prudence are the virtues that governs this arena, 1a2æ.59.a4 .sc & c; 1a2æ.58.a5.c; cf. 1a2æ.60.a2.)

Third, Aquinas explains the formation of intellectual and moral virtues towards lives populated by a variety of interesting virtues. The formation begins naturally, but can only continue *theologically* through what, in Augustine, was love commended and love poured in. Along the way (1a2æ.58.a2), Aquinas disagrees with Socrates and unnamed others who misapply Aristotle's dictum that 'the soul rules the body like a despot'. If the soul is in such command, then on this view only ignorance leads to sin (Socrates), which is remedied by giving knowledge to the soul. Aquinas opposes such an account, countering that reason commands appetite only by a 'politic power'. The soul's requirement for such a 'politic' power highlights how 'the habits or passions of the appetitive faculty cause the use of reason to be impeded in some particular action.' In this way, Aquinas accounts for Augustine's famous reflection that 'sometimes we understand [what is right] while desire is slow, or follows not at all'. Therefore, it follows that:

> for a man to do a good deed, it is requisite not only that his reason be well disposed by means of a habit of intellectual virtue; but also that his appetite be well disposed by means of a habit of moral virtue. (1a2æ.58.a2.c)

Reason needs an appetitive ally. Moral virtue is this ally, and the antidote to concupiscence. Arguably, Thomas nicely anticipates the gravamen of Haidt's rider and elephant metaphor:

> [T]o one who is swayed by concupiscence, when he is overcome thereby, the object of his desire seems good, although it is opposed to the universal judgment of his reason. [. . .] [H]e needs to be perfected by certain habits, whereby it becomes connatural, as it were, to man to judge aright to the end. This is done by moral virtue [. . .]. Consequently the right reason about things to be done, viz. prudence, requires man to have moral virtue. (1a2æ.58.a5.c)

Aquinas reiterates that 'passions are not in themselves good or evil' (1a2æ.59.a1.c). The mood is profoundly Augustinian, with the crucial *City of God* XIX and XIV evident again as Aquinas' key inspiration. 'Virtue overcomes inordinate passion; it produces ordinate passion. It is inordinate, not ordinate, passion that leads to sin' (1a2æ.59.a5.ad1,2). But can virtue simply trample down concupiscence on-call? That would surely be to repeat the error of Socrates (and in Augustinian terms, of the Pelagians). Virtue, in turn, needs assistance, and a quotation from Augustine becomes significant:

> 'the soul needs to follow something in order to give birth to virtue: this something is God: if we follow Him we shall live aright.' Consequently the exemplar of human virtue must needs pre-exist in God [. . .]. (1a2æ.61.a5.c)

That is, virtue springs from the God from whom we all spring:

> [. . .] by a kind of participation of the Godhead, about which it is written (2 Pet. 1.4) that by Christ we are made 'partakers of the Divine nature.' And because such happiness surpasses the capacity of human nature, man's natural principles which enable him to act well according to his capacity, do not suffice to direct man to this same happiness. Hence it is necessary for man to receive from God some additional principles, whereby he may be directed to supernatural happiness, even as he is directed to his connatural end, by means of his natural principles, albeit not without Divine assistance. Such like principles are called 'theological virtues': first, because their object is God, inasmuch as they direct us aright to God: secondly, because they are infused in us by God alone: thirdly, because these virtues are not made known to us, save by Divine revelation, contained in Holy Writ. (1a2æ.62.a1.c)

Famously, the four natural cardinal virtues (of justice, prudence, temperance, and fortitude) are complemented, in an unanticipated and gratuitous way, by God's gifts of faith, hope and love. The complex argument of 1a2æ.63.a2–a3 locks the development of virtue into a net that relies upon God's graceful agency in his divine law and in the infusion of virtue. By this stage in the *Summa*, we are dealing with that same global turning of the heart towards new loves that we saw in Augustine.

XI. Love poured in and commended

What is the logic of the global turning of the heart towards new loves? In Servais Pinckaers's reading of the *Summa*, Thomas' understanding of the relationship between the theological virtues and the 'evangelical law' (1a2æ.106–108) is too often ignored, so that 1a2æ is dissected into its various supposed 'treatises':

> [T]here is hardly anything left but human acts, a smattering of passion, and a small sampling of virtue. The place in the sun is turned over to natural law and

sin. We also note that the most explicitly Christian treatises have been removed from moral theory proper.[419]

Hence a kind of decapitation is often perpetrated, where the action of the Holy Spirit and the New Law – actually 'the entire Gospel capstone of St. Thomas's moral teaching' – has 'been suppressed'.[420] But rather, at the pinnacle of this section of the *Summa*, Thomas mainly deploys Jeremiah, Paul and Augustine, with Aristotle invoked only for some limited procedural and illustrative points. The evangelical law (of which the Sermon on the Mount is paradigmatic) is conceived as internally active, and dependent upon the Spirit's action (following Augustine's logic in *On the Spirit and the Letter*). For Pinckaers, this is a novel development in the Scholastic tradition.[421] That the New Law is a 'grace' correlates it with the treatment of grace to follow (1a2æ.109–114).

The Holy Spirit, first considered in 1a.36–38, reappears immediately after the material on virtue (1a2æ.68–70). The Holy Spirit co-ordinates several gifts together to direct the natural virtues. The section is surprising in its ardent and urgent tone; Thomas seems quite delighted by what these spiritual donations represent. On the Beatitudes, for example, a pattern of both virtue and gift operates in synergy upon both intellectual and sensitive appetite, working to turn a person *wholeheartedly* to the good. This turn to the good is 'by a virtue, so that [passions] are kept within the bounds appointed by the ruling of reason', but now *also* 'by a gift, in a more excellent manner' (1a2æ.69.a3.c). Thus, the virtue of moderation, for example, now joins with a *contempt* for riches and honours; and with a *sorrow* at the irascible passions that beckon. The virtue of justice joins with 'ardent desire' that is signified in the Beatitude's *hunger and thirst*; and with *peace* to the neighbour. Thus, Aquinas sees the Spirit residing among the operations of the sensitive appetite, powerfully to fuel, amplify and vindicate virtue's intellectual task. Virtues are no longer merely natural. They are supernatural because *the loves of the soul have supernaturally been changed.* This is a logic of love poured in: 'All the moral virtues are infused together with love' (1a2æ.63.a2.sc).[422]

The total effect is to describe a person in whom there are natural possibilities to move towards the happiness described in 1a2æ.1–5. But for this trajectory to be realized, natural possibility can only be fulfilled or completed by the Spirit. The Spirit does this by theological virtues, by gifts, by beatitudes and by fruits. These operate at all levels upon the human *syntagma*. In addition (and bypassing Aquinas' consideration of sin, 1a2æ.71–89) comes the evangelical law – a kind of technical term for Christ's own teaching, also called 'New Law' – through which

419. Pinckaers, *The Sources of Christian Ethics*, p. 171.
420. Pinckaers, *The Sources of Christian Ethics*, p. 171.
421. Pinckaers, *The Sources of Christian Ethics*, pp. 176–77.
422. For a similar account, see Stump, 'Non-Aristotelian Ethics', p. 95.

the Spirit works. For Pinckaers, 'Clearly, not only ethics but the whole study of theology converges in the treatise on the evangelical law'.[423]

But a problem for it is outlined in 1a2æ.107.a4.c, arising from a 'difficulty [that] attaches to works of virtue', namely, that 'that a virtuous deed be done with promptitude and pleasure.' Virtue, once inculcated in a person, helps this difficult problem. To act with promptitude and pleasure 'is difficult for a man without virtue: but through virtue it becomes easy for him.' However, the New Law cuts across us; it offers the opposite of promptitude and pleasure, by challenging various 'interior movements of the soul' (such as an adulterous glance, or murderous anger). How can the New Law help at all, then? In it, thinks Aquinas, our 'interior movements are ordered' (1a2æ.108.a3.c) by its address to *human volition*. Rather than merely proscribing external behaviours, evangelical law addresses hearers to refrain 'from internal acts, and from the occasions of evil deeds'. It also interrogates intention, so that 'we should seek neither human praise, nor worldly riches, which is to lay up treasures on earth.' In the actual saying and hearing of it, Christ's teaching reorders a person towards the 'pleasures and promptitudes' of virtue. The same reordering occurs in reference to the neighbour, of whom it is forbidden 'to judge him rashly, unjustly, or presumptuously' or 'to entrust him too readily with sacred things if he be unworthy'. As in Augustine, love poured in merges into love commended, as hearers of the evangelical law are invited (by command) to participate in the divine reordering of love.

> He teaches us how to fulfil the teaching of the Gospel; viz. by imploring the help of God; by striving to enter by the narrow door of perfect virtue; and by being wary lest we be led astray by evil influences. Moreover, He declares that we must observe His commandments, and that it is not enough to make profession of faith, or to work miracles, or merely to hear His words. (1a2æ.108.a3.c)

Thomas has already made it clear that by the Spirit, God is at work to bring the theological virtues; and the hearing of the evangelical law is, apparently, instrumental to the Spirit's work. This hearing adds no new legal precepts. It reorders the heart, and seems also to be the means by which the gifts, beatitudes and fruits come among the elements of the human *syntagma*. Interestingly, it reorders by revealing truth that is consonant with the moral field (for rather than doing violence to natural virtues, it enhances them). Recalling that people are powerless to reorder themselves (given their bondage to voracity and selective sight), then presumably, evangelical law unveils whatever in the moral field was always present but lay hidden, veiled by voracity and selective sight.

This conception of the evangelical law's unveiling task concurs with what, for Pinckaers, is the 'dynamic interconnection' between all the kinds of law in Aquinas. Space forces me to sidestep the important treatise on law (1a2æ.90–105) since it is not directly germane to the investigation. But Pinckaers' summary of Aquinas'

---

423. Pinckaers, *The Sources of Christian Ethics*, p. 178.

on law is sensitive, and worth recounting here to cast light upon my claim that evangelical law somehow unveils the moral field. (Pinckaers' account also frees us from the modern conceit of law as always only a heteronomous imposition upon the unwilling – a misunderstanding that renders, especially for Protestants, the term 'evangelical law' an oxymoron. Anyone struggling under baggage of oppression in words like 'law' and 'legislation' might experiment with substituting them, in the quotation following, with something like 'moral order':)

> [Aquinas] distinguished five kinds of law: the eternal law, divine source of all legislation; natural law, which is the human heart's direct participation in this; then human law, which derives from natural law. Revelation further added the Old Law, centred in the Decalogue and relating to natural law, and the evangelical Law of the New Testament. These different laws were dynamically interconnected, beginning with the eternal law, descending through natural to civil law, and ascending again toward God to reach their summit in the evangelical Law, the most perfect possible participation in the eternal law that can be found on earth and the closest approximation to our final goal.[424]

The supernatural work here remains mysterious, like wind; yet participation in the entire process is entirely accessible, beginning with the hearing of the evangelical law, and continuing in the doing of it (including reflection upon and adjustment of 'interior movements'). Thus, for Pinckaers, Aquinas pictures a 'Christian moral organism', where under the instruction of the evangelical law, evangelical (or supernatural, or 'theological') virtues proceed from the Holy Spirit. Acting through the reason and the will, *and with the assistance of a spiritually reordered sensitive appetite*, these virtues superintend the natural virtues of prudence, justice, fortitude, and temperance, which in turn (especially in the case of the last) govern the sensitive appetites. 'In this way, a new moral organism is formed, which is specifically Christian.'[425]

XII. How Thomas helps

We might almost imagine Thomas telling the familiar Christian story, but inductively. He does not walk the preacher's usual path of a Christian proclamation to which the hearer must commit before they can be further persuaded.

Rather, the first half of the *Summa* quietly and inexorably corrals the Aristotelian reader into an Augustinian corner. If the science of Aristotle is as true as it seemed in thirteenth-century Paris, then to be a good Aristotelian entails a particular anthropology. A succession of implications follows from this anthropology: first for human action and emotion; then for virtue; then for *theological* virtue; and

---

424. Pinckaers, *The Sources of Christian Ethics*, p. 181.
425. Pinckaers, *The Sources of Christian Ethics*, p. 179.

then for the work of the Spirit in the intellectual and sensitive appetites. Finally, the teachings of Christ are seen to fulfil this logic. The *syntagma* that is left is not, as Pinckaers rightly observes, an Aristotelian one: it is a Christian moral organism, a kind of being that answers the deepest aspirations of Aristotle more completely than the best conclusions that thinker could ever give.

'Christian morality [. . .] lies principally in virtues and interior acts' and 'the action of the Spirit through the virtues creates within us a spontaneous, personal movement toward good acts'.[426] Thus precepts are reduced, freedom increased, and the content of the precepts guarded by love. People can even be said to have developed new instincts. Perhaps, on this account, Christ's evangelical law added no precepts to the natural morality of the Decalogue, so that there exists no specifically Christian ethic. But Thomas' ethic 'consisted mainly in virtues and only secondarily in precepts'.[427] There *is* a specifically Christian ethic – constituted in the bringing to being of divinely reordered Christian moral organisms. Distinctive to these Christian moral organisms is their logic of love, by which they approach the moral field under divine tutelage, learning to love those aspects of it previously veiled to them by their voracious selective sight, and participating in new praxis that will further generate reordered love.

I think it worth adding that by 'Christian moral organism' we do not mean to imply that card-carrying Christians are such organisms, while others are not. Sectarian tribalism only obscures the vision in Thomas, where all people may participate in a new way of being – a new gestalt – carried along by gifts natural, theological and christological. Jean Porter neatly summarizes the elementary natural basis of moral order for Thomas. '[H]is theory of the human good is itself grounded in a general theory of goodness, which rests upon a particular theory of nature.'[428] We may each find moral and emotion integration, where the adjective 'Christian' refers not to some sectarian demand, but to the deepest logics of loving human being led to completion in the surprises of God, in Christ.

To this end, we have seen a matrix-like quality at work in Aquinas' grand vision of transformed appetition and renewal of mind. Given that elementary natural basis, certain structures can be discerned within love itself. Love diffracts into a series of emotional responses that reflect the complex array of goods within moral order. Hence a *syntagma* of human being places passion central to human doing – but not so central as to displace will and intellect because, ultimately, passion, will and intellect are all subsumed under appetite, which in turn is conditioned by love. And love will be either that which we love as it stands, unexamined in the moment or, a form of love informed and shifted by the essence of the God who is love (1a2æ.4.a4). The penultimate *telos* of human action is a set of non-passionate (i.e., non-voracious) emotions such as happiness, contentment, joy, and love, all terminating finally in and with God.

---

426. Pinckaers, *The Sources of Christian Ethics*, p. 185.
427. Pinckaers, *The Sources of Christian Ethics*, p. 185.
428. Porter, *The Recovery of Virtue*, p. 32.

Thomas' account effectively interprets some NT parenesis (e.g. 1 Pet. 1.14, 4.2; 2 Pet. 1.4; Rom. 12.2) and seeks to convert Aristotelians to Augustine's account of order: that the problem with passion is the disturbance of voracity and the conflict of goods; that emotions are not in themselves bad, but can be put to bad uses (thus making passions ordinate or inordinate); that the impassibility of God does not impugn the bodily nature of our passions (which I have only touched upon in this chapter, but to which I will return); that we are contentedly to enjoy each other; and that the soul has its weight of love which cannot be ignored. Virtue was understood as the producer of ordinate passion; and the Spirit, working through the evangelical law, was understood as indispensable finally to turn the soul's love to its proper end.

Within this satisfying matrix, we also find a particular emphasis upon the immediacy to us of sensory particulars. No counsellor would disagree. Many distressed individuals and relationships are almost entirely constituted by an indistinguishable succession of reactive moments, each fired by something in the senses. It is the counsellor's living to go about the frail task of reconstruction after events.

Augustine showed the privations of disorder within a good cosmos, where moral reasoning is complicated by our passionate responses to a complex world. But the prospect of reordered love beckons us to an optimistic partial overcoming of several such complications. If theology's understanding of the good can join with the best available science, then perhaps we can discern the order that was lost and reorder love. Something like this was Aquinas' project.

Indeed, to hope for less is to fear the worst: that our passions might be evil, that their irrationality makes them monstrous, that life in a body is fractured, and 'manichean' at best. But thankfully, Aquinas' grand vision triumphantly vindicates Augustine against the Manichees. For Aquinas, there are many reasons joyfully to expect the gospel's promise of reordered love.

However, *all* that we have achieved in this chapter is to begin a kind of meta-analysis our lives. What is it, really, to participate in it? That will be the subject of Chapter 9. Before that, though, a nagging worry needs to be met: Is it that passion is merely human, if God be impassible? That, perhaps, has been the theological conceit at the base of various denigrations of human emotion in its relation to rationality and moral reasoning. Sarah Coakley, among others, thinks this conceit is not, and has never been, true.

Chapter 8

COAKLEY'S INSIGHT

THE GROUND OF ALL DESIRE

In a reflection on contemporary philosophies of mind and emotions, Sarah Coakley addresses the 'currently regnant reductive physicalism' and notes how balkanized, effectively, are the available replies to it. Better replies 'could well be regenerated if new thought experiments were conducted on the supposition of God's existence rather than on the dogmatic presupposition of God's non-existence.'[429]

By extension, the same implication is likely for moral psychology. This chapter seeks to show how God, as described in classical Christian theology, and as finally revealed in Jesus Christ, shapes human being and moral psychology. (*How* that might relate to each of our own lives is the subject of Chapters 9 and 10.)

The chapter begins (I) with the problematization of divine love arising from various accounts of divine impassibility. Then, via Aquinas' account of divine love (II), we will consider how a God blazing with love could also be understood as 'simple' – a long-standing conception the tradition has considered necessary to a proper understanding of God. I will borrow some insights from David Bentley Hart in this discussion.

By way of this roundabout introduction, I will then outline (III) Sarah Coakley's account of how God's love patterns all our desire, including even our sexual desire (V). (I will commend her disagreement with Oliver O'Donovan's recent account of desire in its relation to ethics.) Her *ressourcement* in Dionysius the Areopagite enables us to conceive of how God loves in ways that become elemental to human constitution (IV). Coakley's and Paul Gondreau's conversation with Thomas Aquinas on the passions of Jesus Christ will then enable us then to observe, in Jesus of Nazareth, the human vocation to desire and love well (VI). My conclusion to the chapter (VII) connects its impetus back to moral psychology.

---

429. Sarah Coakley, 'Postscript', in *Faith, Rationality, and the Passions* (ed. Sarah Coakley; Malden, MA: Wiley-Blackwell, 2012), pp. 251–55 (254).

I. Impassibility and its spectre

Only twenty articles into the *Summa* – just after Thomas has drawn breath, as it were – he treats of 'whether love exists in God' (1a.20.a1). The first (erroneous) objection turns on God's impassibility. 'It seems that love does not exist in God. For in God there are no passions. Now love is a passion. Therefore love is not in God' (1a.20.a1.obj1). As is well known to those in the Anglican tradition, two centuries later it adopted such terms in the first words of its Thirty-Nine Articles of Religion: 'There is but one living and true God, everlasting, without body, parts, or passions [. . .]'.

The modern conflation of passion with emotion has triggered a revolt against the Article and other such expressions of divine impassibility. The thin version of it is taken to imply that God has no 'feelings', or no 'emotions'. Should that be true, then the objection at its most florid becomes that this is no God worth believing in. More apposite for our purposes is the anthropological implication of this version of divine impassibility. If God has no emotions, then human beings should presumably aspire to a passionless, reasonable existence, with emotions firmly suppressed – a serious aspiration in various epochs, but nowadays unthinkably inhumane (or so it is assumed). Or, while our emotions might be sanctioned by God as a particularly human gift – like, say, our fingernails – that leaves them to be no part of the image of God. For our moral emotions, then – as we saw in Kant (Chapter 2) – they are at best accidental to our obligations, and at worst irrelevant to them.

For these and other reasons, theology has taken a turn for several decades against divine impassibility. It is being cautiously revisited of late. My visitation of this terrain is not intended to settle every dispute raised between passibilist and impassibilist theologians.[430] However, we must at least have some kind of position

---

430. The following quick assay of a vast literature (listed in descending order of recency) will give an overview of the discussion and its history: Amos Winarto Oei, 'The Impassible God Who "Cried"', *Themelios* 41.2 (2016), pp. 238–47, online at: https://www.thegospelcoalition.org/themelios/article/the-impassible-god-who-cried (accessed 25 September 2021); Paul Helm, 'Impassionedness and "So-called Classical Theism"', in *Within the Love of God: Essays on the Doctrine of God in Honour of Paul S. Fiddes* (eds Anthony Clarke and Andrew Moore; Oxford: Oxford University Press, 2014), pp. 144–54, doi: 10.1093/acprof:oso/9780198709565.003.0011; Jürgen Moltmann, 'The Passibility or Impassibility of God', in *Within the Love of God: Essays on the Doctrine of God in Honour of Paul S. Fiddes* (eds Anthony Clarke and Andrew Moore; Oxford: Oxford University Press, 2014), pp. 108–19, doi: 10.1093/acprof:oso/9780198709565.003.0008; Christiaan Mostert, 'Moltmann's Crucified God', *Journal of Reformed Theology* 7.2 (2013), pp. 160–80, doi: 10.1163/15697312-12341293; Daniel Castelo, 'Continued Grappling: The Divine Impassibility Debates Today', *International Journal of Systematic Theology* 12.3 (2010), pp. 364–72, doi: 10.1111/j.1468-2400.2010.00510.x; Randall Bush, 'The Suffering of God as an Aspect of the Divine Omniscience', *Journal of the Evangelical Theological Society* 51.4

on whether 'God can feel emotions' (to speak colloquially) before we can know the merit of Coakley's insight for human moral emotion.

My generation of theological learners was blooded into the fight via Jürgen Moltmann's *The Crucified God*.[431] Moltmann surveys ancient Hellenistic valorization of *apatheia*, the Greek term behind the Latin root for English impassibility. This term connoted, said Moltmann, unchangeableness, psychological insensitivity, and ethical freedom. In application to God, it followed (on Moltmann's account of Plato and Aristotle) that God is unchanging, has no defects, needs nothing, does not return the love of friendship, suffers nothing, and 'is without emotions'.[432]

We young hotheads drew a direct line from these Greek conceptions to the absurdity of any view, whether Christian or not, of a God without passions. (As hotheads, passions were very important to us.) Moltmann was not so crass, observing how Judaic influences, and the very highly engaged God of the Hebrew Scriptures, combined to give a nuanced reception within the Christian tradition of divine *apatheia*. As Moltmann told it, this Christian adjustment of the Greek heritage held that God 'loves without self-seeking and anxiety', since:

> [. . .] *apatheia* could be taken up as the enabling ground for this love and be filled with it. Love arises from the spirit and from freedom, not from desire or anxiety. The apathetic God could therefore be understood as the free God who freed others for himself. The negation of need, desire and compulsion expressed by *apatheia* was taken up and filled with a new positive content [associating] passion with love out of freedom for others and those who were different, and taught an understanding of the meaning of the suffering of love from the history of the passion of Israel and of Christ.[433]

But even so, asserts Moltmann, those moves cannot suffice as an account of 'the positive side of the new relationship with God'.[434] Famously, Moltmann went on to deploy the suffering death of Jesus to insist upon 'God in Auschwitz, and Auschwitz

(2008), pp. 769–84; Scrutton, 'Emotion in Augustine and Thomas'; David Bentley Hart, 'No Shadow of Turning: On Divine Impassibility', *Pro Ecclesia* 11.2 (2002), pp. 184–206, doi: 10.1177/106385120201100205; Sarot, 'God, Emotion, Corporeality'; and Marcel Sarot, 'Patripassianism, Theopaschitism and the Suffering of God', *Religious Studies* 26.3 (1990), pp. 363–75. The classic English study is J. K. Mozley, *The Impassibility of God: A Survey of Christian Thought* (Cambridge: University Press, 1926), online at: https://archive.org/details/impassibilityofg0000mozl (accessed 25 September 2021).

431. Jürgen Moltmann, *The Crucified God: The Cross of Christ as the Foundation and Criticism of Christian Theology* (trans. R. A. Wilson and J. Bowden; London: SCM Press, 1974).

432. Moltmann, *The Crucified God*, p. 268.

433. Moltmann, *The Crucified God*, pp. 269–70.

434. Moltmann, *The Crucified God*, p. 270.

in the Crucified God' as 'the ground for a love which is stronger than death and can sustain death', and for 'living with the terror of history' while 'remaining in love'.[435]

His discussion leverages passion as emotion in its relation to passion as suffering. The sprawling literature since Moltmann has focused upon the possibility of the Godhead experiencing suffering, so as to be *com*passionate with and for creation and its humans. That focus is both understandable and even laudable in a world riven with suffering. For Christiaan Mostert, 'of all major theologians of the last six decades or so, Moltmann has been most deeply exercized by the problem of suffering' and '*Crucified God* is above all an answer to the "protest atheism" powerfully articulated in Dostoevsky's Ivan Karamazov and echoed silently by millions after him'.[436]

In many respects, Moltmann took his cues from J. K. Mozley's influential 1926 study, where God's 'feeling' is only mentioned in passing, and suffering foregrounded as a species of that genus. Revealingly of Mozley and his milieu:

> It is much easier to form a picture of what thinking and willing mean, when ascribed to God, than of what feeling means. Thought and will seem to have a meaning when use in connexion with God who is Spirit which cannot equally be said of feeling.[437]

This eminently contestable assumption shows where Moltmann was engaged, within a twentieth-century mindset whose subordination of emotion to reason could be no more clearly illustrated than in what Mozley can imagine about thought and will, but not about feeling. To be fair however, Mozley knew that:

> something which is linked up so closely with the whole of human life as is the element of feeling has, presumably, some archetypal perfection of itself existing in God. Even if 'feeling', owing to its associations, is an unfortunate word, it still may be much truer to say that God feels than that he does not.[438]

But Mozley could get no further. When Moltmann sets himself the task of engaging with the matter, God's suffering (or not) had become the primary lens, a starting point that arguably elided the more primary consideration of the nature of God's inner life – the *qualia*, so to speak, of divine love. '[W]hat has surprised me in my study of the debate on the issue of divine impassibility', says Marcel Sarot, 'is that one of the most important arguments Aquinas provides in favour of divine impassibility – the argument that bodily changes are necessarily involved in

---

435. Moltmann, *The Crucified God*, p. 278.
436. Mostert, 'Moltmann's Crucified God', pp. 161–62.
437. Mozley, *The Impassibility of God*, p. 180.
438. Mozley, *The Impassibility of God*, pp. 180–81.

emotion – is almost completely neglected in the contemporary literature on this issue.'[439]

The theological stream represented by Moltmann is chary of speculation about whatever in God remains hidden to us: 'we do not analyse the nature of God, but take as our starting point God's self-identification in his revelations.'[440] His trenchant opposition to the notion of a compassionless God whose love has no identifiably feelingful archetype begins with the many attestations against such a being in the Christian Scriptures (such as the 'grieving' of the Spirit in Eph. 4.30, or the sufferings of the Servant of Isaiah ch. 53).[441] His theological method – working through what can be known of God via revelation and culminating in the life, death and resurrection of Jesus Christ – is axiomatic to several theological approaches, and for this author, cannot be gainsaid.

Less properly, his rebuttal also consists in the quick rejection of what he takes to be medieval theology's preference for divine substance over subjectivity, with Thomas Aquinas a key villain. Moltmann even quotes the objector to Thomas (in 1a.20.a1.obj1, introduced above) as if representing Thomas' own view.[442] He cites this quotation from a secondary source, not directly from the *Summa*, suggesting unfamiliarity with the discourse convention that Thomas' objectors, like Job's friends, usually speak erroneously.

For Thomas Aquinas knows what Moltmann knows, and also knows something of how to parse human language about God (cf. *Summa* 1a.13.). Drawing from across Thomas' corpus, Marcel Sarot observes:

> Aquinas is quite conscious of the fact that on a literal interpretation many biblical texts seem to imply that God is capable of experiencing emotions. In this connection he provides the following examples:
> 'I regret having made them' (Gen. 6.7).
> 'Yahweh is tenderness and pity, slow to anger and rich in faithful love' (Ps. 103.8).
> 'Yahweh's anger blazed out at his people' (Ps. 106.40).
> 'There is rejoicing among the angels of God over one repentant sinner' (Lk. 15.10).
> 'God is love' (1 Jn. 4.16).
> In view of texts like these, Aquinas cannot simply deny that God can experience emotions like repentance, mercy, anger, wrath, joy and love.[443]

When Thomas and apologists for impassibility such as Mozley and Sarot maintain that within God something emotion-like inheres, we have good reason to think that

---

439. Sarot, 'God, Emotion, Corporeality', pp. 62–63.

440. Moltmann, 'The Passibility or Impassibility of God', p. 110.

441. Moltmann, 'The Passibility or Impassibility of God', p. 116.

442. Moltmann, 'The Passibility or Impassibility of God', p. 114.

443. Sarot, 'God, Emotion, Corporeality', pp. 76–77, citing *The New Jerusalem Bible* (London: Darton, Longman & Todd, 1985).

the emotionless god of ancient Greece does not map so easily onto the impassible God of Christianity. The inner life of God may, therefore, prove elemental to human moral emotion. To begin to see how, we need first to see something of how this God loves.

II. Thomas' account of how God loves

Thomas denies the god of Aristotle by pointing out that 'God is love' (1 Jn 4.16), as does Moltmann.[444] 'On the contrary,' Thomas replies to the objection that a God without passions cannot love. 'It is written: "God is love"' (1a.20.a1.sc). He goes on to answer the objector – in the gentlest of terms, it must be said – by making the distinctions seen in Chapter 7 between passions as movements of bodies, and the kind of appetition that is love but not manifested in the sensitive appetite of a human body:[445]

> [I]n us the sensitive appetite is the proximate motive-force of our bodies. Some bodily change therefore always accompanies an act of the sensitive appetite [. . .]. Therefore acts of the sensitive appetite, inasmuch as they have annexed to them some bodily change, are called passions [. . .]. Love, therefore, and joy and delight are passions [but] in so far as they denote acts of the intellective appetite, they are not passions. It is in this latter sense that they are in God. (1a.20.a1.ad1)

To us, this response seems a bit mild. Where the leap, the abandon, the fire, that we believe and experience of love? But in his usual, quiet way, Thomas is deeply hostile to any account of impassibility that entails an absence within God of profound and infinite affection. Buried in his third answer to impassibilist detractors Thomas describes God's love using a logic of intersubjectivity (rather than a logic of substances) of precisely the sort that Moltmann thinks proper to theology.

The article's third answer rebuts the objection that God is too simple to experience love, since love unites and binds (1a.20.a1.obj1), and to unite and bind something logically requires a composition of parts that need binding. That would be complex, thinks the objector, and not simple. The notion of simplicity takes us into arcana of Aristotelian logic. We moderns never really deploy the concept of simplicity in any meaningful way, understanding everything we know in terms of parts and particles all the way down. Indeed, our notion of the simple is the exact reverse of Aquinas', for whom the simple refers to the ultimate wellspring of all complexity, and *all* complexity is ontologically less than simple; whereas for us, anything simple is somehow the lesser for it. (To picture it analogously, perhaps, the undifferentiated *something* that existed prior to everything else in the

---

444. Moltmann, 'The Passibility or Impassibility of God', p. 115.

445. See Sarot, 'God, Emotion, Corporeality', pp. 64–73, for an extensive account of Thomas' reasoning on this matter, and drawn from across his corpus.

picoseconds following the Big Bang, comes closest to helping us imagine Thomas' sense of simple – albeit that his 'simple' goes far beyond even that amazing natural *something*, as David Bentley Hart's elucidation below will insist.) But rather than trying to explain and defend what Aristotle, Aquinas and Aquinas' objectors had in mind by simplicity,[446] it may work better for us to intuit the merit within the objection.

If we imagine God to be a Zeus or a Thor or some such demiurge, then of course God cannot be simple. As is well-known to village atheists everywhere, such projections of ourselves only magnify our tragic, or ridiculous, inner- and intra-conflicts and divisions. Such loves as these gods experience can only be as messy as our own. But the God in whom Aquinas believes is the One described in David Bentley Hart's summary of the tradition. In the first paragraph following, Hart's sense of the word 'simply' is ours ('not simply some craftsman'). In the final sentence, Hart's use of the term 'simplicity' gives an ostensive feel for what Aquinas understood by it.

> [God is] the infinite fullness of being, omnipotent, omnipresent, and omniscient, from whom all things come and upon whom all things depend for every moment of their existence [; . . .] Spirit, incorporeal, not an object located somewhere in space, not subject to the limitations of time, not a product of cosmic nature, not simply some craftsman who creates by manipulating materials external to himself, not composed of parts [; . . .] eternal, omniscient, omnipotent, omnipresent, uncreated, uncaused, perfectly transcendent of all things and for that very reason absolutely immanent to all things.[447]

> In one sense he is 'beyond being,' if by 'being' one means the totality of discrete, finite things. In another sense he is 'being itself,' in that he is the inexhaustible source of all reality, the absolute upon which the contingent is always utterly dependent, the unity and simplicity that underlies and sustains the diversity of finite and composite things.[448]

On this account of God, the objection makes more sense: how could God *do* love, when love longs for what lies beyond? Isn't Thomas' first answer (about passions needing human bodies) therefore simply a fudge? Simplicity is the attempt to name how there exists no such beyond for such a God; so surely it does not matter for Thomas to delineate God away from the bodily passions of the human's sensitive appetite. Surely God's intellective appetite still entails a going beyond that simplicity denies.

---

446. For an excellent introduction and overview, see D. Stephen Long, 'Thomas Aquinas' Divine Simplicity as Biblical Hermeneutic', *Modern Theology* 35.3 (2019), pp. 496–507, doi: 10.1111/moth.12510.

447. David Bentley Hart, *The Experience of God: Being, Consciousness, Bliss* (New Haven, CT: Yale University Press, Kindle edn, 2013), pp. 7, 9, 29.

448. Hart, *The Experience of God*, p. 30.

Thomas admits (1a.20.a1.ad3) that love indeed binds disparate being together. 'An act of love always tends towards two things; to the good that one wills, and to the person for whom one wills it: since to love a person is to wish that person good.' So far, this insight into how love works appeals to how we take any delight in good relationships, although Thomas first demonstrates it by reference to our immediate individual aspirations: 'Hence, inasmuch as we love ourselves, we wish ourselves good; and, so far as possible, union with that good.' 'So', he continues, love is indeed 'called the unitive force'.

And this is so 'even in God, yet without implying composition' – because at this point Thomas sees an implication that initially, we moderns abhor: 'for the good that He wills for Himself, is no other than Himself, Who is good by His essence'. Here we flip easily into the notion of God as a contemptible cosmic egoist, another favourite trope of the village atheist. But for this God, in whom inheres eternity and perfection, it can be no other way than that God knows and revels in the excellence of that. That was somehow the intuition of Aristotle, and (says Hart) of Orthodox Judaism, Islam, Sikhism, Hinduism, Bahá'í and others.[449] Nicholas Lombardo gives us some insight into how Thomas construes God:

> God's appetite aims at what is perfective and completing – which, ultimately, is nothing other than God's own being, since nothing else can satisfy desire for infinite good – [but] it never strives toward it as though it were an end not yet attained. [. . .] God is his own appetite, just as he is his own intellect, his own act of loving, and his own act of knowing. [. . .] Consequently, for Aquinas, the claim that God is love is not poetry; it is a technical claim about God's identity. God is identical with a movement of the intellectual appetite: the intellectual affection of love.[450]

Again, our reflex is recourse to some jibe against God as the self-absorbed cosmic solipsist. (We are all more suppurated in Nietzsche than we know.) But in his next sentence, Thomas returns to *relationally intersubjective* reasoning to help us see God:

> And by the fact that anyone loves another, he wills good to that other. Thus he puts the other, as it were, in the place of himself; and regards the good done to him as done to himself. [. . .] [L]ove is a binding force, since it aggregates another to ourselves, and refers his good to our own. (1a.20.a1.ad3)

The God who is simple, and who must of necessity revel in being God, turns out to revel in being God by regarding good done to another 'as done to himself'. It is a transcendent way of being simple. 'And then again the divine love is a binding force, inasmuch as God wills good to others; yet it implies no composition in God.'

---

449. Hart, *The Experience of God*, p. 29.
450. Lombardo, 'Emotion and Desire', p. 114. Cf. *Summa* 1a.19.a1.ad2.

Somehow, the God who knows all good, in Godself, 'refers his good to our own', as also 'done to himself'.

(In passing, we may observe that such a claim about God becomes warranted per the unveiled Holy Trinity, whose Persons perpetually glorify one another. Hence Thomas, like many before him, is no mere speculator upon hidden substances. After an extensive investigation and defence of the tradition, my colleague Jacqueline Service uses the term 'divine self-enrichment' to describe these simple and eternal ways of love.[451] The intersubjectivity inherent to the simplicity of the one God becomes an astonishing new possibility for the human race to encounter, once God becomes known within human history as Trinity.)

David Bentley Hart is a trenchant opponent of (almost everyone, but especially) Moltmann. His critiques are several, but two need recounting here. First, rather than 'rescuing' God by imagining God's 'becoming' as somehow contingent upon Auschwitz, all such applications of Hegel only succeed in dignifying evil by 'describing a God who is the metaphysical ground of Auschwitz.'[452] It has precisely been God's *apatheia* and the tradition's insistence upon it, Hart argues, that secures divine love and our joyful hope. His account of the Christian reception of the term[453] goes into more detail than does Moltmann's. Some highlights must suffice.

It is by taking us beyond our habits of immediate reactivity that *apatheia* enables 'a condition of radical attachment.'[454] It envisions love 'without restraint,' 'a love so perfect that no perturbation or pathos can obviate its intensity.'[455] 'Obviously, at this point, one is not talking about the sort of austere impassivity or want of feeling one would ascribe to Aristotle's or Plotinus's "God," or of some sort of pure and dispirited indifference.'[456]

> [L]ove is not primordially a reaction, but the possibility of every action, the transcendent act that makes all else actual [. . .]. This is so because the ultimate truth of love is God himself, who creates all things solely for his pleasure, and whose act of being is infinite. And this is why love, when it is seen in its truly divine depth, is called *apatheia*. [. . .] [L]ove is not, in its essence, an emotion

451. Jacqueline Service, 'Divine Self-Enrichment and Human Well-Being: A Systematic Theological Inquiry, with Special Reference to Development and Humanitarian Aid', (unpublished Ph.D. dissertation, Charles Sturt University, 2018), pp. 84–130, online at: https://researchoutput.csu.edu.au (accessed 28 September 2021). See further Jacqueline Service, *Triune Wellbeing: The Kenotic-Enrichment of the Eternal Trinity* (Maryland: Fortress Academic, forthcoming).

452. Hart, 'No Shadow of Turning', p. 192.

453. Hart, 'No Shadow of Turning', pp. 192–205.

454. Hart, 'No Shadow of Turning', p. 193.

455. Hart, 'No Shadow of Turning', p. 194.

456. Hart, 'No Shadow of Turning', p. 194.

– a pathos – at all: it is life, being, truth, our only true wellbeing, and the very ground of our nature and existence.[457]

In Anastasia Scrutton's linguistically oriented solution,

> [. . .] re-appropriating the Augustinian–Thomist distinction between passions as extreme and overpowering feelings, and affections as feelings that are in accordance with reason and the will, might elucidate the argument more aptly than recourse to the category of emotion. In speaking of God being able to experience affections, the concerns of the passibilist would be in some ways compatible with the impassibilist [. . .]. A model of the divine 'emotional life' that includes affections but excludes direct experience of passions, may unite some of the concerns of both passibilist and impassibilist theologians.[458]

There is a great deal more to consider in the debate over impassibility. I can say no more here about its Trinitarian dimensions, nor examine the various proposals for how human suffering connects meaningfully to the divine life. It suffices here to have seen that only in caricature does 'God' have no bearing on the human propensity to love. Human loving springs from God's love, as elemental to our own being as to God's (even though we experience passions, whether ordered or disordered).

III. Coakley's extension

It will seem somewhat roundabout to have arrived at Sarah Coakley's work via a survey of impassibility. But I wanted no misinformed notion of it to compromise the implications of her insights for moral psychology.

She has characterized her *God, Sexuality and the Self*[459] as a work that has 'made "desire" the key anthropological category, and prayer (especially prayer-in-the-Spirit as understood by Paul in Romans 8) the axis around which the whole doctrinal discussion revolves'.[460] We have already seen the importance of that anthropological key in Augustine and in Aquinas. In the remainder of this chapter, we will see how Coakley envisages it, both in far-reaching extent, and in further relation to God.

Starting a little further back than her account of desire, I note her provocative suggestion that philosophies of mind (and so by extension, moral psychologies)

---

457. Hart, 'No Shadow of Turning', p. 195.

458. Scrutton, 'Emotion in Augustine and Thomas', pp. 176–77.

459. Sarah Coakley, *God, Sexuality and the Self: An Essay 'On the Trinity'* (Cambridge: Cambridge University Press, 2013).

460. Sarah Coakley, 'A Response to Oliver O'Donovan's *Ethics as Theology* Trilogy', *Modern Theology* 36.1 (2020), pp. 186–92 (192 n 28), doi: 10.1111/moth.12561.

'could well be regenerated if new thought experiments were conducted on the supposition of God's existence rather than on the dogmatic presupposition of God's non-existence.'[461] Her utterance is not made in a vacuum. 'My own faculty at Cambridge is physically poised between the faculties of philosophy, law, and criminology. I also have close relations with colleagues in the natural and medical sciences, and in philosophy of science [and] an intense commitment to continuing the conversation with my secular (even atheistical [*sic*]) colleagues in philosophy, the natural sciences, and the social sciences.'[462]

Her suggestion is therefore quite serious – that in other words, should it become 'properly basic'[463] to regard God's simplicity also as love, and the cosmos and we participants in it as springing from such a One, how might then we parse moral psychology? David Burrell, in a treatment of Aquinas' reception of other writers, summarizes this core aspect of the tradition in a way that throws further light on Coakley's thought experiment:

> [T]he creator ever acts by constituting the order which inheres in each existing thing, in the measure that it is. [. . .] Yet since 'order' is a consummately analogous term, we can never be sure we have detected the originating divine order in things, though our conviction that there is one, *inscribed in their very being and our intentional attitudes towards them*, will continue to fuel our inquiry.[464]

On Burrell's account, Aquinas follows one 'Dionysius the Areopagite', a figure also of interest to Coakley. Dionysius 'prefer[s] to characterize human beings as "good-seeking animals" (like "heat-seeking missiles") rather than as "rational (or speaking) animals"'.[465] That operation, within the 'order' Burrell mentions, under the God whom Aquinas, Bentley Hart, Coakley, Dionysius and others seek to name, gives reasons all the way down for why our moral psychology cannot but zero-in on our predilections for moral intuitions that often take the form of emotional dispositions manifesting as some expression of love.

In this respect, Coakley takes issue with the usually reliable Oliver O'Donovan, a monumental figure in recent theological ethics. In an otherwise appreciative review of his mature work, she queries his marginalizing of desire in relation to

461. Coakley, 'Postscript', p. 254.

462. Sarah Coakley, 'On Why *Analytic Theology* Is Not a Club', *Journal of the American Academy of Religion* 81.3 (2013), pp. 601–08 (607), doi: 10.1093/jaarel/lft040.

463. An allusion Coakley makes to so-called 'Reformed epistemology'; Coakley, 'Postscript', p. 214.

464. Burrell is named (p. 251) as the author of this section of C. S. C. David Burrell and Isabelle Moulin, 'Albert, Aquinas, and Dionysius', in *Re-thinking Dionysius the Areopagite* (eds Sarah Coakley and Charles M. Stang; *Directions in Modern Theology* series; Chicester: Wiley, 2011), pp. 215–50 (227); emphasis mine.

465. Burrell and Moulin, 'Aquinas and Dionysius', p. 224.

moral decision-making. Beginning with a citation of O'Donovan, she summarizes his view as follows:

> 'We cannot live without desire; but we cannot live with desire alone. Its pangs are indispensable as motivations . . . but they are by no means adequate for decision'. Both faith and agency, then, are outside its purview. It has become an 'emotion', (or as we might put it in its modern, Humean understanding) a 'passion', no longer a 'power' in the earlier scholastic sense, integrating body and soul.[466]

She disagrees:

> [Desires are] not necessarily a 'superficial' distractor from questions of agency and faith, but closely and intrinsically and *analogically* aligned to a more primary longing for God. Such of course is the perception of the long Jewish and Christian tradition of commentary on the *Song of Songs*; but it is no less the implication of an integrated theory of 'appetite', such as Thomas Aquinas's, which allows at the outset that we have an inborn longing for God manifested both in the sensual and the psychic dimensions of the self, and which is – under grace – progressively purified, integrated and guided by will and reason.[467]

Further remarks by O'Donovan[468] elucidate his position on desire. (I will quote these at length since they are not available in print at the time of writing.) O'Donovan confines desires to their future-wards orientations, whether or not the outcome is practicably achievable:

> [D]esire may still assist deliberation by pointing it in the direction of belief, of hope, of prayer, so that even where it cannot resolve on any other action, it still finds something significant to be done. Desire must always have some object that can be judged possible. [. . .] [Y]et at the same time, the object of a desire is a good that is absent. Desire implies wanting – in the literal sense, that is, being without.

> There is always a temptation to lose sight of this, and to expand the limits of desire too far. Desire does not include every kind of appreciation of the good. If it did, it would embrace the present good as well as the absent good, and the price paid for such an expansion of desire is to lose sight of its distinct character as an affection. Desire is different from liking, enjoying, willing, and so on.

---

466. Coakley, 'A Response to Oliver O'Donovan's *Ethics as Theology* Trilogy', p. 190, ellipsis and emphasis hers. The quotation is from Oliver M. T. O'Donovan, *Entering into Rest* (*Ethics as Theology* series, Vol. III; Grand Rapids: Eerdmans, 2017), p. 27.

467. Coakley, 'A Response to Oliver O'Donovan's *Ethics as Theology* Trilogy', p. 190, emphasis hers.

468. Oliver M. T. O'Donovan, *Lecture 2, The Missing Frontier: Time* (*Gifford Lectures 2021: The Disappearance of Ethics*) (University of St Andrews, 2021), 44'56"–54'05".

Desire is a specialized emotion. We can do deliberately what we feel no desire to do, and while desire may be a precipitating factor that carries us to deliberation and action, it is only one possible precipitating factor. There are others: a sense of duty, for example; and other strong emotions may replace desire in prompting action, as when we strike out in anger, weep in sorrow, shout in jubilation – sometimes in the teeth of a strong desire to control ourselves. [...] [G]ood excites desire, in particular. It promises more of itself. The promise is central to desire. There's a great difference between desire satisfied, and a pleasant surprise. In the one case, the good was present to the mind, anticipated, promised, looked-for. In the other, it is an unexpected discovery. What allows these ideational presences is the capacity of real goods to generate promises of their own further realisation. The object of desire is desirable because it is implied within a good already known. Desires are unintelligible, unless they are born out of a constellation of goods that we already appreciate.[469]

As is often the case with O'Donovan, these comments serve a more subtle point. (Desire is 'a distinct emotional response to temporality',[470] with O'Donovan's main concern being the bearing of time upon moral thought and practice, and also the bearing upon it of theological revelation about history.) Given the quotation above as it stands, it would be tempting to resolve the disagreement between O'Donovan and Coakley as a merely semantic one: that desire for O'Donovan is only a term for proximate near-term longings, whereas for Coakley it is an all-encompassing term, like for Augustinian love.

But O'Donovan goes on to notice that desires are, in fact, *not* only future-ward: they are also 'reminders of things that were good, and have passed away.'[471] Desire, therefore, expresses both as hope and as sadness. In this respect, we may add, it is therefore akin to appetition in Thomas' *syntagma*, and is as elemental. What, then, is the problem in his account, if any? In order better to locate the focus of Coakley's challenge to O'Donovan, and although it may not be fair to borrow O'Donovan's impromptu answer to a question after his lecture, his explication of disordered desire deserves further attention:

All feelings – and desire is a feeling, part of our affectual resources – [are] capacities that generate the possibility of action within us, in general terms.

---

469. O'Donovan, *Lecture 2, The Missing Frontier*, 47'08"–50'49".

470. O'Donovan, *Lecture 2, The Missing Frontier*, 52'49–53". Interestingly, a related claim is made by Roy F. Baumeister, 'Emotions: How the Future Feels (and Could Feel)', in *Homo Prospectus* (eds Martin E. P. Seligman et al.; Oxford: Oxford University Press, 2016), pp. 207–23. The psychology and theology of moral emotions in their relation to future-oriented temporality – with special reference to O'Donovan's later work, and this new departure in psychology (in which emotions are fundamentally prospective) by Seligman *et al.* – would be another fascinating conversation.

471. O'Donovan, *Lecture 2, The Missing Frontier*, 53'05–09".

All feelings have to be subject to thought. Not that thought [. . .] is some kind of an abstract, beautiful commander, and feelings a kind of jumble and mess of vitalities, and there is a kind of imposition. The meaning of our feelings is immanent to them, they tell us something of themselves. But we can remain in ignorance of what they are telling us.

Disordered desire is [. . .] an experience of desire that doesn't understand itself: that something is lacking in our lives. That we're deeply aware of something lacking in our lives can be an intense feeling, a quite preoccupying feeling, without our having the first idea really what it is that's lacking, or how to set about finding out.

That is, I think, the meaning one gives to disordered desire: it has nowhere to go, the desire comes, the feeling can be on its own, it is not self-interpreting. We need to be able to interpret it, which we have to do by placing it alongside everything else we know about the world, besides the fact of our desire.

And of course, the problem about very strong feelings is that they hide from us all the other things we know about the world. They push them out. So, we get to a state where the only thing we're aware of is how much we desire something; and the realities surrounding that situation don't appear to us with the weight that in other states of mind, they would obviously have. So recovering them is, as it were, the recovery of the truth of the desire that we have.[472]

There is Augustinian nuance here, in the recognition of our voracity and selective sight, and in the need to 'recover' reality beyond fixated desire. Perhaps the point at issue, though, is that despite the attempt here to mitigate against the conceit that 'thought' is the 'beautiful commander' of the 'mess of vitalities' – a neat summary of what Solomon called the 'myth of the passions' – O'Donovan is surely too suspicious of the way 'very strong feelings [. . .] hide from us all the other things we know about the world'. There seems little room here for intuitions that arise directly from love. Correspondingly, he is flat-footed both in the means by which 'thought' recovers truth and wider realities; and in the previous long quotation, by which the intelligibility of desire consists in the 'appreciation' of a constellation for goods. *For even these acts of 'thought' are acts of love* – as he well knew in his early work on the aspects of love, rehearsed in Chapter 6. Coakley suggests that 'those aspects of Augustine's thought on desire that should entrance him, fail to do so'.[473]

O'Donovan's early work was marked by close attention to Augustine's logic of love, surveyed in Chapter 6, and worth reprising here. Recalling my claim that Augustine shows how *love has an ordinant logic* and *deliberative logic has its love(s)*, O'Donovan went on to analyse these logics as a series of aspects, making plain the centrality of love to our participation in the cosmos. As love becomes divinely reordered, we love according to each of these aspects. To notice Augustine's

---

472. O'Donovan, *Lecture 2, The Missing Frontier*, 1.03'57" – 1.06'13".
473. Coakley, 'A Response to Oliver O'Donovan's *Ethics as Theology* Trilogy', p. 190.

aspects of love is to discriminate between love's various *responses* to the complex order of moral field, since 'the loving subject stands in a complex and variable relation to the reality which his love confronts.'[474] O'Donovan showed how the mature Augustine constantly moves between these four aspects of love:

> The choice of means to ends, the admiration of the neighbor's goodness, the pursuit of the neighbor's true welfare, all these are the subjective aspects of a single movement of the soul which reflects the one dominant cosmic movement, the return of the created being to its source and supreme good.[475]

That conclusion is closer to Coakley's view, as witnessed in her work below. O'Donovan's later comments on desire are hard to align with his earlier account of the primacy of love within our being, constitution, and epistemology. To put it another way: these nuanced aspects of love in O'Donovan's earlier work seem not to have relegated it to desire's 'pangs' that must next be brought to the court of (underspecified) 'thought'. Almost certainly, a scholar of O'Donovan's stature will be well able to explicate how cosmic love, and daily desire, are related; perhaps, we have misunderstood his distinctions. A possible defence may be offered in terms, say, of the traditions to be described in Chapter 9: that a purgation of false loves that manifest as 'desire' must logically precede union with the love of God that will also manifest as different, proper 'desire'. But given what we know, Coakley is correct to press him on the point. To reiterate, even the appreciations and recoveries of properly truthful thought are, finally, enacted love, and manifestations of desire.

IV. Our participation in divine 'ecstasy and return'

Coakley's work may be characterized as a relentless pursuit of the logic and implications of the created soul's subjective movements in love as it returns to its source and supreme good. She finds themes not unlike those of Aquinas in the late fifth-century writer Dionysius the Areopagite. Like Thomas, Dionysius struggles adequately to describe how God loves:

> [T]he very cause of the universe in the beautiful, good superabundance of his divine yearning for all, *is also carried outside of himself* in the loving care he has for everything. He is, as it were, beguiled by goodness, by love, and by yearning, and is enticed away from his transcendent dwelling place and comes to abide within all things, and he does so by virtue of his supernatural and ecstatic capacity to *remain, nevertheless, within himself.*[476]

---

474. O'Donovan, *The Problem of Self-Love in St Augustine*, pp. 12–13.
475. O'Donovan, *The Problem of Self-Love in St Augustine*, pp. 35–36.
476. Dionysius, *Divine Names*, IV.13; cited in Coakley, *God, Sexuality and the Self*, pp. 314–15.

Coakley's added emphasis highlights a kind of ecstasy-and-return in God, and in this classical Christian tradition, people participate within and are further swept up into this ecstasy-and-return. (In passing, we should note while it has almost become a truism in theology to bewail Christianity's convergences with neoplatonism, Coakley is not embarrassed by these. Neoplatonism articulated a fundamentally coherent universe that includes an intelligible moral weave, which is reflected in Dionysius's account. Coakley suggests a genealogy of his thought that includes several overtly neoplatonic thinkers, and Christians so influenced, including Augustine and even St. Paul in Romans ch. 8.) Here is another attempt by Dionysius to portray the ecstasy-and-return in God, as cited by Coakley:

> [God] is yearning on the move, simple, self-moved, self-acting, pre-existent in the Good, flowing out from the Good. [The divine yearning] . . . shows especially its unbeginning and unending nature travelling in an endless circle through the Good, from the Good, in the Good, and to the Good; unerringly turning, ever on the same centre . . . always proceeding, always remaining, always being restored to itself.[477]

For Coakley, 'the divine ecstasy returning to itself allows redeemed creation to participate in it.'[478] But given the divide between creature and creator, how can such participation be? As Bentley Hart puts it, the One who donates to us our very being 'resid[es] in all things while remaining perfectly one, present to us in the depths of our own beings [. . .] not only *superior summo meo* – beyond my utmost heights – but also *interior intimo meo* – more inward to me than my inmost depths.'[479] 'Infinite being, infinite consciousness, infinite bliss, from whom we are, by whom we know and are known, and in whom we find our only true consummation.'[480] For Coakley, 'To know God is unlike any other knowledge; indeed, it is more truly to *be* known, and so transformed.'[481]

This becoming 'swept up into' the life of God is nicely pictured by Eleonore Stump as a 'second-personal connection with God', wherein 'it is possible for there to be as-it-were mind-reading or social-cognition between a human person and God'.[482] There is a pneumatological impetus to this conjoining with God, and (for Aquinas) the various virtues are the form of it, as is the experience of joy. But the connection needs primarily to be parsed intersubjectively. Aquinas:

---

477. Dionysius, *Divine Names*, IV.14; cited in Coakley, *God, Sexuality and the Self*, p. 315.

478. Coakley, *God, Sexuality and the Self*, p. 317.

479. Hart, *The Experience of God*, pp. 9, 10.

480. Hart, *The Experience of God*, p. 30.

481. Coakley, *God, Sexuality and the Self*, p. 45.

482. Stump, 'Non-Aristotelian Ethics', p. 98.

[There is] a happiness surpassing man's nature, and which man can obtain by the power of God alone, by a kind of participation of the Godhead, about which it is written (2 Pet. 1.4) that by Christ we are made 'partakers of the Divine nature' (*Summa* 1a2æ.62.a1.c).

God is happiness by His Essence: for He is happy not by acquisition or participation of something else, but by His Essence. On the other hand, men are happy [. . .] by participation (*Summa* 1a2æ.3.a1.ad1).

Whoever has the love of God [. . .] already has what he loves, as is said in 1 Jn 4.16: 'whoever abides in the love of God abides in God, and God abides in him.' And joy wells up from this.[483]

When [Paul] says 'The Lord is near [Phil. 4.5],' he points out the cause of joy [Phil. 4.4], because a person rejoices at the nearness of his friend.

V. Divine desire and human eros

Coakley's unconventional extension of this reasoning is to show how divine desire meaningfully interprets even our moments of intense sexual desire. Her insights here are not novel, by intention. Her project of *ressourcement* brings to bear an entirely conventional association, found in early Christian thought, of divine desire with human *eros*. The association begins earlier than that, such as in this cheek-reddening exultation: 'as the bridegroom rejoices over the bride, so shall your God rejoice over you' (Isa. 62.5). Similarly, Coakley regularly points to the long tradition of Christian commentary on *Song of Songs*, which was unembarrassed to connect its expressions of human ardour to divine love. Obviously, over the centuries, though, some in the tradition have studiously sought to delineate *eros* away from the things of God. (Coakley critiques the work of Anders Nygren as a case in point.)

Of course, she does not envisage some simple correspondence between our physiology and the being of God: 'no one can simply move from earthly, physical love (tainted as it so often is by sin and misdirection of desire) to divine love – unless it is via a Christological transformation.'[484] She also draws her insight from Gregory of Nyssa and Augustine, who know 'of the *infinite* difference between the divine, trinitarian life, and the human life of sexual temptation and struggle.'[485] Even so:

---

483. This paragraph and the following are Stump's citations of Thomas' commentaries on St Paul's Epistles to the Galatians and Philippians respectively. Stump, 'Non-Aristotelian Ethics', p. 99.

484. Coakley, *God, Sexuality and the Self*, p. 316.

485. Coakley, *God, Sexuality and the Self*, p. 268.

Instead of 'God' language 'really' being about sex, sex is really about God – the potent reminder woven into our earthly existence of the divine 'unity', 'alliance', and 'commingling' that we seek.[486]

That conclusion can also straightforwardly be demonstrated from, say, Eph. 5.32, where Christ's love for the church is the primary (as also in Rev. 21.2-3), of which human marriage throughout Eph. 5.25-33 is a derivative. Another favoured theological source for Coakley is Gregory of Nyssa, who also wrote in the 'Song-commentary tradition', and for whom *eros* 'is agape (as he puts it) "stretched out in longing" toward the divine goal.' Gregory's vision is of 'desire as thwarted, chastened, transformed, renewed, and finally intensified in God, bringing forth spiritual fruits of agape and *leitourgia* [i.e., service] in a number of different contexts.'[487]

Coakley's proximal interest in some of her writing is to break open stalemates over sexual ethics in interesting new ways. Her contribution is more profound than those issues of the moment, however. She presses the logic of love to its conclusion. Our age regards *eros* as its most precious existential experience. Christian culture responds with much nervous, stern or earnest limitation of it. But for Coakley, *eros* witnesses to Augustine's realization that humanity is constituted in love. We are made out of divine love, and for love, as seen also in *eros*. '[S]exual desire is not necessarily a "superficial" distractor from questions of agency and faith, but closely and intrinsically and analogically aligned to a more primary longing for God.'[488] Coakley's insight reminds me of exasperated conversations I have had with young evangelical men who, fixated on seeking freedom from their lustful fixations, found it difficult to see how these are amplified by the *absence* of other love for beauty within the nature, and supernature, of their lives.

In whatever reactions to the world we care to scrutinize, *eros* included, we see refractions of divine love and human participation within it.

VI. *The Passions of Jesus Christ*

No account of the divine can, in Christian thought, be complete without consideration of Jesus Christ. The divine inhabitation of an incarnation has proven ontologically taxing, to say the least, which should of course be expected given the magnitude of the premise. That is, attempts to imagine how christology works pivot upon attempts to comprehend God, such as we have glimpsed in this chapter. Even so, generations of Christians have known God and known themselves after the advent of Jesus Christ, and ontological speculation only arises derivatively from that encounter.

---

486. Coakley, *God, Sexuality and the Self*, p. 316.

487. Sarah Coakley, 'Pleasure Principles: Toward a Contemporary Theology of Desire', (*Harvard Divinity Bulletin*; Autumn 2005), online at: https://bulletin.hds.harvard.edu/pleasure-principles (accessed 21 September 2021). This article has no pagination.

488. Coakley, 'A Response to Oliver O'Donovan's *Ethics as Theology* Trilogy', p. 190.

Coakley addresses what we know of Christ in conversation with Thomas Aquinas' treatment in the *Summa*, III.1–59.[489] In Thomas' account, the first twenty-seven articles in this section contemplate Christ's inner life in conversation with the tradition of ontological speculation on Christology. The remainder of the section proceeds more inductively, looking to what was remembered of Christ in the four Gospels.

Neither Thomas' nor Coakley's reflections on Christ should be regarded as determinative, since after all, interlocutors in the tradition insist that the Gospels make Christ accessible to everyone who reads them. Even so, Thomas and Coakley's reflections on Christ are important to this enquiry, since these reflections extend their analysis of human and divine passions and desires. If indeed Christ is 'God with us' and 'Word made flesh', it should be expected that what is known of him becomes the test of coherency in the rest of their thought. In this matter, Coakley also points to an extraordinary study by Paul Gondreau[490] (inspired in turn by his professor, Jean-Pierre Torrell). These thinkers have rejuvenated attention to Thomas' magisterial treatment of the person of Christ.

Between them, we are reminded of some key terms in christology. The tradition has come to the conclusion that Christ is 'truly human' yet not 'purely human'.[491] Christ has not merely *appeared* to be human; he was and is human, with a human nature. Yet, he was also of divine nature. However, these natures are unified as one *person* (in what came to be known as the hypostatic union); and that *person* is continuous with the Second Person of the Trinity, the eternally begotten Son. Various mistakes – more harshly denoted as heresies – arise, it has been held, when the natures morph into two distinct persons (as in Nestorianism); or when divine person-and-nature is primarily held as determinative of Christ's being (as in Docetism and its cousin, Apollinarianism); or when human person-and-nature is primarily held as determinative of Christ's being (as in Arianism). Yet, furthermore, in order actually to be human, this nature is not generic: it is individuated into a particular human,[492] Jesus of Nazareth. This human nature is taken up into divine nature, in a way that perfectly preserves it, and does not involve a change of divine nature.[493] (When language fails at this point, as always it seems to, various heresies are implied!)

489. Sarah Coakley, 'Person of Christ', in *The Cambridge Companion to the Summa Theologiae* (eds Philip McCosker and Denys Turner; *Cambridge Companions to Religion* series; New York, NY: Cambridge University Press, 2016), pp. 222–39.

490. Gondreau, *Passions of Christ's Soul* (see n 395 above).

491. Paul Gondreau, 'Life of Christ', in *The Cambridge Companion to the Summa Theologiae* (eds Philip McCosker and Denys Turner; *Cambridge Companions to Religion* series; New York, NY: Cambridge University Press, 2016), pp. 240–54 (245), borrowing a phrase from Jacques Maritain.

492. See further Coakley, 'Person of Christ', pp. 226, 230.

493. Coakley, 'Person of Christ', p. 228 (drawing on the *Summa* III.2).

We seem a long way from what matters to modern people. Even those interested in theology share a modern tendency to smirk at the distinctions. Putting aside such lightweight cynicism, the literature is complex and not for the faint-hearted. But I persist with it here because if it is true that divine love functions somehow as the wellspring of all reality; and if human loves, even in damaged and disordered forms, are consequentially fundamental to moral reality; then an apprehension of Jesus Christ's inhabitation of desire becomes important for how we may inhabit our own desires, and hence our moral impulses and thoughts. Gondreau cites Thomas (who drew in turn upon other thinkers) to offer some insight into how Christ proceeded:

> Jesus could be tempted only by 'outward suggestion' [. . .] as this can happen 'without sin', whereas interior temptation results from disordered impulses of the flesh [and] from disordered affective movements (concupiscence), 'which cannot be without sin' [. . .]. [T]o explain how Jesus could be genuinely *drawn toward* a desirable though unlawful object, and thus be genuinely tempted [entails] the useful distinction that experiencing a good as *desirable* (such as the stone being turned to bread [Lk. 4.3]) is quite distinct from *desiring* that good; we can affirm the first in Jesus but not the second, which implies sin.[494]

For our purposes we may expatiate in Augustinian terms. In Christ it is known, both of God and within the humanity of Jesus, that the divine Person blazes with love: his being drawn towards anything proves, with Augustine, that we humans are constituted with a love that instantiates the divine yearning, 'pre-existent in the Good, flowing out from the Good'.[495] Even a casual reader of the Gospels sees that: Jesus' acuity about what matters is powerfully interwoven with expressions of desire. His response to the city of Jerusalem is an example among dozens: 'As he came near and saw the city, he wept over it, saying, "If you, even you, had only recognized on this day the things that make for peace!"' (Lk. 19.41-42.) 'How often have I desired to gather your children together as a hen gathers her brood under her wings, and you were not willing!' (Lk. 13.32).

At the same time, Jesus seems able to effect love of what is desirable that is not tunnel-visioned and intermittently voracious. The absence of his susceptibility to concupiscence consists, perhaps, in that capacity for a wide-ranging topography of affection. When he sees a woman victimized by legal purists, he can love their law while knowing how to love the woman as much, and differently, and appropriately (and not, note, the 'more' or 'better' *we* would reach for in *our* tunnel-vision). In his rages against injustice, he never crosses into violence against persons (even, arguably, in the temple-cleansing episodes). His disagreements are manifold, yet people still follow, presumably because they know he loves them too. It is

---

494. Gondreau, 'Life of Christ', p. 250. These crisp assertions summarise the more extensive argument in Gondreau, *Passions of Christ's Soul*, pp. 350–64.

495. Dionysius, *Divine Names*, IV.14; cited in Coakley, *God, Sexuality and the Self*, p.315.

no stretch for us to regard his loves as *eros*: they are absolutely as intense as that word connotes. As a species of that genre, he would of course have known the desirability of the overtly sexual; yet at the same time, whatever was that awareness is framed by such loving respect for the integrity of others as to entail, as far as we know, that he never actioned it (and if with the tradition Gondreau is correct, did not concupiscently desire to do so). Amid this landscape of properly ordered loves arises other pinnacles of properly located desire: 'With *desire I have desired* to eat this Passover with you, before I suffer', to gloss clumsily by italics the original emphasis of Lk. 22.15.

His inhabitation of human desire is never more apparent than in biblical depictions of what, most significantly of course, become denoted as his Passion. This datum must loom massively in any account of how a human, with all our desires, may participate in the cosmic scale of what God loves. The upshot of Coakley's assessment of Jesus, per the lenses Thomas provides, will strongly inform the subsequent monastic traditions' accounts of how to participate well in divine love.

> [I]t is in [Christ's] prayers that we see [. . .] yearning towards the full knowledge of beatitude being worked out, and worked out on behalf of others. The result is a rich and dynamic account of struggling human desire as intrinsic to the act of prayer and as gradually conforming human selfhood to the will of the Father [. . .].[496]

VII. Conclusion

Jesus does not represent an exemplar for us – an overworked concept (*pace* Thomas) that relies too much on our willpower, and too little on the reshaping of our love. Jesus was as individuated as are each of us, so it is not some copying the exact contours of his life, experiences and reactions that came to be understood as the proper way to participate with him in divine love. Christian theology has expounded on that participation in several ways, beginning with his redemption of humanity – an operation that invites us all to start again with God, no matter what we have done or become. There then exists in theology several descriptions of what participation 'in Christ' – to point to the canonical Pauline mystical phrase – then entails.

But it was his own life of prayer, such as noted by Coakley above, that became a clue for the many following who took seriously his way of reshaping desire. A final word from Coakley (commenting on Gregory of Nyssa) signals our next stop in Chapter 9:

> Gregory ends [. . .] with an insistence on ascetical *practices* as means of transformation, and of the indispensable spiritual power of one from whom one may *mimetically* 'catch the halo', as he puts it, of rightly ordered desire. In other

---

496. Coakley, 'Person of Christ', pp. 235–36.

words – and this is surely a point of great spiritual significance for today – right-channelled Eros, whether married or celibate, is impossible without deep prayer and ascetic perseverance; but it is even more impossible, interestingly, without shining examples to emulate.[497]

In other words, Gregory nudges us towards 'a training of desire, a lifelong commitment to what we might now call the "long haul" of personal, erotic transformation, and thereby of reflection on the final significance of all one's desires before God.'[498] In the chapter that follows, it will not so much be the concept of emulating holiness directly that interests us as the possibility of emulating intentional participation with God's love, through various contemplative practices.

It will seem very odd, in a book that began with the naturalistic milieu of clinical and experimental psychologies, to converge upon 'ascetical practices' and time-worn notions of purgation, illumination and so on. For so many reasons, we have been conditioned to avoid such talk. On the modernist side, we have learnt to sneer at Hume's 'train of monkish virtues' and (particularly in my archly utilitarian Australian context), only to esteem whatever will get to the most crassly valorized consequentialist value, be it the economy, my identity, my passion, or whatever. In such a milieu, spirituality must rigorously be sequestered to that private, optional space where predilections are stored. Overlaid onto that milieu – indeed, some (such as Charles Taylor) would argue,[499] setting the conditions for it – is a largely Protestant contempt for anything smacking of Catholic contemplation, mysticism, or ascetic practice.

However, the psychological may inexorably home in on the spiritual, as Haidt intuits, and as my own psychologist believes (see my introduction to the book). For if with Coakley's thought-experiment we concede that essential to God, who sustains all natural being, is love, we are better equipped to conceive with Augustine of how elemental to human being, including to human moral being, is love. The *prospect* of this participation has been our task within this chapter, but not yet the *means* of it.

The means of it, however, has been the burden of an enormous volume of Christian thought, often inculcated into and then indebted to Christian monastic and contemplative traditions. It has been the gift of Joan Chittister to induct the uninitiated into these traditions, so that we who have no real concept of them apart from the polemics we have heard, may yet benefit from their wisdoms. We will assay these traditions a little in the chapter that follows. Chittister's mediation to non-monastics of one of them helps us imagine a path to different loves.

497. Coakley, 'Pleasure Principles'.
498. Coakley, 'Pleasure Principles'.
499. I am thinking here, if I may be permitted to gesture towards it only loosely, of an aspect of the argument in Charles Taylor, *A Secular Age* (Cambridge, MA: Belknap Press of Harvard University Press, 2007).

Chapter 9

CHITTISTER'S GIFT

AN EVERYDAY SCHOOL

When Haidt gestures towards a spirituality that may or may not be 'trans-natural' (Chapter 3), he exemplifies a growing suspicion that something has gone wrong in Western conceptions of humanity that have excised the spiritual. The matter is of course fraught and contested. When Johann Hari lists the reconnections people need if to overcome depression and anxiety, he notes with some honesty that one psychological change people can make 'is prayer – there's evidence that people who pray become less depressed.' He quickly adds, 'I'm an atheist, so that's not on the table for me.'[500] But what might happen if we viewed such evidence, with Coakley, 'on the supposition of God's existence rather than on the dogmatic presupposition of God's non-existence'?[501]

The deliberately vague notion of spirituality is in key respects an accommodation to Western political pluralism, and its liberal polity. The broadness of the following consensus definition shows the expanse of human experience we are now trying to name:

> Spirituality is a dynamic and intrinsic aspect of humanity through which persons seek ultimate meaning, purpose and transcendence, and experience relationship to self, family, others, community, society, nature, and the significant or sacred. Spirituality is expressed through beliefs, values, traditions and practices.[502]

There is no doubt that every effort must be made to notice the varied range of what seems 'spiritual' to people. But at the same time, on any serious account, the term is also a direct descendant of thick Christian mystical ontologies whereby the Holy

---

500. Johann Hari, *Lost Connections: Why You're Depressed and How to Find Hope* (London: Bloomsbury, 2018), p. 224.

501. Coakley, 'Postscript', p. 254; see further Chapter 8.

502. Christina M. Puchalski, et al., 'Improving the Spiritual Dimension of Whole Person Care: Reaching National and International Consensus', *Journal of Palliative Medicine* 17.6 (2014), pp. 642–56 (646), doi: 10.1089/jpm.2014.9427. I am thankful to my doctoral student, the Rev'd Mark Layson, for introducing me to this definition.

Spirit mediates God to the human spirit – 'that very Spirit bearing witness with our spirit that we are children of God' (Rom. 8:16), to choose one New Testament example of that ontology from among dozens. David Tacey makes a related point most trenchantly:

> [T]he West will have to dust off the late medieval tomes on the interior life, dig up the lost and forgotten traditions of mysticism, and make these available to the starving masses. The way forward for Western religions is to bring the monastic traditions out of the cloisters and into the streets. Secularism has alienated us so fully from religious forms that when the spirit stirs again we will not be content with hearing stories about holy people, but we will want to taste holiness ourselves.[503]

Towards precisely that end, then, this chapter will gesture towards thousands of people who have been deeply interested in moral psychology, albeit in a different register than our own. I have in mind generations of monastics and contemplatives, both Eastern and Western. The chapter will alert us to such lives, and eventually converge upon the ministry of Joan Chittister. She has also lived such a life, yet engagingly draws modern people into living our own version of it. We easily underestimate how several streams of Christian monastic and contemplative tradition *practically* engaged with love commended and poured in, such as was articulated in Augustine's and Aquinas' more abstract accounts.

But I do feel fundamentally out of my depth, and as if trespassing on others' terrain. I come from a background of Christian formation that was heavily impacted by forms of positivism and empiricism, which found their way into various portrayals of theology and biblical studies. Similarly, I was also impacted by polemical (and often ill-informed) stances against monastic and contemplative traditions, wherein the term 'mystical' was held in contempt. The critique was that these traditions sought to excise the mediatorial work of Christ, echoing Augustine's complaint against the Pelagians that their scheme made Christ to die 'for nothing' (Gal. 2:21; see Chapter 6). But all Christian traditions find ways to do that, and the better articulated mystical traditions (like, arguably, that of St. Paul) are not so easily negated.

Ultimately, I blame no one for these deformations. My own confirmation biases meant I noticed and internalized what suited me at the time. Even so, I am not alone in having been misled in these ways, and hope at least to begin a task of translation for people like me. For those familiar with these millennia of tradition, my account may seem childishly simplistic. I take heart in the wisdom of self-proclaimed 'Imperfectionist' Oliver Burkeman, who advises that one's to-read pile should be treated more like a river to be dipped in to, rather than a bucket to

---

503. David Tacey, 'Contemporary Spirituality', in *Oxford Textbook of Spirituality in Healthcare* (eds M. Cobb, C. M. Puchalski, and B. D. Rumbold; Oxford: Oxford University Press, 2012), pp. 473–79 (476).

be emptied.[504] No truer word could be spoken of the vast domain of monastic and contemplative thought, and any corrections and additions springing from others' expertise can only be welcomed. I will sample testimonies from the 'East' (I); from the 'West' (II); from Joan Chittister (III); and will offer one of my own (IV). Although the chapter only samples this river of imaginative practices and rich insights, the small vials lifted from it are necessary to show how theology's logic of love is made substantive, with practices embedded in the theology of the God who is love (Chapter 8) rather than in vague and politically liberal notions of spirituality.

I. From the 'East': The testimony of The Philokalia

There has been a renaissance of interest in Eastern Christianity among Western theologians. A tangential note is in order for the uninitiated. The term 'Eastern' here does not refer to East Asia. The 'Western' church was centred on Rome, but from around the fifth century after Christ, the Eastern churches diverged on linguistic, cultural, and theological grounds into various subgroups centring on other major cities of the eastern Mediterranean. The largest Eastern church centred on Constantinople and later Moscow – what we today call Greek or Russian Orthodox – but smaller communities also formed in Egypt as the Coptic Orthodox Church, and in Syria and further east to Central Asia as the Antiochene Orthodox and the Assyrian Church of the East. Eastern Christianity includes theologians who wrote predominantly in Greek rather than Latin (though some small traditions also wrote in Coptic, a form of Egyptian influenced by Greek; Amharic, the language of Ethiopia; and Syriac, a later form of Aramaic, the language spoken by Christ; and eventually, in Russian and other Eastern European languages). Today, Eastern Christianity can be divided into various eastern European Orthodox Christian denominations and other Middle Eastern Christian communities, including the Coptic Orthodox Church, the Maronite and Melkite Catholic Churches, and the Assyrian Church of the East. Distance, linguistic differences, and even warfare, meant Eastern and Western churches increasingly stopped talking to each other, and when they did, would dispute at cross-purposes, often mis-hearing the different languages used for similar theological concepts.[505]

Our task here is to register an Eastern classic of monastic wisdom, *The Philokalia*,[506] which sits squarely at the intersection of moral evaluation and affective experience. The title can be glossed as 'Love of the Good', clearly reflecting

504. Oliver Burkeman, 'Treat Your To-Read Pile Like a River, Not a Bucket', online at: www.oliverburkeman.com/river (accessed 13 December 2021).

505. I am indebted to my colleague Dr Bernard Doherty for clarifying these Eastern distinctives, and for introducing me to Orthodox sources used in this chapter.

506. I will sample here the first volume of a recent four-volume translation: St Nicodemus of the Holy Mountain and St Makarios of Corinth (eds), *The Philokalia: The*

a preoccupation with what we would call the psychology of morality. It is an eighteenth-century compilation of two-millennia of Eastern Christian wisdom that includes discourses, reflections, and easily accessible advice on how to fall in love with the good, so as to inhabit it.

'If your heart comes to feel a natural hatred for sin,' advises St. Isaiah the Solitary, 'it has defeated the causes of sin and freed itself from them.'[507] A plethora of advice follows, such as Evagrios the Solitary's systematic desensitization of loss-aversion: 'When buying or selling you can hardly avoid sin. So, in either case, be sure you lose a little in the transaction.'[508] But this literature also insists that such advice can only function in proper perspective within communion with God expressed via prayer. St. Isaiah again:

> In storms and squalls we need a pilot, and in this present life we need prayer; for
> we are susceptible to the provocations of our thoughts, both good and bad. If our
> thought is full of devotion and love of God, it rules over the passions.[509]

These vignettes exemplify how generations of monastics and contemplatives remediated false loves, and trained new loves, using a slew of practices to participate in the love of God. In the case of the *Philokalia* we see several conceptions that map roughly onto Aquinas' *syntagma*. Intellect in these authors corresponds to Aquinas' rational powers, both cognitive and appetitive, which is capable of attention to universals (the 'bigger picture', as we might say). Passion is roughly equivalent to Aquinas' sensitive appetite. There is an incensive power or appetite in the soul, similar to Aquinas' irascible power. St. Isaiah's first assertion is that 'There is among the passions an anger of the intellect, and this anger is in accordance with nature. Without anger a man cannot attain purity [. . .]'.[510]

The *Philokalia* is ably introduced in Rowan Williams's *Looking East in Winter*, effectively a commentary on it.[511] Williams notes that some readings of the compilation do conduce to what Solomon called the 'myth of the passions' – that simplistic and dualistic conceit where cool thoughts oppose hot passions. While Williams once held to such a reading of the *Philokalia*, his recent work recants that view, and expounds subtle and wholistic anthropological philokalic themes.[512] For example:

Complete Text (trans. G. E. H. Palmer, Philip Sherrard, and Kallistos Ware, Vol. I; London: Faber & Faber, 1979).

507. St Isaiah, 'On Guarding the Intellect: Twenty-Seven Texts', *Philokalia*, p. 23 (text 6). (This figure is not to be confused with the much earlier Hebrew prophet Isaiah, after whom a book of the Bible is named.)

508. Evagrios, 'On Asceticism and Stillness', *Philokalia*, p. 35.

509. St Isaiah, *Philokalia*, p. 27 (text 14).

510. St Isaiah, *Philokalia*, p. 22 (text 1).

511. Williams, *Looking East in Winter*.

512. Williams, *Looking East in Winter*, pp. 6–7.

Human awareness is initially and primitively just the registering of the image of an object without either meaning or craving attached. [. . . But] this bare 'human' consciousness becomes diabolical, becomes bound to the acquisitive mode of perceiving; and the implication is that what will stabilize the mind is the infusion of angelic awareness, seeing the things of the world in their true – that is, symbolic – significance and using them accordingly. This is a 'natural' state in that it relates human consciousness to the real significance of things. And this allows us to say that the world as it is has nothing in it that is intrinsically evil, whether in soul or body: everything has the capacity to convey the divine intelligence and so to be related to human intelligence in its proper state. For the human intelligence – and thus the life that intelligence organizes – to be natural is to perceive the world as comprehensively significant; and because the world is significant in relation to God, it cannot take its significance from its potential for self-directed or self-serving human use.[513]

In other words, and to conflate with a little of Augustine's language, a properly natural human state is to learn and discern the actual meaning of things by reference what they mean to God, and to attach to them in love. To return to that nature is no simple atavism. The quest is spiritual. The following long quotation is Williams's adroit description of that quest, laced with reorientations of the affections, as envisaged in the Philokalic tradition:

We are not yet natural. [. . .] Created with certain capacities, we have in one sense irretrievably lost our starting point. We have known division and cannot behave as if the divided intelligence could be ignored or overcome by wishing it so. We are as a consequence living in some degree of unreality; we are not really here. The body's habitual response to stimuli has become either defence or absorption (anger or lust), so that we are chronically unable to exist as part of an interdependent created order. To learn to do so requires us to be educated in how we identify destructive behaviour (keeping the commandments) and so to check these habitual responses. In the process, something begins to happen to the instinctive life of aggression and desire, which reconstitutes it as a positive discontent with the present state of slavery. We recognize that we actively and profoundly want something other than the life of passion and fantasy. And that uncovered or reconstituted wanting is our opening up to the life for which we were made and that is made accessible to us once again in baptism, in the identification of ourselves with the self-giving Word of God incarnate. Beyond this, it is the Spirit who acts for the transformation of our awareness, physical and mental, so that the simplicity for which we were designed may pervade our intelligence. Throughout that lifetime's labour, the awareness of the gulf between what we may be and what we have made of ourselves continues to act as a goad

---

513. Williams, *Looking East in Winter*, pp. 13–14. Williams cites Maximos in support of these ideas.

to preserve the habit of self-questioning and penitence. We do not simply stop being divided; we learn to use our very dividedness to cast into a stronger light the possibility of a proper presence in and to the world and its maker. The intelligence that has not yet remembered itself is not yet truly embodied.[514]

Williams has seen into the way these authors noticed, like Augustine, a kind of negation at work in the operation of evil. But they convert this realization into concerted, existential practices of remediation. Williams continues:

> Our problem, if this reading of the Philokalia is correct, is not that we are embodied spirits, but that we are incompletely embodied spirits – that is, that we are as yet unable to live in this material and mutable world without clinging to our impressions, distorting our impressions, or compulsively marking out our territory. The things of the world – and our human neighbours in the world – appear either as food or as threat to the ego. Unless we become able to receive the truth of what is before us as it stands in relation to God, not to us, we are failing to be embodied in the sense of being properly part of creation: we are caught in an implicit idolatry, the effort to separate ourselves from the order of which we are a part.[515]

Comparing to my own dawning awareness of other Christian contemplative traditions, this description of the Philokalic tradition could equally describe the journeys of Western Benedictine or Ignatian spiritualities, and probably others. But we will retain focus for a little longer on this Eastern account, using as our lens an intriguing manual of 'Orthodox psychotherapy'.

Archimandrite Hierotheos S. Vlachos published his *Orthodoxi Psichotherapia* in 1986 (translated to English as *Orthodox Psychotherapy*[516]). This psychotherapy connotes a cure of the soul, the original meaning of the term, but theologically understood. It is a synthesis of the *Philokalia* and other Orthodox literature, and for our purposes, represents an explicit reply to psychology from the perspective of theology. It offers a 'theanthropology' – that is, an account of human being that cannot be abstracted from within the greater Being of the God who loves. It also illustrates another energetic account of human being where the loves and hates that drive us are elemental to us (and to what we now conventionally, and very boringly, denote as values, morality, and ethics).

Vlachos contends that 'many psychological illnesses are caused by the anxiety of death, the lack of meaning in life, a guilty conscience and the loss of communion with God'; and although some neurological and pathological anomalies sit rightly within the domain of psychiatric and neurological expertise, 'Orthodox theology

---

514. Williams, *Looking East in Winter*, p. 19.
515. Williams, *Looking East in Winter*, pp. 19–20.
516. Hierotheos S. Vlachos, *Orthodox Psychotherapy (The Science of the Fathers)* (trans. Esther Williams; Levadia, Greece: Birth of the Theotokos Monastery, 1994).

cures the deeper causes that engender' these more regular travails of our inner life.[517] He draws upon and summarizes the philokalic tradition in a manner that explicitly exemplifies a movement from human thoughts, loves, and passions into 'divinization' – a term particularly understood in the Orthodox tradition to name proper human inhabitation within God's own love.

This term has biblical antecedents in the human *telos* of 'fellowship with divine nature' (2 Pet. 1.4). Similarly, we are 'created according to the likeness of God', as we may gloss the Greek construction of Eph. 4.24, and are renewed into 'the image of' the Creator (Col. 3.10). Each of these later New Testament anthropologies list quotidian virtues that express and then terminate upon love.

Vlachos leverages the ancient parallelism of 'image' and 'likeness' (Gen. 1.26) to assert that while humanity retains the 'image' of God, in the absence of communion with divine love we have 'lost completely the likeness of Him'.[518] 'Deification is identical with "likeness", that is, to be like God.'[519] Here, theanthropology is premised on God as 'a living Person Who is in organic communion' with humanity, expressed not primarily individualistically, but through the *primarily* therapeutic ministry of the Church.[520] In its *primary* task, the Church assists divine grace to heal the soul.

It is not easy to summarize the nuances of Vlachos's account of the philokalic tradition without distorting it. For example, there is a *nous* and a heart on view, but these do not connote the now tired trope of thoughts pitted against feelings. Rather, 'in patristic theology these two are joined together.'[521] These both need to be purified, but that term connotes neither other-worldly superiority, nor spiritualized self-deception, nor self-punishment or related kinds of self-abnegation. Rather, forms of redirection of attention and energy are on view. The path to healing is typologized according to three stages: 'practical philosophy or purification of the heart, natural theoria or illumination of the nous, and mystical theology or communion with God through theoria.'[522]

These three stages correspond to concepts of purgation or purification, illumination, and contemplative union common to the Western tradition, a typology that originated with Dionysius the Areopagite. This typology developed into 'an account of spiritual progress conceived in terms of the three "ways", beginning with the eradication of bad habits and the cultivation of the virtues, moving on to the illumination of the mind by meditation and contemplation, [and] culminating in unitive love.'[523] A critique and 'pelagian' risk of this conception

---

517. Vlachos, *Orthodox Psychotherapy*, p. 12.

518. Vlachos, *Orthodox Psychotherapy*, p. 11.

519. Vlachos, *Orthodox Psychotherapy*, p. 26.

520. Vlachos, *Orthodox Psychotherapy*, pp. 25–26.

521. Vlachos, *Orthodox Psychotherapy*, p. 39.

522. Vlachos, *Orthodox Psychotherapy*, p. 40.

523. F. L. Cross and Elizabeth A. Livingstone, *The Oxford Dictionary of the Christian Church* (Oxford: Oxford University Press, 3rd edn, 2005), *s.v.* 'purgative, illuminative, and unitive ways'.

(especially in a performance- and merit-obsessed culture such as ours) becomes for the path through purification, illumination and communion to represent a kind of spiritual 'levelling up' (like mastering a spiritual computer game) that inevitably creates in-groups and abusive hierarchies.

As Vlachos sees these authors, though, that is not the case. The stages simply note aspects of what happens for a sick soul to be healed. It is not even the case that they always occur in a set order. Maximus intuits that 'in the case of the more learned, theoria precedes praxis, whereas with simpler people praxis comes first'.[524]

In the theological tribes of Christendom, those of Reformed Protestant ilk are bound to hear overtones of salvation by works in this language. Arguably though, the gift of divine grace to justify people irrespective of their past lies just as firmly at the base of these thinkers' approaches. Their language and terms are a more granular account of Reformed theology's expansive, umbrella concept of sanctification, with the Orthodox tradition having a great deal more to say about the discrete steps the distortedly loving human might begin to dance with the loving, saving God. Something like that can be seen in the detailed and penetrating analysis found in the tradition on *logismoi*, or 'thoughts', and on the passions.

The Orthodox conception of *logismoi* is more in the nature of a sensorium than a verbal apparatus. These occur to us as images, and are straightforward enough until tinged with passion. Right at the outset then in Orthodox conception, there is no basis upon which to compartmentalize a thought away from a feeling or an emotion. Thoughts, in this understanding, are readily tinged with passion. A thoroughgoing assessment of what makes an evil thought evil will entail evaluative mindsight about the passion underlying it, and a further account of passion as such.

In this tradition, passions generally have a morally negative connotation, which is not to say that the tradition derides emotion or valorizes cool rationality. (Williams's change of reading, above, probably pivots on this point.) For Vlachos, the Orthodox tradition insists (much as did Aquinas and Augustine) that passions are 'natural powers of the soul which have been corrupted by sin and by our withdrawal from God'.[525] That is as opposed to them having illicitly entered the soul and needing to be rooted out. It follows, then, that we will look for and here find another explanation of love as elemental to human being, with its fractured and distorted manifestations bedevilling our daily existences (and in this tradition, thereby termed 'passions'). Love is already encoded into the incensive and appetitive aspects of the soul (and in different respects, also into its intellectual aspect). Passions occur when the soul habitually inclines towards what is lesser for it – such as pleasure, and other manifestations of self-love – instead of what is greater for, such as various virtues and engagements with God. Vlachos quotes and paraphrases St. John of the Ladder:

---

524. Cited in Vlachos, *Orthodox Psychotherapy*, p. 40.
525. Vlachos, *Orthodox Psychotherapy*, p. 247.

'We have taken natural attributes of our own and turned them into passions' [...]. 'The seed for childbearing' is natural in us, but we pervert it for fornication. The anger which God gave us against the serpent, to wage war against the devil, is natural, but we have used it against our neighbour. We have a natural urge to excel in virtue, but instead we compete in evil. Nature stirs within us the desire for glory, but that glory is of a heavenly kind, for the joy of heavenly blessing. It is natural for us to be arrogant – against the demons. Joy is ours by nature, but it should be joy on account of the Lord and for the sake of doing good to our neighbour. Nature has given us resentment, but that ought to be against the enemies of our souls. We have a natural desire for food, and not for profligacy.[526]

The mention of the devil and demons in this quotation illustrates that in this tradition, those evil beings remain partially causative but not determinative. I have stepped lightly past the role they play in the tradition's account of evil thoughts; and the extensive literature on Orthodox demonology, and its function within Orthodox theanthropology, is beyond our scope. Suffice perhaps to say, with Bentley Hart, that 'a kind of "provisional" cosmic dualism' is on view in this language – 'not an ultimate dualism, of course, between two equal principles, but certainly a conflict between a sphere of created autonomy that strives against God on the one hand and the saving love of God in time on the other.'[527]

What should probably be far more offensive to the modern reader is the embedded notion that our passions are, in fact, *unnatural* – *not* in respect of them being 'emotional', but in that they cast us into the realm of 'un-nature' by robbing us of proper love:

[T]he passions of the body are distorted energies of the soul. When the soul lacks love and self-control, the passions of the incensive and appetitive part of the soul are distorted. And these passions are aroused through the senses. The passions of the carnal life, in the sense of the absence of the Holy Spirit, are an unnatural movement of the soul and are therefore its dying, death and sickness.[528]

As Williams describes this properly natural state, 'the essential activity of the intelligence is always and already grounded in the indwelling Word of God, so that what baptism does is to set free the indwelling Word to shape as it ought the life of the human agent.'[529]

The Orthodox treatment, in a nutshell, is to regard and learn Christian doctrine as an account of spiritual sickness and health; to promote self-knowledge, by accepting that one is ill, and (alarmingly for moderns) to thereby engage in

526. Vlachos, *Orthodox Psychotherapy*, p. 249.

527. David Bentley Hart, *The Doors of the Sea: Where was God in the Tsunami?* (Grand Rapids: Eerdmans, 2005), pp. 62–63.

528. Vlachos, *Orthodox Psychotherapy*, p. 252.

529. Williams, *Looking East in Winter*, p. 21.

appropriate forms of self-reproach; to participate with a therapist (for Vlachos, the self-aware priest, who is on the same road of spiritual healing); and then to practice asceticism (in the form of self-control, patience, stillness and love – often beginning with astute practices in relation to the consumption of food; and with attention to the commands of God); to engage in sustained and intentional stillness and prayer; and to participate in the life of Church and sacrament.[530] This tiny summary of the 'Orthodox Way', as Vlachos terms it, belies literally thousands of its practices, tips and other wisdom peppered through the *Philokalia* and beyond, an Eastern monastic wisdom that is a comprehensive moral psychology in its own right, and which remains scalable to modern lives.

II. From the 'West': The testimony of Benedict's Rule

A similar set of concerns and approaches can be seen in an influential strand of Western monasticism, even if some modes of expression differ. It was my doctoral supervisor, the Rev'd Prof. Michael Banner, who first alerted me to the significance for theological ethical reflection of Benedict's *Rule*. This sixth-century Western document drew upon and significantly altered earlier such attempts, and prescribed the life of a monastic community. Banner shows how the *Rule* offers a substantive vision of a Christian moral life, as opposed to philosophical notions of ethics that have 'rather forgotten about the ordinariness of ethics'. 'Moral philosophy demands rules, principles, and rationales which are enunciated out loud and if it doesn't find them straight off, it finds no ethics at all.'[531]

In contrast, Benedict's *Rule* 'can plausibly be seen as Christianity's paradigmatic framing and answering of the question of ethics'.[532] It is, therefore, an apposite introduction to living in Christian perspective. The *Rule* '[keeps] company with the classical tradition in addressing and answering the broad question, "What is it to live well?"', and despite its monastic occasion, is 'in effect, addressed to all'.[533] Concomitantly, the *Rule* addresses moral psychology in multiple ways.

It not really possible for a brief written account comprehensively to convey this address, since after all, the *Rule* sets the conditions for a community's whole life, a shared life that shapes each member's psychology and moral conceptions. We do them a disservice to imagine that academic description can name adequately their profound process of reshaping moral conceptions and psychology. Later in this chapter, we will defer to the work of a contemporary Benedictine, Joan Chittister, who makes the rhythms and intentions of the monastery accessible to everyday non-monastics, taking seriously that these rhythms and intentions are, 'in effect, addressed to all'. But I borrow first the work of a colleague, the Rev'd Dr

---

530. Vlachos, *Orthodox Psychotherapy*, pp. 42–55.
531. Banner, *The Ethics of Everyday Life*. Kindle edn, loc. 5888.
532. Banner, *Christian Ethics*, p. 10.
533. Banner, *Christian Ethics*, p. 11.

Jane Foulcher,[534] whose account of the monastic tradition highlights the *means* it envisaged for reshaping of moral conceptions and psychology. It begins to show what participation in the love of God, and its renovations of our passions and actions, might look like.

Jane Foulcher's *Reclaiming Humility: Four Studies in the Monastic Tradition*[535] positions her as an authority on the theology of humility.[536] Here, I shall mainly use her work as an introduction for the uninitiated to the logic of monasticism, albeit that humility will come to the fore from time to time as an illustration of its approach to morality and its psychology. Foulcher works with four instances of monastic life in an exercise of theological *ressourcement*. The four are the early Desert Fathers, Benedict's *Rule*, Bernard of Clairvaux, and Christian de Chergé and the monks of Tibhirine. Her method, a diachronic assay of monastic thought and practice, makes her work a useful introduction to it.

The modern urban person, and particularly those primed in Protestant thought, may wonder how the Christian movement could move to desert monasticism so quickly after the world of the New Testament, in which Christians are highly embedded in secular urban environments. The answer becomes apparent in the landscape of ancient Egypt, where small cities abruptly give way to expanses of desert. For a person struggling to retrain their passions amid the excesses of the city, the desert straightforwardly beckons – probably a mere few blocks away, in our way of measuring distance – as a place of quiet, undistracted thoughtfulness.

Conversely, when this movement took on a momentum that valorized lonely splendour over the call to communal love, another corrective came to the fore. Foulcher amusingly recounts the lot of one Valens, who conceived of himself as freed from the need either of community or of Eucharist, having seen Christ and been visited by angels. Upon declaring this to the local church, he was very lovingly bound in irons for a year, to enable 'an ordinary unbusied life'. After this intervention and the prayers of the local church, he was 'cured of the disease of conceit', and rejoined monastic community.[537] Correctives like this (without the

---

534. For this section, I have drawn on material published previously in Andrew J. B. Cameron, 'Humility and the Middle-Aged Man: A Reflection on Foulcher's Wisdom', *St Mark's Review* 256 (2021), pp. 26–41.

535. Jane Foulcher, *Reclaiming Humility: Four Studies in the Monastic Tradition* (Cistercian Studies series 255, Collegeville, MN: Cistercian Publications, 2015), p. 124.

536. See also Jane Foulcher, 'Response to Norman Wirzba', in *The Joy of Humility: The Beginning and End of the Virtues* (ed. Drew Collins, Ryan McAnnally-Linz, and Evan C. Rosa; Waco, TX: Baylor University Press, 2020), pp. 122–25; Foulcher, 'Response to Don E. Davis and Sarah Gazaway', pp. 155–59, same volume; and Jane Foulcher, 'Ageing, Humility, and the Monastery', *Journal of Religion, Spirituality & Aging* 26.2–3 (2014), pp. 148–59, doi: 10.1080/15528030.2013.857380.

537. Foulcher, *Reclaiming Humility*, p. 87. (The story comes from Palladius' fifth century *Lausiac History*.)

irons) coalesced into communal forms. A precinct with a gatehouse, a guesthouse, a church, an infirmary, a dining hall, private rooms, and a refectory, became a layout reflecting various conceptions of the human good in physical, architectural form.[538] The thinking behind such places can be found in Benedict's sixth-century *Rule* and its antecedents, which mapped a path for Christian living that trained love for God in concert with love for the near-neighbour, and for the created order. Such passions and virtues as spring from these loves take their form in this style of life. Foulcher outlines four key elements of it.

The first important element emerges in the materiality of monastic life. These communities paid close attention to diurnal and seasonal rhythms; to practices of bodily care towards each other; and to the orderly handling of money, food, beverages, and other items. In her response to Norman Wirzba's framing of human life as within a meshwork of interrelated entities comprising the planet's ecology,[539] Foulcher shows that the monastery's 'stripping back of material life to its bare essentials sharpens the monk's perception of their "entanglements" – with soil, with creatures human and nonhuman, and with the divine creator.'[540] 'Wood and stones will teach you what you can never hear from any master.'[541]

'Monastic life is not a *container* for some other purpose, a stage for the spiritual journey of the individual, but rather a meshwork in which relationships are reordered.'[542] Foulcher's comment here gestures towards the second important element in the monastic form of life – the many practices that enable human relations to flourish. '[W]e are going to establish a school for the service of the Lord's service', the *Rule*'s Prologue[543] famously puts it, and 'Benedict immediately plunges into the tough mechanics of monastic life'.[544] This 'school' includes services to the neighbour that signal 'a care and regard for the good of the community and for the individuals within and without it [but] in various ways subversive of practices, expectations and patterns of behavior likely as common then as now.'[545]

---

538. Foulcher, *Reclaiming Humility*, p. 88. For an outstanding example, visit the ruins of Rievaulx Abbey near Helmsley, North Yorkshire, United Kingdom.

539. Norman Wirzba, 'Creaturely Humility', in *The Joy of Humility: The Beginning and End of the Virtues* (ed. Drew Collins, Ryan McAnnally-Linz, and Evan C. Rosa; Waco, TX: Baylor University Press, 2020), pp. 107–21 (113) and *passim*.

540. Foulcher, 'Response to Norman Wirzba', p. 125.

541. Foulcher, 'Response to Norman Wirzba', p. 122, citing Bernard of Clairvaux.

542. Foulcher, 'Response to Norman Wirzba', p. 124.

543. Many versions and translations of the *Rule* can be round online, but the online version of the following translation, updated with gender-inclusive language, is a useful starting point: Benedict of Nursia, *Saint Benedict's Rule for Monasteries* (trans. Leonard J. Doyle OblSB; Collegeville, MN: Order of Saint Benedict, 1948, 2001), online at: www .archive.osb.org/rb (accessed 9 December 2021). Further useful background and literature can be found at www.osb.org/our-roots.

544. Foulcher, *Reclaiming Humility*, p. 134.

545. Banner, *Christian Ethics*, p. 14.

Skills of perspective-taking are practised, daily and hourly, in myriad finely grained postures and attitudes and acts towards others that both constitute and train love for each other. Foulcher explores several of these practices in detail, including (for the parsing of humility) a close analysis of the *Rule*'s handling of rank and hierarchy in relationships.[546]

The third relevant element of monastic life is that service and love towards God expressed in worship and praise. As Banner puts it, 'the *Rule* enjoins a round of worship so full as to astonish all but the most avidly devout', in the seven famous three-hourly Hours of prayer (Lauds, Prime, Terce, Sext, None, Vespers and Compline). 'This service of God [. . .] is thought to be that which enables the service of neighbour'.[547] 'The goal is ascent, the movement towards God', suggests Foulcher; 'but ascent simultaneously requires that one place oneself before God, for judgment, aware of the infinite distance between the human and divine.'[548] Regular worship reclaims us in truth about ourselves, and then in truth about our relationship to our neighbour. In Foulcher's study, humility is therefore emergent, rather than striven toward. The double-entendre of her title is that we do not get to 'reclaim' it. It will only 'reclaim' us when we properly reorient to our place within the cosmos, under God, with the neighbour – and once encountering Christ.

The fourth important element of monastic life is, therefore, worshipful encounter with Christ. Technically, it could be regarded as subsumed within the third element of monastic life, worship of the Triune God. But a Christian's engagement with Christ attends to his human nature (on which see my brief summary of Gondreau, in Chapter 8). Moreover, this engagement is not merely that Christ can be *copied*, as uninformed popular accounts of Christian piety tend to suggest. Again using humility as our lens, more important in Christ is the self-disclosure God:

> [I]t is God, in the person of Christ, who shows us that humility comes from God's very being: his self-emptying (Gk. *kenosis*) leads to and finds expression in the extreme humiliation of death on the cross. In the words of an ancient Christian hymn, 'being found in human form, he humbled himself and became obedient to the point of death – even death on a cross'. (Phil. 2.6-8)[549]

That is to say, in Christ we reacquaint to the actual substrate of human being. (As the Baptist theologian Tyler Wittman nicely puts it, Christ 'embodies the truth of human nature and its corresponding vocation.'[550]) The humility that 'comes from

---

546. Foulcher, *Reclaiming Humility*, pp. 134–59.

547. Banner, *Christian Ethics*, p. 14.

548. Foulcher, 'Ageing, Humility, and the Monastery', p. 156.

549. Foulcher, 'Ageing, Humility, and the Monastery', p. 158.

550. Tyler R. Wittman, 'Belonging to Another: Christ, Moral Nature, and the Shape of Humility', *Studies in Christian Ethics* 33.3 (2020), pp. 392–410 (394), doi: 10.1177/0953946818822276.

God's very being' in Christ, is a diffraction of the 'divine yearning for all' wherein God '*is also carried outside of himself* in the loving care he has for everything',[551] which Coakley found in the thought of Dionysius. A commentator on Foulcher, Heather Thomson, summarizes these large theological thoughts with some implications for human moral psychology:

> Pondering ourselves in relation to a humble God, we see the ridiculousness of human pride and vanity. God's humility undercuts the whole foundation of our socially constructed selves in relation to others, our grasping after power, privilege, wealth and status. These measures of our self-worth lead to rivalry and violence rather than the cultivation of 'selfless receptivity' that is a hallmark of humility.[552]

By this stage we have moved a long way from the limited premises of modern empirical psychology. It is worth noting what is delivered by a richly theological account of humanity, as exemplified in these four elements of monastic life. Modern empirical accounts, because of their methodological commitment to naive naturalism (whether or not that reflects an ideological commitment *per se* to naturalism) must of necessity terminate upon the operation of the will if to move, bend, or challenge our unexamined moral psychologies. The discipline may go further, noting the social and psychological conditions that affect us,[553] albeit that even those can only be corrected by further acts of will. Even when theorists such as Haidt gesture coyly towards spirituality as somehow beneficial to moral life and general well-being, there can be no room within the discipline for *how* the effects of spirituality are effective. This domain is inherently 'pelagian', the theological ethicist's term for systems that terminate upon the muscularity of human will in programs of self-improvement.

In contrast, these theological approaches rest elsewhere. They present a cosmic canvas that decodes each life within echelons of being that long predate us and will long outlast us. Christ becomes the apotheosis of how to inhabit that canvas, in whom (by the Spirit, whose operation I have only touched on via Augustine and Aquinas) we reorient to that entire ontological terrain. This kind of approach does watch the will, but from the corner of the eye as it were, leveraging it where

---

551. Dionysius, *Divine Names*, IV.13; cited in Coakley, *God, Sexuality and the Self*, pp. 314–15.

552. Heather Thomson, 'On the Humble God', *St Mark's Review* 236 (2016), pp. 86–90 (88–89).

553. I am reminded of a thorough work that, should space have permitted, deserved further analysis within these pages. In Hari, *Lost Connections* (cited above, n 500), the author finds seven major *aporia* that have opened up in modern lives, and that set the conditions for *anomie* and *acedia*. While the book ostensibly focusses upon mental health, it is in reality a work of moral psychology, broadly understood. It is also a book about the human *telos*, as witnessed by the title's terminus in 'hope'.

possible to set the conditions under which to move better within that cosmic canvas, as practices of love.

To make this rather abstract point more concretely, we can see it in the early Christian *locus classicus* on the matter of humility – the so-called Christ-hymn and its prefatory comments in Phil. 2.3-4 (already mentioned in Foulcher's work, above). English translations of these verses regularly include three imperatival verb-forms that sound like direct appeals to the will: 'do nothing' from conceits of ambition or rivalry; 'regard', 'value' or 'consider' others above oneself; and 'look to' the interests of others.[554] Upon reading this list of prescriptions, the reader may then set about reclaiming humility through the willpower of various doings, valuings and lookings-to.

But worth attending here is a subtle grammatical point, and a translational error of sorts, which goes to how we might regard the will theologically. For importantly, this second part of St. Paul's complex sentence includes only *one* Greek imperative (*phroneite*), rendered in the English clause '*Let the same mind be* in [or "among"] you that was in Christ Jesus, who [. . .]' (2.5, emphasis added). The Greek basis of the English verbs above ('do nothing', 'regard'/'value'/'consider', 'look to') are participles. Roughly (although inaccurately) we could imagine translating them as 'doing nothing', 'regarding'/'valuing'/'considering', 'looking to'. Even those renderings do not obviously entail, for the English reader, anything other than acts of will. But that they occur prior to the main imperative obscures that they are conceived as *outcomes* of it, and therefore as *responses to* meditative encounter with Christ. Such sentence construction is easy to parse in Greek. Word order is far more significant for thinkers-in-English, so it becomes hard for us to imagine how preludes to the main exhortation in fact signal outcomes of it. But the gravity of the sentence is for us to gaze meditatively upon the Christ, via the lengthy description of him that follows, so that a humble demeanour then arises within us. The kind of 'will' that arises within us is akin to what we saw in Chapter 6: the inexorable enaction of a revised love.

To rephrase the claim: the participial verb-forms are the turns-of-phrase most apt to indicate participation and response, rather than the primacy of human willpower. Rather than emphasizing strenuous emulation of Christ's acts, the construction expressly emphasizes a kind of mindset *arising from* meditative encounter with the Christ of the hymn that follows. Again, humility is emergent, but this time, from a relationship with Christ that blossoms into a kind of like-mindedness. ('Mind' here is not some thin cognitivism, either; it is a probably inadequate translation for a whole-of-self-identification with Christ's own being, knowledge and loves.)

Hence in this biblical vignette we see illustrated the point made above. A cosmic canvas decodes our life, with Christ the apotheosis of how to reorient to that entire

---

554. I have constructed this sentence using the *New Revised Standard Version*, the *New International Version,* and the *Holman Christian Standard Bible.*

ontological terrain, and with the will operative only to set the conditions under which we may move responsively within it.

If a Christian complaint to moral psychology is that it is inherently 'pelagian', this is not to say there is no wisdom in the various cognitive reframings recommended by psychology (of which in the case of humility, it turns out, there are many useful ones[555]). But they are bound to fail, argues Foulcher, in the absence of locating oneself upon the same cosmic and divine canvas as did these monastics. The four elements we have seen offer a clue to how one may relocate. Another word from Rowan Williams, arising from Eastern monasticism, further illuminates the outcome of such relocation, and its divine wellspring:

> Freed from the distortions of anger and possessive desire, we embrace in love and thanksgiving a world and a divine reality that are literally nothing but gratuitous gift or bestowal. And in entering such a state [. . .] we come to see something of what the exchange of life and goodness might be in that divine life that necessarily and eternally knows nothing of self-possession or self-withholding, nothing of the fear of loss or of absorption, but is the loving and joyful apprehension of sheer otherness.[556]

The monastic life has given itself over to *that* kind of apprehension. To recall Banner's comment on jejune modern moral philosophy, here is not an ethics that 'demands rules, principles, and rationales which [. . .] if it doesn't find them straight off [. . .] finds no ethics at all.'[557] Rather, we find in these monastic sources 'hard-won wisdom tried and tested over years, decades and centuries of practice, reflecting and building upon what has gone before.'[558]

III. Chittister's gift: Monasteries for the masses

But even if we concede that the *Rule* is 'in effect, addressed to all',[559] and includes the training of life and its loves, what are we non-monastics to do? Modern empirical moral psychology at least assumes the quotidian givens of modern life – its frenetic pace, its relentlessly demanding overload, its capitalist underpinnings, and its manifold other challenges thrown upon us by centuries of cultural history. Of what more than antiquarian use can it be for moderns, to see that Christian monastics had their ways?

---

555. See e.g. Cameron, 'Humility and the Middle-Aged Man', pp. 16–19.
556. Williams, *Looking East in Winter*, p. 24.
557. Banner, *The Ethics of Everyday Life*, Kindle edn, loc. 5888.
558. Thomson, 'On the Humble God', p. 86.
559. Banner, *Christian Ethics*, p. 11.

Joan Chittister's *The Monastery of the Heart: An Invitation to a Meaningful Life*[560] is her flagship work that offers an account of Benedictine spirituality for the non-monastic masses. In it, she makes more accessible to everyday people the renewed interest in Benedict's *Rule* that has been seen in academic theological ethics. But since Benedictine monastic reasoning makes less sense without a community, this work also functions as a gateway to 'Monasteries of the Heart', 'an online movement sharing Benedictine spirituality with contemporary seekers'.[561] Chittister's approach is an elegant simplification of the *Rule* and a mediation of it that makes it thinkable and doable, in effect, for all. In my short description following, it is important to remember how the monograph is conceived not only as a means of individual edification, but also as an entrée to a communal experience. 'The function of Benedictine life, with its community commitment, is *not* to hide from the world. It is to make community for others around it, to enable others to also draw from its well.'[562]

Chittister leads with the Benedictine priority of the persistent reading of Scripture:

> As monastics of the heart we must
> read the scriptures day in and day out,
> till they ring in our ears,
> and fill our hearts,
> and become the very breath
> we breathe.[563]

The logic of this contention is not that we read in order to imbibe deontic prescriptions. Rather, we read with a view to reframing our awareness towards that of Christ's, and away from 'the worship of our private little idols of money and power and status that lure us away from the real treasures of life',[564] 'to turn consciously now and here toward the God to whom our entire lives are geared'.[565] She then introduces the *Rule*'s induction into the practice of prayer, both alone, but also as a community – 'the bond and constant source of inspiration and purpose and glue that holds us together, the touchstone of everything that has meaning to us.'[566]

560. Joan Chittister, *The Monastery of the Heart: An Invitation to a Meaningful Life* (Katonah, NY: BlueBridge, 2011).

561. 'Monasteries of the Heart', (Benedictine Sisters of Erie, PA, 2011), online at: www.monasteriesoftheheart.org (accessed 3 December 2021).

562. Chittister, *The Monastery of the Heart*, p. 28. Chittister formats her writing in stanzas, like a poet. I will not always reproduce that formatting here.

563. Chittister, *The Monastery of the Heart*, p. 5.

564. Chittister, *The Monastery of the Heart*, p. 4.

565. Chittister, *The Monastery of the Heart*, p. 9.

566. Chittister, *The Monastery of the Heart*, p. 26.

The elemental nature of prayer in these traditions is hard to overstate, and equally hard for the modern mind to comprehend. Prayer has a decisive effect upon a person's moral psychology: 'Prayer is the conversion of the self-centered self to the conscious contemplative, to the prophetic witness of the radical spiritual life.'[567] Importantly, however, these effects upon moral psychology are incidental to its main purpose:

> Benedictine prayer,
> the heartbeat of Benedictine spirituality,
> is always about
> the presence of God in time –
> this time, our time, my time.
> Benedictine prayer is not mindless repetition
> of endless formulas.
> It is about the immersion in the mind of God
> that living the God-life requires,
> if we are to be faithful to it
> all our living days.
> Prayer restores the soul
> that is dry and dulled
> by years of trying
> to create a world
> that never completely comes.[568]

The last stanza highlights the Benedictine's growing awareness of the limitations of human willpower, and of self- and social improvement. Steeped in the Psalms and conducted according to the famous thrice-hourly Hours of prayer, it 'becomes for us the pulse of the day, the rhythm of a life that might otherwise be caught in the drumbeat of ambition or profit or self-centeredness.'[569] '[W]e do not pray merely to pray. We pray to become more a sign of the mind of God today than we were yesterday.'[570]

Chittister mediates an older conception of human life and flourishing, of a being who emerges from and finds sustenance within the wider cosmos, and beyond that, from and within the loving mind of a personal God who upholds all that. 'There is in the Benedictine spirituality of prayer, then, as much a consciousness of content as there is a choice of prayer forms and formats.' She continues:

> In thirteen chapters on prayer,
> the ancient Rule, in its specification

---

567. Chittister, *The Monastery of the Heart*, p. 37.
568. Chittister, *The Monastery of the Heart*, p. 34.
569. Chittister, *The Monastery of the Heart*, p. 36.
570. Chittister, *The Monastery of the Heart*, p. 38.

of the psalms for the day,
lays out the concepts on which Benedictine spirituality rests:
that good overcomes evil,
that God is our strength,
that God is present in every part of life,
that God is our refuge,
that God is merciful,
that sin is destructive of both the self and the world,
and that praise of God is the purpose of life.
In those ideas and that consciousness we rest,
secure in the presence of God,
certain of the love of God,
convinced that our trust in God
is never, ever in vain.[571]

This responsive inhabitation of Scripture through prayer is, in essence, the core of this spirituality. Individual practices arise from it, such as intentional silences[572] and retreats,[573] and habits of focused reading ('lectio').[574] But so also do communal practices, in some ways the cauldron within which moral psychologies are retrained. Regular and meaningful interaction between members of this community:

[. . .] is the process of creating
and sharing common bonds:
the faith life that underpins a group,
the personal life and affections
of each member,
the emotional life that forms
and fluctuates and drives each of us
at different times
at different levels,
and the undercurrents and ideas and concepts
that stir our attitudes and hopes
for the human enterprise.[575]

She goes on to observe how the *Rule* inculcates at its heart a radical version of equality. Although we think of equality as *de rigeur* for modern political life, we are in fact beset by severe inequalities. In contrast, the *Rule* outlines how are community's life may, on the one hand, attribute excellence and authority where

---

571. Chittister, *The Monastery of the Heart*, pp. 38–39.
572. Chittister, *The Monastery of the Heart*, pp. 41–47.
573. Chittister, *The Monastery of the Heart*, pp. 57–63.
574. Chittister, *The Monastery of the Heart*, pp. 49–55.
575. Chittister, *The Monastery of the Heart*, p. 69.

due, while on the other hand recognizing no ontological distinctions based on race, age, gender, or wealth.[576] It schools its participants in the proper essences of political life.

It, therefore, also schools its participants in practices of direction, counsel, and 'leadership',[577] and in the communicative logic of sharing, with attention to each member finding sufficiency.[578] That in turn reframes our perception of consumption, for both the nourishment of personal need, and for the reciprocal nourishment of others.[579]

Consequent upon this landscape of shifting affection is a renewed apprehension of the nature and purpose of work. The *Rule* pays a great deal of attention to labour and its purposes, and Chittister expatiates on these:

> The Benedictine heart knows that
> simply staying close
> to the mechanical functions
> of what it means to get through a day –
> running the vacuum,
> washing the dishes,
> shoveling the snow,
> doing the laundry,
> peeling the vegetables,
> cleaning out the car,
> making the bed,
> bathing the children–
> keeps us all, men and women,
> aware of the struggles
> embedded in every dimension of life.
> [. . .] Whatever kind of work it is –
> professional or technical,
> physical or intellectual,
> financial or social –
> it is to be *good* work,
> whatever makes the world
> a better, more just, more fair
> and more human place
> for everyone.[580]

---

576. Chittister, *The Monastery of the Heart*, pp. 73–79.
577. Chittister, *The Monastery of the Heart*, pp. 81–88.
578. Chittister, *The Monastery of the Heart*, pp. 89–94.
579. Chittister, *The Monastery of the Heart*, pp. 95–101.
580. Chittister, *The Monastery of the Heart*, pp. 107, 109.

Indeed, her brief account of daily work deserves more attention than can be given here, and should be regarded as elemental to any Christian theology of work. Suffice for our purpose to note that this monastic foundation apprehends for work different motivations and loves than are often the case: 'It is done for the sake of the soul, not for the punishment of the body or for the gratification of the ego [but] in praise of what it is to be alive, to redeem creation from chaos and our souls from apathy.'[581] More granularly, this good work takes the form of seeing ourselves as co-workers with God, as loving carers of others and of the natural environment, and as givers of hospitality.[582] A coda to *Monastery of the Heart* draws readers back to wisdom's task of ongoing listening; to an ongoing disposition for the conversion of attitudes and emotions; to the growth of a kind of spiritual stability, and of humility; and to tools and sacred arts for the journey.[583]

In a sense, this brief digest of Chittister's gift can do little good other than to alert the reader to its existence. Her account is itself a summary of a summary, where the *Rule* is a summary expression of an entire life, shaped by community and shared participation in the Christian narrative of the well-lived life. I can only gesture here, somewhat inarticulately, at the way these Benedictine traditions offer an entire program for the renovation of what we regard as our moral psychology, but with foci and emphases quite unlike our modern attention to neurological and psychological processes. By proper inhabitation of the divinely generated landscape, and by the retraining of love – using all the tools of Benedictine life – our moral psychology looks after itself. (We are now a long way, for example, from Sidney Callahan's cumbersome if well-intentioned advice that we saw in Chapter 1.)

IV. Coda

After completing this chapter, I began a program of spiritual direction with Micheál Loughnane, coordinator of the Arrupe Program of Ignatian Spirituality at the Jesuit College of Spirituality in Melbourne, Australia. I note this development simply to highlight yet another profoundly influential movement in the retraining of love, which to my novice eye, makes moves similar to those profiled in this chapter. A snapshot:

> The Spiritual Exercises contain a method of encountering God's action in our universe in an ordered progression. People [. . .] let God strip them of their inordinate affections so that they can find God's will and thus become more and more attuned to God's redemptive intention in creating this universe. Ignatius himself cites the purpose of his Spiritual Exercises as overcoming 'oneself, and to

---

581. Chittister, *The Monastery of the Heart*, pp. 109–10.
582. Chittister, *The Monastery of the Heart*, pp. 115–42.
583. Chittister, *The Monastery of the Heart*, pp. 145–219.

order one's life, without reaching a decision through some disordered affection'. For Ignatius, union with God meant union with a God who is always actively bringing about God's reign in this universe. Union with God meant ordered desires and action.[584]

But rather than attempting to introduce the Ignatian tradition,[585] I want simply to conclude with a point arising from my experience of it. The retraining of love does seem to entail some ongoing, existential participation in intentional spirituality, and as far as I can testify, in a Scriptural and overtly Christian framing of it. Such a program with another (in the person of a director) is, in its own way, communal, which also seems to me a necessary element. At no point have I found the experience to entail notions of strenuous moral self-improvement, nor any denial of the prevenience of divine grace and the totality of divine gift that culminates in Christ's saving work. It is, rather, an exercise in the deep appropriation of what is announced in the gospel.

If any reader of this chapter has been moved by it, I could not recommend such a program more highly. I am deeply thankful to Micheál Loughnane for his direction, and for Paul Ruefli who referred me to him.

584. William A. Barry, *Letting God Come Close: An Approach to the Ignatian Spiritual Exercises* (Chicago, IL: Jesuit Way/Loyola, 2001), pp. 2–3; thanks to Micheál Loughnane for this reference.

585. For an excellent short introduction that reprises several themes we have seen so far, see Thomas V. Frederick and Timothy P. Muldoon, 'Ignatian Spirituality and Psychotherapy', *Journal of Psychology and Christianity* 39.1 (2020), pp. 12–23.

Chapter 10

AFFECTIONS, PASSIONS AND MODERN LIFE

In some ways the task of this book is done. But the intention of this chapter is to bring into the present the contention that love resides at the base of all moral intuitions. The chapter will return to some shabby malfunctions of unexamined love, and the gesture towards themes that have emerged in the book for addressing them.

I will return to where I began, to consider how even anxiety may be construed as a form of disordered love (I). An odd dream then vignettes its daily deceptions (II), resonating perhaps with anyone who has reflected on the pettiness of some loves and the enormity of what is missed. I will go on to say a little about our shared public life (III); our values and virtues (IV); Christian preaching (V); and on how we might proceed (VI).

I. Anxiety's logic of love

I prefaced this book with an exercise of oversharing, where I related my own experiences of anxiety, and problematized it with reference to the vice of cowardice. While preparing the book, I have been struck by thick conduits of anxiety thrumming through several aspects of our *shared* social experiences, which have been marked by political polarizations; surging racial enmities; manifold and ongoing environmental concerns; war near NATO's border; Chinese geopolitical ambition; and of course, a global pandemic with its urgent mitigations. In early 2022, we are struck in turn by micro-manifestations of these events: inflation; supply-chain disruption; increases in all-cause death statistics (for whatever as yet undetermined reasons); a so-called great resignation, as people abandon pre-pandemic work practices; and the myriad family and personal disruptions and breakdowns that continue to attend it all. It is a truism to say that we live in anxious times.

While it will seem uncaring to predicate cowardice of anyone during these times, it is certainly clear that various deleterious moral stances have erupted through them. Unseemly jockeying for vaccine supplies might be a candidate. The right accuses various polities of draconian overreaction in relation to vaccine mandating, overriding principles of informed consent once considered elementary to bioethics in a liberal order, all in the name of public safety. The left accuses various interest groups of reifying and inflaming racial tension, in atavistic efforts to shore up goods of national identity and group affinity. Both right and left decry any possibility of finding truths that are not tainted by ideology. Narratives of scarcity drive and distort markets in oil, food, housing, labour, rare earths, industrial precious metals – and, of course, arms.

It is not really possible to judge where, if at all, the cap of cowardice fits any human moral agent within these aggregated masses of decision and action. It is, however, important to notice how these disputes and anxieties are driven by forms of love that, at first, are almost entirely veiled. If Augustine is correct, we are constituted in our loving as much as in our existing and our knowing; and I suggest that now as in his day, we remain as illiterate about these loves. They are hidden in plain sight, driving our conceptions of scarcity, our prognostications about the future, and our enmities. In other words, love, counterintuitively, lies at the base of anxiety (and of cowardice). Yet, both as individuals and as political communities, we are generally not well schooled in naming the good we wish to defend or procure, or at noticing how our reactivity arises from those aspirations, or at comparing and evaluating them alongside other legitimate candidates for our love. Without that meta-discussion, life simply tears along, with our unevaluated love for that which is legitimate within the goods (for example) of public safety or technocratic intervention so dominating discourse and policy that other legitimate and important goods remain hidden.

I think of a chaplain describing how the goods of physical and social contact were deprived to the dying. These were eclipsed by the love of public safety, entailing that the dying be kept in an empty ward, and separated by layers of personal protective equipment. In hindsight, such treatment was a form of neglect and abandonment in the name of another legitimate love. Similarly, a highly polarized opposition to the Canadian truckers' strike in protest of mandatory vaccination seemed incapable to evaluate whatever legitimate loves drove their concerted position. Something about toilet paper – definitely a good worth loving, along with clean bottoms presaged by it – became a love that completely demented urban Australians early in the pandemic. There were brawls over ample supplies of it. In each case, some good was totalized in a manner that distorted our common life.

If such a claim is too complicated and contestable in the public arena, it is perhaps easier to see when scaled down to the private and personal domain. Over the years, I have journaled my various anxieties, not realizing that in each of these moments I was capturing some proper good to which my anxiety had attached with some initial legitimacy. One such entry serves as example. Going back some twenty or more years, I was having an anxious day about one of my then-children's teeth. Apparently, some news from a dentist had not been good; I cannot recall the detail at this distance. It transpired that both then and now, said person has entirely functional teeth, and there never was a problem. The good, of course, of intact and functional teeth is hardly to be doubted, and to want that was a form of proper love both for my child and for teeth in general. The 'wanting' in that sentence is simply love – love of the good, and of my child – in another of its myriad disguises. It drove whatever actions I took in consequence: working for a living, planning in a diary, driving the car to a dentist, paying their bill.

The problem is not that I was anxious about those teeth. The problem emerges as I read month after month, year after year, in these episodic entries, of my anxieties attaching to this, then that, then something else. Anxiety is a tricker: it attaches to goods as if each is a receding scarcity, and *never* holds itself to account when the last such evaluation turned out to be in error. It is simply on to the next, then the next, then the next. And if I were to have examined some rolling average of the effect of this habit, I would have seen its real harm. It robbed me of the capacity to love with thanks the real goods before my eyeballs, including presence and connection to my wife, my children, my colleagues, my students, and so on. In this way legitimate loves become false and disordered, and in turn, a form of distorted worship. The chronically anxious person degenerates into a person whose main gestalt becomes that of a martyred victim, who in their own conception should be lauded for their defence, pursuit, avoidance, upholding, and so on, of very valuable mirages, when in fact they run from what is before them. As these habits and patterns of feeling and action cascade and reify, we eventually become frightened of our shadow, and the cap of cowardice does fit. That is the moral judgment against it, which only seems cruel until we realize that such a judgment is not condemnatory, but evaluative, seeking within a long tradition to remind us that bad outcomes can arise from seemingly good loves. (A similar kind of analysis could be put to chronic anger, or sadness, or longing, or ambition, and so on. The parade of characters in C. S. Lewis's *The Great Divorce*[586] are portrayals of people who lose themselves by doubling down on their fixations, reifying them to the point of imbecility.)

It would be a denial of the wisdoms I have assayed in this book to offer here some quick fixes to these malfunctions of love. The observations I am making are the stuff of the Proverbs, and the stuff of cognitive-behavioural therapy. They are the stuff of Eastern monasticism, and the stuff of emotionally focused therapy. They are the stuff of Western monasticism, and the stuff of acceptance-commitment therapy.

Therefore, there is nothing to denigrate about the granularity of diagnosis offered by the modern psychologist. But neither is there reason to spurn the yoke of ancient spiritual disciplines, as long as these are properly theologically framed, under the safety of God's steadfast, merciful love. Both kinds of intervention need to be honest and careful about their implicit and substantive moral stances. Modern approaches, and approaches in the Christian tradition, are implicitly complementary, and fundamentally moral in that they cannot ever evade our human embeddedness in evaluations of good, right, wrong, and maturity (or not) of character.

586. See above, n 10.

The reader could stop here, then, and further explore these psychologies, those biblical and contemplative traditions, perhaps also undergoing some psychological counsel and spiritual direction, and forge ahead under God. If the false distinctions between them have been blurred, then this book may have completed its limited task. But I will presume to say a little more – about our shared public life (III); about values and virtues (IV); about Christian preaching (V); and about what to do next (VI). I will proceed by way of a strange tangent (II) – a dream I had, which handily highlighted the shabby malfunctions of unexamined love in everyday life.

II. A very quotidian dream

While preparing this book, I was recovering from a small operation. Sleeping it off one day, I had the most extraordinarily detailed dream. I will take the odd step of sharing it. It is laced with morality and emotion within a not-quite everyday scenario. I'll say at the outset that it doesn't reflect well on me, nor, it seems, on my attitude to women. I am embarrassed by that. But I hope you will bear with it nonetheless, since it highlights important themes examined in this book, now set within the tawdriness of everyday life.

It was a sunny day in the eucalypt-shaded public carpark of my local supermarket. Approaching my vehicle after shopping, I became aware of a boy aged around 11, wearing studded football boots, running up and down over the hood, the roof, and the trunk of the car, and even jumping along its windscreen pillars. As a result, the whole surface was now pitted and dented, as if from hail damage. In Australia, we call a vehicle's shiny exterior its 'duco', and we love it a *lot*. I was, therefore, dismayed, and very quickly became quite angry.

Sitting in the vehicle parked alongside was his pregnant mother, with two other small children. She looked up at me sheepishly, and said, 'I'm sorry for what he's done to your car.' But I sensed, as one only can in dreams, that she had no intention to pay for any damage. I demanded – somewhat churlishly, as can only a man with damaged duco – 'Well I'll expect you to pay for it. Can I have your details?' She became evasive and withdrawn, and (shifting magically as people do dreams) was now sitting kerbside in the gutter, gaze averted. But two of her adult friends – her 'posse' – had now materialized. 'You can't prove he did it,' the mother hesitated. 'You don't have video.' The posse fronted me menacingly.

I became angrier. 'Oh come on. Don't play games. When I left the car, it was as smooth as the day I bought it. And anyway, don't you think you should have stopped him doing that?' They all snorted in derision. 'How do you expect her to do *that*?' spat her friends. 'He's an eleven-year-old boy.' I was incredulous. Who were these people, I thought, who considered this scenario acceptable, and that *I* was somehow in the wrong for expecting reparation of my property?

But the situation was escalating. 'I take seminars for retirees,' one of the friends said importantly. She showed me some advertising for said seminar. 'We educate the elderly in how their vision tunnels down into fixations on gardening, health, and travel.'

'What,' I retorted; 'are you saying that I am one of these because I have a fixation on my car?' It was clear this was her implication: I was old, and petty, and should leave her beleaguered pregnant mother-friend alone. But *I* knew I was not old, only middle-aged, and easily six- or eight-years junior to her petty seminar demographic. And in any case, my concern with my car was an obviously more elemental cause than that of gardens, health, and travel. I was incensed by the comparison.

The verbal shoving match continued a few more minutes. But sensing I was not going to get a change of heart nor any contact details, I prepared to drive away. My huffy parting shots satisfied me, at least. 'I think you are a bit ashamed,' I said to the boy's mother. 'You said you were sorry, then you got all evasive. I just think you ought to own this, and take some kind of responsibility.' The dream meandered on for a while, with some angry driving and cogitations over insurance. Then I awoke.

The dream included a recognizable kind of daily dispute about morality, and the banal emotions that go with it. The totally unshared value about the good of smooth duco was its narrative's main driver – a value that is near-sacred among most (men) in modern Australia. My rising anger and fighting words to get back this lost good are also clearly evidenced. The escalation in the scenario was telling. Within seconds, the matter was complicated by the friends' love of the pregnant person, and their discounting of myself as an older person with petty fixations (and incidentally, my implicit agreement with this discounting, since I had no interest in identifying with such people). My anger as I left the scene became less about the duco and more about being discounted as a human being with interests, cares and concerns. I was angry that these others had no care nor interest – no love for – me and what mattered to me. (There is a kernel of truth in our instant reactivity in such situations, since God loves us, and we do therefore matter. Dreams, of course, are a time-honoured route for unearthing those deeper truths about ourselves.)

Further layers of irony revealed themselves to me upon waking. Because what was the case in this woman's world – three children to care for, another on the way, and an uncontrollable boy – obviously occupied her horizon. On any account, these four beings were proper loves for *her*, and could have become part of *my* moral horizon. But in my dream, my only moral horizon was the sanctimonious Australian male's value of a sleek car.

The further shock when I awoke was that the vehicle concerned was one I no longer owned. In real life it had been bought in 1993, and long ago been sold. The realization of that, on waking, flooded me with relief, as often upon waking; the thing wasn't real, the loss was illusory, therefore sadness and anger – the emotions associated with the loss of a good and its retrieval – were not needed.

On further reflection, a final irony emerged. This was a vehicle I had dinged and dented dozens of times. There was almost *never* a day when it was 'as smooth as the day I bought it'. Indeed in 1998 a friend had laughed mockingly, 'it looks like the Starship Enterprise!' He was referring to the spaceship of television fame, after battle. That it did. I had these dings repaired at considerable cost, when another accident involving an old wardrobe and a gust of wind resulted in another massive dent on the bonnet and a further trip to the head-shaking panel beater.

But somehow, in some final arch hypocrisy, it was OK when *I* was the one being careless with the car, but not when the difficult son of a beleaguered pregnant woman was.

Had I inhabited a different character in that dream as a more compassionate person (i.e., a person with more expansive loves), I would have parsed the scene and interrogated the reactions more mindfully – or better, with more attention to the first stirring and movements of my thoughts and their passions, and to their hierarchy of attachments. On arriving back at the car, instead of the usual stereotypical indignance that is valorized for the modern Western car-owner, a more compassionate man may have seen the first movements to anger, and noticed that they arose from a trivial attachment to a modern conceit of perfection – shiny duco. He may then have noticed a woman so overwhelmed as feebly to be unable to stop her son. After all, if the themes of this book are correct, compassion arises from the loves *within the other* that drive their sufferings, and (as Augustine said) is a kind of fellow-feeling with them (popularized today by appeal to our 'mirror neurones'). Even a slightly expanded imaginative horizon might have noticed that a lot of love is invested by such a woman in those three, nearly four, children, with untold numbers of losses and disappointments and threats and yearnings absorbing her along the way. Even had there been some place for discussing reparations, it could have taken a very different path. 'It looks like you are having a very difficult time today. He's just been to football, I see. Is he a bit of a handful?' The compassionate act of feeling, to some extent, what is hard for her, may have meant her posse of defenders did not need to materialize nor impress upon me the pettiness of my puny loves. Compassionate-me may have been able to say, 'Look, I wonder if we can discuss your making the damage good on another occasion, but I can see that will be a burden for you right now. Could we do that another time?' A reframing of the matter might even have made for some revision of love: away from duco, away from the preciousness of my own ego, towards a struggling family, and in the direction of grace. I might have let the damage go – which, after all, I was entirely willing to do in real life, for several years, as I careened about in the Starship Enterprise.

I concede that something loathsome about my ego is revealed in this dream, and possibly of the male ego in general. Its disturbingly gendered elements can stay between me and my therapist. But I have been thinking a lot of late about the purely heinous, self-righteous, self-enclosed, self-justifying excesses of men, particularly as we age, whether we are religious or not, all predicated upon monstrous forms of love for this or that overvalued good, and the torrents of interpersonal and social damage caused by it all. A book for another day, perhaps.

For the purposes of this book, though, the dream usefully highlights those quotidian experiences where a kind of moral and emotional illiteracy rules. Moral imaginations are shrunken to the most emaciated shared value, derived from the group and concerning nothing very substantial (like the shininess of shiny a car's paint job). It shows how with neither thought nor reflection, we rush to our corner, and how self-righteousness is the most thickly moral-emotional stance that we can conjure in an instant. Social media did not figure in the dream; for a dreamer of a different generation, it would have (and nearly did, in the mention of video proof). But had it, gangs of duco-loving men versus mother-loving women would have coalesced immediately, inflaming and enraging into the kinds of 'othering' firestorms we see every day; and just as certainly, with all those players totally de-skilled in stepping from within those horizons to any apprehension of what loves may drive the other. Perhaps my alternative response of compassion has become literally unthinkable for most of us on most days.

III. The anxious city: The logic of love in public

Yet, we remain constituted in love. That is to say, if Augustine is correct, other people each have their loves that are as real to them as are our own to us, and each of these loves has more than a grain of truth to it. If Aquinas are right, it behoves us to notice the trajectory of our moral emotions before making moral conclusions, evaluating what loves they represent. If Coakley, Chittister and the monastics are right, a habit of worship, contemplation, and prayer may just give us what it takes to participate properly in the love of God towards, say, a pregnant woman on a bad day in a car park (and at a stretch, even to whatever love evinces an 11-year-old's running up and down over cars). In a Western world with more such literate people, car parks would operate differently, as would social media, and politics itself.

Augustine has famously said[587] that none of us need to be taught to love our own body (nor, by extension perhaps, our car and its paint job). 'But the need remain[s] for us to receive commandments about what is above us, and what is next to us.' He then recounts the two great commandments (Mt. 22.37 and vv. 39-40), and the principle that *all* Christian commands are for the purpose of love (1 Tim. 1.5). '[I]f you understand yourself as the whole of you, that is your spirit and body, and your neighbour as the whole of him, namely his spirit and body [. . .] then no kind of things that are to be loved has been overlooked by these two commandments.'

It follows for him that when 'love of God is put first, and the manner of that love is clearly prescribed,' 'everything else is to converge on it.' Here in a nutshell is Augustine's conviction that to participate in the love of God is then to find how to love what surrounds me. His bedrock position on the relation between love and ethics then follows:

> [L]iving a just and holy life requires one to be capable of an objective and impartial evaluation of things: to love things, that is to say, in the right order, so that you do not love what is not to be loved, or fail to love what is to be loved,

---

587. I am recounting here and in the quotations following the argument in Augustine, *Teaching Christianity (On Christian Doctrine)* (trans. O. P. Edmund Hill; New York: New City Press, Kindle edn, 2014), I.26–29 (loc. 3059 and following).

or have a greater love for what should be loved less, or an equal love for things that should be loved less or more, or less or greater love for things that should be loved equally.[588]

(That statement is arguably a more straightforward way to parse the connection between our emotions and our ethical deliberations than the guidance we saw in Callahan or Clore in Chapter 1.) Knowing that there are degrees of connection between and differing responsibilities towards different people, all of whom 'are to be loved equally', Augustine nonetheless offers sage advice to my dream-self in that carpark. '[T]reat it as the luck of the draw when time and circumstance brings some [person] into closer contact with you than others.'[589]

But in carparks with property damage at stake, his advice has become conventionally unthinkable. It is in the nature of disorder that some forms of thought refuse to participate in the reordering of love. In his epic *City of God*, Augustine extends upon biblical metaphors to tell Rome of two 'cities' or societies mingled in that place, competing for cultural space, whose citizenry live respectively for self (in disordered love) or for God (participating in the divine reordering of love).[590] 'Each desires its own kind of peace, and, when they have found what they sought, each lives its own kind of peace.' The full quotation is instructive:

> Though there are many great nations throughout the world, living according to different rites and customs, and distinguished by many different forms of language, arms, and dress, there nonetheless exists only two orders, as we may call them, of human society: and, following our Scriptures, we may rightly speak of these two as cities. The one is made up of men who live according to the flesh, and the other of those who live according to the spirit. Each desires its own kind of peace, and, when they have found what they sought, each lives its own kind of peace.[591]

---

588. Augustine, *On Christian Doctrine*, I.27–28. I am thankful to Dr Bernard Doherty for alerting me to this passage: Bernard Doherty, 'Christ-haunted but not Christ-centred: Ghosts of the Christian South in HBO's *True Detective*', *St Mark's Review* 257 (2021), pp. 46–69 (57).

589. Augustine, *On Christian Doctrine*, I.29.

590. The view is not confined to one biblical author. Cf. Ps. 119.19-20 and v. 54; Mt. 5.13-16 (perhaps); Rom. 12.2; 2 Cor. 6.14-18 and 10.2-3 (but noting 'entanglement' as a given in 1 Cor. 5.10); Eph. 2.19; Phil. 3.20; 1 Pet. 1.1, v. 17, and 2.9-11; Heb. 11.13.

591. Augustine, *City of God*, 581, XIV.1. This concept is evident from the start of *City of God* (p. 3, I.pref); but the second half of the work sees particular emphasis upon this 'entanglement' of one among the other: e.g. pp. 448 (X.32); 450 (XI.1); 498 (XII.1); 511 (XII.9); XIV.1 (581); cf. 587 (XIV.4) & 632 (XIV.28).

The uneasiness of their coexistence follows from differing logics of love concerning what brings peace – whether that be unmarked shiny car paint, or some temporary or permanent abdication from disciplining an unruly boy. His binary may seem too extreme: it is manifestly the case that those who profess to theology's logic of love sometimes abandon themselves to alternative accounts of peace, such as sleek cars. (Or, far more horribly and importantly, that endless succession of self-gratifying sexual exploitations by those 'who pervert the grace of our God into licentiousness and deny our only Master and Lord, Jesus Christ', Jude v. 4.) But Augustine's heuristic set in train an account of moral psychology that at least asks us to interrogate from whence is formed our narrative of what will give us peace, and whether participation in the love of God is having any bearing upon it, or not.

It is a heuristic that straightforwardly names the anxieties and conflicts of the city that lives according to the flesh. Contrary to caricature, flesh here is not some reference to sexuality. To gloss St. Paul and Augustine, it is a biblically derived code word for those manners of life that orient themselves to the immediate responses of the moment, and to the striving, longings, anger, and grief that arise from narratives of scarcity, needs real or imagined, and threatened goods. It is a manner of life unconditioned by the reframing that worship brings (and into which even worshipping people regularly regress). In Chapter 6, we saw how it is the body of disordered love.

As we have already observed, the world has lately been beset by rising tensions over the threats and losses, real and imagined, attending a global pandemic. These have been magnified by various otherings concerning vaccination status or not, or mask-wearing or not, all overlaid upon the perennial strivings concerning race, gender, sexuality, economics, and the rest. I may have been beset by anxiety personally, but people like me are affected within an already anxious milieu, where anxieties are multiplying.

The irony, however, is that if Augustine is to be believed, at the base of each position represented in this anxious landscape are goods worth loving, and people who love them. These may be fixated loves, to be sure, and not always loves that take the neighbour seriously. But our shared moral illiteracy in this landscape takes the form of a general incapacity to notice how what we each regard as self-evident is indeed a form of love, and consequently, then to engage imaginatively with the loves another person has.

I had hoped that *A Politics of Love*, a recent offering by US political activist Marianne Williamson, might offer a way forward along such lines.

> I've seen how the energy in a room can change profoundly when we drop into our hearts for a meaningful, sober, sincere conversation about things that matter most. The political atmosphere shifts when the spiritual atmosphere shifts, and that is as true among the masses as it is in a small room.[592]

---

592. Marianne Williamson, *A Politics of Love: A Handbook for a New American Revolution* (New York: HarperCollins, Kindle edn, 2019), p. 217.

That we are constituted in love, and that at the base of our soul is an attraction to what and who matter, is evidenced here in the language of 'our hearts', 'meaningful', and 'things that matter most'. The conjoining of the spiritual with the political is a welcome relief from the usual posturing. She continues, 'I have witnessed and experienced what happens when love has joined two people's hearts together. I have also witnessed and experienced what happens when love has joined the hearts of two thousand.'[593] On the whole, the book is an extended exhortation for us to join together, like this, in love. Her tone is almost Johannine: 'you must love one another' (although without the ontic premise 'as I have loved you,' Jn 13.34, or that 'the love you have for me may be in them', Jn 17.26).

There is merit to this exhortation. But it elides Augustine's point that the hard and intervening step must be the close interrogation of the 'what matters', those things that make for peace as each sees them – the loves proximal to us that then cause conflict, well before we can see and hear our neighbour aright. In *City of God* XIX.5-8, Augustine rehearses the melancholic consequence when voracity and selective sight are to the fore in our social and political experience (introduced in Chapter 6). Families experience conflict; the judiciary malfunctions horribly; and even friendships are uncertain and prone to treachery. We prefer pets to strange others: 'a man would more readily hold a conversation with his dog than with another man who is a foreigner.'[594] So severe is this disorder that the ontology of a good universe peopled with those who love all its varied goods almost seems submerged. Instead, a series of vices and woes seem to rule as the finally real. 'The earth is full of this great mass of evils.'[595]

For travellers towards the City of God, then, the hard task becomes living among the calamity while allowing the City of God's final peace to inform, shape and guide settled habits and patterns of action and feeling – that is, our virtues. Such travellers recognize that peace as the soul's proper gravity, reshaping the soul's loves. Thus, they 'maintain their identity not by withdrawal, but by something far more difficult: by maintaining a firm and balanced perspective on the whole range of loves of which men are capable in their present state'.[596] It is only by attention to this whole range of loves – a close parsing of them, and even an empathic, if transient, imaginative inhabitation of how they are manifesting within others, that we may engage across the battle lines to find something approaching the love for the other that Williamson enjoins upon, in her case, American politics.

But I note in passing an insight by Canadian political philosophers Jonah Goldstein and Jeremy Rayner, on how the tasks of political negotiation are complicated of late by existential needs within identity politics. 'Identity-claims depend on others for their viability', because (citing philosopher Charles Taylor) 'there is "a close connection between identity and recognition," and [. . .] "we

593. Williamson, *A Politics of Love*, p. 217.
594. Augustine, *City of God*, p. 928 (XIX.7).
595. Augustine, *City of God*, pp. 929–30 (XIX.8).
596. Brown, *Augustine*, p. 325.

become full human agents, capable of understanding ourselves, and hence of defining our identity," only through dialogue with others.' However,

> this fact is rarely acknowledged by the claimants, for to do so would be to acknowledge dependency, and this is precisely what the claimants want to deny. This helps explain why the politics of identity fosters grievances that are so difficult to resolve: identity-claims often involve demands that cannot be made transparent to either side without threatening the self-esteem of those seeking recognition.[597]

Even more problematically, identity-disputes 'characteristically lack clear focus':

> They may simmer on and on without resolution, not just because 'identity-claims' are poorly articulated, but because identity-claimants often resist clarifying what they really want, even to themselves. Indeed, the negotiating process in identity disputes is often typified by denial and mystification, and its outcome is frequently ambiguous: no matter what I get (what interests are satisfied), I may continue to wonder if what I get really recognizes who I am.[598]

As a result, suggest Goldstein and Rayner, we find ourselves in regimes that entail 'deep acting' towards identity claimants – presumably the opposite of what those claimants desire and need. In other words, there is now within informal and formal political processes an unacknowledged yearning to be seen, known, and loved; yet indeed, we do more readily hold converse with our pets.

Ever since New Testament Christians lived in tangled proximity to pagan neighbours, Christian theology has known that openness about its logic of love will not sweep all before it. Yet, even so, it may sometimes offer a crack of light into the most entrenched social and political nightmare. A heuristic that examines what is at the white-hot core of each claimant's loves, in moments that bypass deep acting and engage in authentic weighing of what matters to the other, even if we cannot then agree on what matters most, would be a step away from 'this great mass of evils' and a step towards 'meaningful, sober, sincere conversation about things that matter most'.

IV. Against values, towards the affections of theological virtue

Peeping throughout the book has been the modern West's go-to term of art for some notional connection between morality and affection: our 'values'. This term

---

597. Jonah Goldstein and Jeremy Rayner, 'The Politics of Identity in Late Modern Society', *Theory and Society* 23.3 (1994), pp. 367–84 (371), available online at: https://link .springer.com/article/10.1007%2FBF00993835, doi: 10.1007/bf00993835.

598. Goldstein and Rayner, 'The Politics of Identity', p. 367.

would seem elementary to any discussion of the connection between emotion and ethics. As Robert Solomon once semi-famously put it, 'Reason makes contact with human values only through the passions.'[599] As Nietzsche more famously put it, '[E]very table of values, every "thou shalt" known to history or the study of ethnology, needs first and foremost a *physiological* elucidation and interpretation, rather than a psychological one; and all of them await critical study from medical science.'[600] By this he intends almost precisely the task of modern moral psychology: the correlation of moral stances with the physiological responses inherent to emotions, to determine what we actually value.

But I have, on the whole, avoided the language of values, because I find it confused in modern parlance to the point of dysfunction. In brief, my complaint is that the term is regularly deployed to claim as valuable what hearers do not, in reality, love much at all. In other words, it has become a term that asserts of our loving attachment what is often not really there at all. We need only cast our mind back to the last lamentable seminar in a church, a school, or a workplace, where we were tasked to list 'our' values. The meetings are interminable, and the resulting lists are always variations on the same master list – something like 'respect', 'tolerance', 'diversity', 'professionalism', 'justice', 'inclusion', 'sustainability', 'accountability', 'transparency', and if we are lucky, maybe 'care' or 'honesty'. And so on.

The problem is not that these words don't prescribe actions. For those, we turn to industrialized codes of ethics, which are moralistic enough to signal corporate rectitude; prescriptive enough to enable punishment; capacious enough to assuage insurers; and so incessantly hyperlinked as to make the most committed ancient Gnostic seem frank and to the point. Rather, they gesture towards a preferred style of life, not unlike older language of virtue. That function, in itself, need not be problematic. Nor is the problem that these words are vague, if we can accept that substantive realities can be described by terms that do not have bright, clear lines of demarcation.

But these seminars are so uniformly denervating because we suspect no one *actually* values (loves) whatever these nouns signify, except for a few enthusiasts, and the management who regard them rather as members' or employees' duties. In reality at these events, enthusiasts and management are simply telling us who to become. In organizational settings, it is of course proper to set expectations of 'what we do around here', and to indicate aspirations for organizational culture. But to couch these as 'our values' is a debasement of what, after all, Nietzsche thought needed to become the term of art for what *actually* matters to each individual and so engages their emotions, irrespective of what anyone else thinks *should* matter to them.

---

599. Solomon, *The Passions*, p. 58.
600. Nietzsche, *On the Genealogy of Morality*, p. 37 (§I.17, concluding note).

What we choose for ourselves, he thought, 'has to be *our* invention, *our* most personal defence and necessity'.[601] In this matter, Nietzsche quite definitely touted a diminution of value's more admirable cousin, the concept of virtue (which has made various cameo appearances throughout this book). The slide from the language of virtue to the language of value is of a piece with a slide from moral realism to moral constructivism.[602] That is, a virtue presents itself as a settled habit and pattern of action and feeling to which all of us are called, since all are called to love and act towards what actually matters (and is aligned to the human *telos*), as opposed to those immediate fixations conveyed to us by our passions. If corporate-speak were simply to say, here are the virtues we expect workers to cultivate, I would have no complaint. But that, of course, would be seen to threaten diversity by imposing a substantive account of moral order. So, managers resort to doublespeak, implicitly promoting aspects of an objective moral order by means of a language invented to deny it. Corporate values language does not work, only creating cognitive and emotional dissonance and lashings of jejune cynicism among those who must endure it.

We can drill a little further into my complaint using an observation by philosopher Charles Taylor. In Taylor's understanding of modern identity, a disengaged self employs procedural reasoning to generate conceptions of value that are then projected upon a fundamentally mechanistic order (i.e., moral constructivism). The ancient view, which he outlines in contrast, relies upon a moral order beyond us, as also does theology's logic of love. On this ancient view, an engaged self employs substantive reason, in response to a real and already morally ordered order (i.e., moral realism). Taylor seeks to defend this ancient view against the modern view, believing that 'ontology' is an 'ontic logos' (as is the logic of love). On the ancient account, what is valuable is already located in the cosmos, not merely in subjects.[603] The virtues we saw in Aquinas (Chapter 7), and the many virtue words in the New Testament,[604] share an appeal to our common inhabitation of an objective moral order.

---

601. Nietzsche, *The Anti-Christ*, p. 133 (§11).

602. A related argument has been made by Himmelfarb, *The De-Moralization of Society*, pp. 8–12.

603. Taylor, *Sources of the Self*, pp. 163 and 86–87 for brief summary statements.

604. There are approximately twenty each of virtue- and vice-lists in the New Testament, depending on how they are counted. There is more to its language of character, virtue, and vice than these lists, but they are an important element. Of course, each has its own occasion and purpose (see further Cameron, *Joined-up Life*, pp. 194–202):

Virtues: Rom. 13.13; 1 Cor. 13.4-7; 2 Cor. 6.6-7; Gal. 5.22-23; Eph. 4.32, 5.9, and 6.14-17; Phil. 4.8; Col. 3.12; 1 Tim. 3.2-12 and 6.11; 2 Tim. 2.22, v. 24, and 3.10; Tit. 1.8-9, 2.2-5, v. 7, v. 9, and 3.1-2; Jas 3.17; 1 Pet. 3.8; 2 Pet. 1.5-7.

Vices: Mk 7.21-22; Rom. 1.29-31; 1 Cor. 5.10, 6.9-10, and 13.4-7; 2 Cor. 12.20; Gal. 5.19-21; Eph. 4.31 and 5.3-5; Col. 3.5 and vv. 8-9; 1 Tim. 1.9-10, 3.2, and 6.4-5; 2 Tim. 3.2-5; Tit. 1.7, 2.3, vv. 9-10, and 3.3; 1 Pet. 4.3; Rev. 21.8 and 22.15.

It is interesting to note that when Jonathan Edwards (whom we glimpsed in Chapter 1) finally determines a genuine religious affection, he settles on manifestations of virtue, with New Testament virtue lists used in support of the thesis that 'Truly gracious affections differ from those affections that are false and delusive, in that they tend to, and are attended with, the lamb-like, dove-like spirit and temper of Jesus Christ.'[605] Under this heading is treated a serviceable account of virtue and character (including, handily, a close dissection of proper and illicit forms of 'fortitude' within expressions of Christian piety).[606]

Shouted value-nouns cannot sustain a life together. Moreover, a virtue cannot only be a settled habit of action, but entails a particularly schooled affection. Whether or not that affection is in easy human reach, the key acknowledgement becomes that a virtuous existence needs to attend to what is loved, or not loved, at least in the first instance. The utility of the traditions examined in Chapter 9 is their sustained examination of what is loved, and the retraining of love that takes the form of lived virtues arising somewhat indirectly from sustained, intentional practices of prayerful and Scripturally informed contemplation.

V. The problem with preaching

I reserve my final salvo for a kind of preaching I have long endured (and have also delivered). I well remember Matthew Elliott's description, while listening to a sermon, of 'a knot in the pit of my stomach; I was afraid the turn was about to happen.'[607] The 'turn' in question was that moment where some vibrant biblical language of feeling was flipped by the preacher to become some will-propelled task of thinking. Elliott offers a compendium of quotations from various Christian preachers and thinkers, all of whom assert that biblical emotion words such as love, joy, and hope, are not primarily feelingful, but are basically thoughts. (This repeated conceit, it should be noted, is *not* a cognitivist account of emotion, where emotions and thoughts are complexly interwoven. Elliott cautiously approves such accounts.) The bait-and-switch sermon in question dealt with joy, where a biblical promise of joy to sustain us in hard times was finally interpreted as a kind of thinking, and an effort of mental will.

Elliott is primarily in dialogue with Reformed Protestantism, the theological tribe I know best, so his account struck a chord. In a focused study of eight evangelical Protestant preachers with Reformed convictions, Andrew Katay has found that although all affirmed that preaching should affect the heart, almost all had little or no anthropological account to inform that aspiration, and therefore

---

605. Edwards, *The Religious Affections*, pp. 272–85.

606. Edwards, *The Religious Affections*, pp. 277–80.

607. Elliott, *Feel*, p. 100. I also highly recommend, and should in this book have paid more attention to, the scholarly work upon which *Feel* is based: Matthew Elliott, *Faithful Feelings: Emotion in the New Testament* (Leicester: Inter-Varsity, 2005).

'little engagement in the actual dynamics of [. . .] transformation.'[608] What has followed, in Katay's estimate, is 'a bare moralism in preaching, that simply states and explains the obedience called for in Scripture, and then appeals to the listeners to exert greater willpower in performing it.'[609] We may cautiously infer that the problem is not confined to his eight.

Obviously, handling of the affective domain constitutes a major difference between recent Reformed and Pentecostal or charismatic Christianity. For Pentecostal and charismatic Christians, it would seem that the presence or not of good feelings directly results from the presence or absence of the Holy Spirit. My impression is that for some of these believers, emotions are not even finally a function of being human: good emotions arrive when the Holy Spirit arrives.[610] If that account also leads to malfunctions in preaching, as is likely, it is not for me to address them. In stark contrast, Reformed Christians imagine that the Holy Spirit primarily affects thoughts and actions, and that emotional states bear no direct correlation to the Spirit's presence or absence.

In this connection, Elliott collates comments from various dialogue partners for whom feelings about their faith and their life are quite disconnected from their thoughts. This gap is not at all capable of being bridged by the further thought or instruction that they should feel differently. If it is true, with Kant, that emotions cannot be commanded, preachers ministering to this gap are well-intentioned when they try to protect us from such a task. 'Bait-and-switch' sermons such as described by Elliott perhaps seek to do us a service, by not creating a load too great for us to bear. If an emotional state is a given and basically beyond our control, such preaching seeks to address what the preacher judges to be within our control: our cognition and rationality. On such an account, this aspect of ourselves can be moved, shifted, and altered through preaching and persuasion, whereas emotions cannot be so moved – even should not be so moved, since that would be manipulative.

608. Andrew P. Katay, 'Preaching to the Heart: Investigating Theory and Practice Among Sydney Anglican Preachers', (unpublished D.Min. dissertation, Trinity Evangelical Divinity School, 2019), p. 58.

609. Katay, 'Preaching to the Heart', p. 59.

610. For a vastly more nuanced (and actually knowledgeable) account positing the emotional and embodied salience of the Holy Spirit's work, see Simeon Zahl, *The Holy Spirit and Christian Experience* (Oxford: Oxford University Press, 2020); and the sympathetic review (with some demurral) by Oliver M. T. O'Donovan, 'Book Review: Simeon Zahl, *The Holy Spirit and Christian Experience*', *Modern Theology* 38.1 (2022), pp. 144–47, doi: 10.1111/moth.12715. In this review, an intriguing comment by O'Donovan casts some light on the preacher's inexorable habit of seeking to force a bare will that has little or no connection to Augustinian 'will' as enacted love. The habit may have begun a very long-time ago. With his typical penchant for exhuming modern tropes from medieval turns, O'Donovan describes 'a failure to envisage human agency clearly [whereby] responsive affections were displaced by the "will" of medieval theory, an uncaused cause supposed to lie behind every attributable act' (140). O'Donovan is a fellow traveller with Zahl in lamenting this turn.

What is anticipated is a kind of trickle-down effect, with theology offering the kind of cognitive reframing that may result in the altered emotional profile. Not that there any guarantees such an altered profile will result in the present: it may prove only to be the God's gift in the eschaton. (Again, I note in my experience the total preponderance of male preachers espousing this line of reasoning.)

Elliott is utterly hostile to this trickle-down view, and seeks to offer alternatives. While I am not convinced by all of them, his infectious style and tone offers a clue as to the most promising route by which to retrain love. The book is laced with stories, exhortations and examples that enable us to visualize and imagine new attachments as we vicariously participate with others of whom we read. Elliott describes precisely such an experience in the company of the quadriplegic Christian Joni Earickson-Tada, whose words he could not quite remember, but whose hopeful presence filled him with hope.[611] In turn, his own description of her serves to affect the reader. The cumulative effect of many such descriptions, all written with an urgency that remonstrates with us for what we can trust is our good, is powerfully helpful. There is a clue here for an alternative approach to preaching that does not devolve the language of love into a 'pelagian' project of thinking and willing alone.

It reminds us of Augustine's handling, outlined in Chapter 6, of the tricky pastoral gap for those who have not yet experienced the reordering of affection towards the love of God. Using the example of the infectious nature of the sporting arena, a deep love for the sportsmen and the sport grows. It is mysterious, yet accessible.[612] This analogy is applied to what Augustine thinks comes upon us as we engage in prayer and in humility.

In teaching on homiletics, I have been struck by how fluidly ancient preachers conveyed God's love, and effected responsive love for God and each other, in precisely such an infectious way. A single example must suffice – an excerpt from John Chrysostom's famous Paschal homily (to be read on Resurrection Sunday):

If any be a devout lover of God,
    let him partake with gladness from this fair and radiant feast.
[. . .] If any have laboured from the first hour,
    let him receive today his rightful due.
If any have come after the third,
    let him celebrate the feast with thankfulness.
If any have come after the sixth,
    let him not be in doubt, for he will suffer no loss.
If any have delayed until the ninth,
    let him not hesitate but draw near.
If any have arrived only at the eleventh,
    let him not be afraid because he comes so late.
For the Master is generous and accepts the last even as the first.

---

611. Elliott, *Feel*, pp. 182–83.
612. Brown, *Augustine (new edn.)*, pp. 448–49.

He gives rest to him who comes at the eleventh hour
    in the same was as him who has laboured from the first.
[. . .] Enter then, all of you, into the joy of our Lord.
First and last, receive alike your reward.
Rich and poor, dance together.
You who fasted and you who have not fasted, rejoice together.
The table is fully laden: let all enjoy it.
The calf is fatted: let none go away hungry.
Let none lament his poverty;
    for the universal Kingdom is revealed.
Let none bewail his transgressions;
    for the light of forgiveness has risen from the tomb.
Let none fear death;
    for death of the Saviour has set us free.
He has destroyed death by undergoing death.
He has despoiled hell by descending into hell.
He vexed it even as it tasted of His flesh.
[. . .] Christ is risen! And you, o death, are annihilated!
Christ is risen! And the evil ones are cast down!
Christ is risen! And the angels rejoice!
Christ is risen! And life is liberated!
Christ is risen! And the tomb is emptied of its dead;
for Christ having risen from the dead,
is become the first-fruits of those who have fallen asleep.[613]

It might be objected that Chrysostom has an unfair advantage in his subject matter, since any preacher can make something of the Resurrection. But it is instructive to see how theological content, with moments of biblical exegesis, is imbued with infectious exhortations to be swept up into the Lord's own joy. In this respect, it effects a logic of responsive participation. But prior to that, the opening stanza takes the time to name compassionately the affective blockages to such joy, all framed within an accounting of divine grace that overwhelmingly accepts each person despite their doubt, hesitation, or fear. In the manner of many a Psalm, it skilfully moves us to a new affective state, by subtle redirections of love.

VI. Coda: *The logic of love, every day*

We love, and cannot help but to love. We love even when we are not aware that we are loving. We love sleek cars, football, babies, success, intriguing insects, works of art. We love friends, beautiful actors, playful children, and stories.

613. Translator unknown; available online at: http://www.orthodoxchristian.info/pages /sermon.htm.

We love colouring in, investigating, Tai Chi, kite flying, and podcasts. We love staring at our phone, because we love news of the new, or the prospect of connection, or the mastery of some task. We love that clever friend who seems to be able to see into who we are. We love mountains, mountain climbing, sports-fishing, and needlepoint. We love academic enquiry, rollerblading, opera, and freedom. We love the house painter, who glides with clean professional ease around cornices and corners. We love pet dogs, new kitchens, happy children, molecular biology, and Sudoku. We love spouses, lovers, elders, saints, and baristas. We love focus, unfocus, attachment, separation, serenity, solitude, and excitement. We love fat bank accounts, prettily wrapped parcels, news of kindness, generosity, an email from a long-lost friend. We love sleeping, waking, exercising, lazing, rain, shine, snow, warmth, cool. We love Eucharist, Bible study, prayer and praise, quiet contemplation. Or we love relief from any of the above.

Every waking moment, and some sleeping ones, mediate to us evaluations based in love that in turn power our hates, griefs, anxieties, despairs, and our every moral conundrum. It was Augustine's genius to synthesize from Scripture's witness how far down into us it all goes, and how deeply from within God it all comes. The thinkers we have surveyed all, in their own way, are seeking to comprehend and enact the logic of love. It has been my contention that what we habitually call ethics and morality is more fruitfully construed as manifestations of love, or at least as forms of grappling with its logic.

The book has been an imperfect attempt to encompass the deep logic of love, but I am convinced that the logic of love offers the best account of morality and moral identity. God sustains a plurality of goods, ordered towards ends and as discrete kinds, where humanity is constituted in being, knowledge and love. Humanity responds in love to the moral field, which elicits love, and gives love its logic. This love generates passions such as joy, sadness, hope and fear, and anger, and our emotions point us to loved goods. Our complex moral emotions build inexorably upon these, as do our moral claims and counterclaims. But confounding all of that is voracity and selective sight, wherein humanity regularly perceives the plenitude of the moral field as a problem of scarcity. At our worst, in faithless unconcern towards God, love and its subsequent reasoning is comprehensively misdirected to ends less than the enjoyment of God and of one another in God, giving us instead our concupiscent will to power.

But divine love poured in by the Spirit offers change, and the settled intention of divine holy affection towards us is also indicated to us by the life and death of Christ; and what may seem chancy and adventitious is made accessible in the invitation (by command) to love commended. The Spirit uses the teachings of Christ, the Old Law, and other aspects of revelation to shape our participation. Under this reordering – and perhaps with an assist from focused and intentional practices of prayerful contemplation of the gospel – all of love's aspects find their proper home.

I have sought to unmask some conceits arising from dubious dichotomies, even if we must retain some linguistic distinctions in order to do business with our lives in the world. My main hope, however, is that we might deploy the logic of love to unveil our personal moments of stuckness, moral failure, despair, distraction, or the like; and to better assess, discuss, and at least understand our shared disputes and moral conundrums.

I hope also to have put the case (notwithstanding the predictable charge that to do so is monolithic) that for each and every one of us, a path forward exists wherein we might find again the God who is love, as revealed in Christ, to then participate anew in Triune love. While not a panacea for every moral firefight, the more of us who so re-engage will coalesce into moments of mutual understanding at least, with increasing bouts of something approaching peace. Goods such as those I listed above can more likely be sustained within their proper home, and all the goods of ordinary life affirmed when loved appropriate to their place within the moral field. Harmonious communities may even form, who live a little more in like-mindedness, and like-heartedness, concerning these goods. Journeying together in joyful affections, and participating in the reordering of our passions, we may then hold forth God's 'yes' to a disordered world, also showing forth God's forgiveness and help, with voracity towards scarcity becoming contentment with abundance.

We might even be able to show how a coward might learn quiet, consistent resolve; and how every other restless heart can find rest, in him.[614]

---

614. Cf. Augustine, *Confessions*, p. 21 (I.1).

BIBLIOGRAPHY

'About ISRE', Online at https://www.isre.org/page/ISRE101.

Adomaityte, Vaiva, 'Emotions and Ethics: A Conversation with Martha C. Nussbaum and Thomas Aquinas', *Dialogue and Universalism* 25.2 (2015), pp. 92–103; doi: 10.5840/du201525242.

Aquinas, Thomas, *Summa Theologica* (trans. Fathers of the English Dominican Province, London: Benzinger Brothers, 1937).

Aquinas, Thomas, *Summa Theologica: Purpose and Happiness (Vol. 16, 1a2æ.1-5)* (London: Blackfriars and Eyre & Spottiswoode, 1969).

Aquinas, Thomas, *Summa Theologica: The Emotions (Vol. 19, 1a2æ.22-30)* (trans. Eric D'Arcy, London: Blackfriars and Eyre & Spottiswoode, 1967).

Audi, Robert, *The Good in the Right: A Theory of Intuition and Intrinsic Value* (Princeton and Oxford: Princeton University Press, 2004).

Audi, Robert, *Moral Perception* (Princeton and Oxford: Princeton University Press, 2013).

Augustine, *The City of God* (trans. Marcus Dods; *NPNF 1* series, vol. II, including *On Christian Doctrine*, Grand Rapids, MI: Eerdmans, 1988).

Augustine, *The City of God Against the Pagans* (trans. R. W. Dyson, Cambridge: Cambridge University Press, *Cambridge Texts in the History of Political Thought* edn, 1998).

Augustine, *Confessions* (trans. R. S. Pine-Coffin, Harmondsworth: Penguin, *Penguin Classics* edn, 1961).

Augustine, *De Civitate Dei Contra Paganos* (ed. J. E. C. Welldon; Vol. I, 2 vols, London: SPCK, 1924).

Augustine, *De Civitate Dei Contra Paganos* (ed. J. E. C. Welldon; Vol. II, 2 vols, London: SPCK, 1924).

Augustine, *Homilies on the First Epistle of John* (trans. H. Browne; *Homilies on the Gospel of John; Homilies on the First Epistle of John; Soliloquies* series, *NPNF 1*, vol. VII, Grand Rapids, MI: Eerdmans, 1986).

Augustine, *On Marriage and Concupiscence* (trans. Peter Holmes and Robert E. Wallis; *NPNF 1* series, vol. V, *Writings against the Pelagians*, Grand Rapids, MI: Eerdmans, 1987).

Augustine, *On Nature and Grace* (trans. Peter Holmes and Robert E. Wallis; *Writings against the Pelagians* series, *NPNF 1*, vol. V, Grand Rapids, MI: Eerdmans, 1987).

Augustine, *On the Good of Marriage* (trans. C. L. Cornish; *On the Holy Trinity; Doctrinal Treatises; Moral Treatises* series, *NPNF 1*, vol. III, Grand Rapids, MI: Eerdmans, 1988).

Augustine, *On the Morals of the Catholic Church* (trans. Richard Stothert; *Writings against the Manichaeans and the Donatists* series, *NPNF 1*, vol. IV, Grand Rapids, MI: Eerdmans, 1989).

Augustine, *On the Spirit and the Letter* (trans. Peter Holmes and Robert E. Wallis; *Writings against the Pelagians* series, *NPNF 1*, vol. V, Grand Rapids, MI: Eerdmans, 1987).

Augustine, *Teaching Christianity (On Christian Doctrine)* (trans. O. P. Edmund Hill, New York: New City Press, Kindle edn, 2014).

Babcock, William S., 'Augustine and the Spirituality of Desire', *Augustinian Studies* 25 (1994), pp. 179–99; doi: 10.5840/augstudies1994259.

Banner, Michael C., *The Ethics of Everyday Life: Moral Theology, Social Anthropology, and the Imagination of the Human* (Oxford: Oxford University Press, Kindle edn, 2014).

Banner, Michael C., *Christian Ethics: A Brief History* (Chichester: Wiley-Blackwell, 2009).

Barclay, Katie, 'State of the Field: The History of Emotions', *History* 106.371 (2021), pp. 456–66; doi: 10.1111/1468-229X.13171.

Barry, William A., *Letting God Come Close: An Approach to the Ignatian Spiritual Exercises* (Chicago, IL: Jesuit Way/Loyola, 2001).

Baumeister, Roy F., 'Emotions: How the Future Feels (and Could Feel)', in *Homo Prospectus* (eds Martin E. P. Seligman, Peter Albert Railton, Roy F. Baumeister, Chandra Sekhar Sripada, Oxford: Oxford University Press, 2016), pp. 207–23.

Beauchamp, Tom L., and James F. Childress, *Principles of Biomedical Ethics* (New York: Oxford University Press, 7th edn, 2013).

Ben-Ze'ev, Aaron, 'Describing the Emotions: A Review of *The Cognitive Structure of Emotions* by Ortony, Clore & Collins', *Philosophical Psychology* 3.2–3 (1990), pp. 305–17; doi: 10.1080/09515089008573006.

Benedict of Nursia, *Saint Benedict's Rule for Monasteries* (trans. Leonard J. Doyle OblSB, Collegeville, MN: Order of Saint Benedict, 1948, 2001). Online at www.archive.osb.org /rb.

Bonner, Gerald I., 'Libido and Concupiscentia in St Augustine', in *Studia Patristica: Papers Presented to the Third International Conference on Patristic Studies (Oxford 1959)* (ed. Frank Leslie Cross, Vol. VI, Berlin: Akademie-Verlag, 1962), pp. 303–14.

Brinkmann, Svend, *Psychology As a Moral Science: Perspectives on Normativity* (New York: Springer, 2011); doi: 10.1007/978-1-4419-7067-1_6.

Brown, Peter, *Augustine of Hippo: A Biography* (London: Faber, 1967).

Brown, Peter, *Augustine of Hippo: A Biography (A New Edition with an Epilogue)* (London: Faber, 2000).

Burkeman, Oliver, 'Treat Your To-Read Pile Like a River, Not a Bucket', Online at www .oliverburkeman.com/river.

Burrell, David, C. S. C., and Isabelle Moulin, 'Albert, Aquinas, and Dionysius', in *Re-thinking Dionysius the Areopagite* (eds Sarah Coakley and Charles M. Stang; *Directions in Modern Theology* series, Chicester: Wiley, 2011), pp. 215–50.

Bush, Randall, 'The Suffering of God as an Aspect of the Divine Omniscience', *Journal of the Evangelical Theological Society* 51.4 (2008), pp. 769–84.

Callahan, Sidney, 'The Role of Emotion in Ethical Decisionmaking', *Hastings Center Report* 18 (1988), pp. 9–14.

Cameron, Andrew J. B., 'Humility and the Middle-Aged Man: A Reflection on Foulcher's Wisdom', *St Mark's Review* 256 (2021), pp. 26–41.

Cameron, Andrew J. B., *Joined-up Life: A Christian Account of How Ethics Works* (Nottingham: IVP, 2011).

Castelo, Daniel, 'Continued Grappling: The Divine Impassibility Debates Today', *International Journal of Systematic Theology* 12.3 (2010), pp. 364–72; doi: 10.1111/j.1468-2400.2010.00510.x.

Cates, Diana Fritz, *Aquinas on the Emotions: A Religious-Ethical Inquiry* (*Moral Traditions* series, Washington, DC: Georgetown University Press, 2009).

Cavanaugh, William T., *Theopolitical Imagination: Christian Practices of Space and Time* (Edinburgh: T&T Clark, 2003).

Chittister, Joan, *The Monastery of the Heart: An Invitation to a Meaningful Life* (Katonah, NY: BlueBridge, 2011).

Clore, Gerald L., 'Psychology and the Rationality of Emotion', in *Faith, Rationality, and the Passions* (ed. Sarah Coakley, Chichester: John Wiley & Sons, Ltd, 2012), pp. 209–22.

Coakley, Sarah, *God, Sexuality and the Self: An Essay 'On the Trinity'* (Cambridge: Cambridge University Press, 2013).

Coakley, Sarah, 'On Why *Analytic Theology* Is Not a Club', *Journal of the American Academy of Religion* 81.3 (2013), pp. 601–08; doi: 10.1093/jaarel/lft040.

Coakley, Sarah, 'Person of Christ', in *The Cambridge Companion to the Summa Theologiae* (eds Philip McCosker and Denys Turner; *Cambridge Companions to Religion* series, New York, NY: Cambridge University Press, 2016), pp. 222–39.

Coakley, Sarah, 'Pleasure Principles: Toward a Contemporary Theology of Desire.' *Harvard Divinity Bulletin*, Autumn, 2005. Online at https://bulletin.hds.harvard.edu/pleasure-principles.

Coakley, Sarah, 'Postscript', in *Faith, Rationality, and the Passions* (ed. Sarah Coakley, Malden, MA: Wiley-Blackwell, 2012), pp. 251–55.

Coakley, Sarah, 'A Response to Oliver O'Donovan's *Ethics as Theology* Trilogy', *Modern Theology* 36.1 (2020), pp. 186–92; doi: 10.1111/moth.12561.

Costall, Alan, 'From Darwin to Watson (and Cognitivism) and Back Again: The Principle of Animal-Environment Mutuality', *Behavior and Philosophy* 32.1 (2004), pp. 179–95.

Cranfield, Charles Ernest Burland, *A Critical and Exegetical Commentary on the Epistle to the Romans (I-VIII)* (vol. 1; 2 vols, Edinburgh: T&T Clark, 1975).

Cranfield, Charles Ernest Burland, *A Critical and Exegetical Commentary on the Epistle to the Romans (IX-XVI)* (vol. 2; 2 vols, Edinburgh: T&T Clark, 1979).

Cross, F. L., and Elizabeth A. Livingstone, *The Oxford Dictionary of the Christian Church* (Oxford: Oxford University Press, 3rd edn, 2005).

Curry, Oliver Scott, Daniel Austin Mullins, and Harvey Whitehouse, 'Is It Good to Cooperate? Testing the Theory of Morality-as-Cooperation in 60 Societies', *Current Anthropology* 60.1 (2019), pp. 47–69. Online at https://dx.doi.org/10.1086/701478; doi: 10.1086/701478.

Dixon, Thomas, '"Emotion": One Word, Many Concepts', *Emotion Review* 4.4 (2012), pp. 387–88; doi: 10.1177/1754073912445826.

Dixon, Thomas, '"Emotion": The History of a Keyword in Crisis', *Emotion Review* 4.4 (2012), pp. 338–44 doi: 10.1177/1754073912445814.

Dixon, Thomas, *From Passions to Emotions: The Creation of a Secular Psychological Category* (Cambridge: Cambridge University Press 2003).

Dixon, Thomas, 'Preface', in *Before Emotion* (ed. Juanita Feros Ruys, et al., New York: Routledge, 2019), pp. xi–xvi.

Dixon, Thomas, 'Theology, Anti-Theology and Atheology: From Christian Passions to Secular Emotions', *Modern Theology* 15.3 (1999), pp. 297–330.

Doherty, Bernard, 'Christ-Haunted But Not Christ-Centred: Ghosts of the Christian South in HBO's *True Detective*', *St Mark's Review* 257 (2021), pp. 46–69.

Edwards, Jonathan, *The Religious Affections* (Edinburgh and Carlisle, PA: The Banner of Truth Trust, 1961).

Elliott, Matthew, *Faithful Feelings: Emotion in the New Testament* (Leicester: Inter-Varsity, 2005).

Elliott, Matthew, *Feel: The Power of Listening to Your Heart* (Carol Stream, IL: Tyndale House Publishers, 2008).

Errington, Andrew, *Every Good Path: Wisdom and Practical Reason in Christian Ethics and the Book of Proverbs* (*T&T Clark Enquiries in Theological Ethics* series, London: Bloomsbury and T&T Clark, 2020).

Evans, Dylan, *Emotion: The Science of Sentiment* (Oxford: Oxford University Press, 2001).

Floyd, Shawn D., 'Aquinas on Emotion: A Response to Some Recent Interpretations', *History of Philosophy Quarterly* 15.2 (1998), pp. 161–75.

Foot, Philippa, 'Nietzsche's Immoralism', in *Nietzsche, Genealogy, Morality: Essays on Nietzsche's Genealogy of Morals* (ed. Richard Schacht, Berkeley; Los Angeles and London: University of California Press, 1994), pp. 3–14.

Foulcher, Jane, 'Ageing, Humility, and the Monastery', *Journal of Religion, Spirituality & Aging* 26.2–3 (2014), pp. 148–59; doi: 10.1080/15528030.2013.857380.

Foulcher, Jane, *Reclaiming Humility: Four Studies in the Monastic Tradition* (*Cistercian Studies* series 255, Collegeville, MN: Cistercian Publications, 2015).

Foulcher, Jane, 'Response to Don E. Davis and Sarah Gazaway', in *The Joy of Humility: The Beginning and End of the Virtues* (ed. Drew Collins, Ryan McAnnally-Linz, and Evan C. Rosa, Waco, TX: Baylor University Press, 2020), pp. 155–59.

Foulcher, Jane, 'Response to Norman Wirzba', in *The Joy of Humility: The Beginning and End of the Virtues* (ed. Drew Collins, Ryan McAnnally-Linz, and Evan C. Rosa, Waco, TX: Baylor University Press, 2020), pp. 122–25.

Frederick, Thomas V., and Timothy P. Muldoon, 'Ignatian Spirituality and Psychotherapy', *Journal of Psychology and Christianity* 39.1 (2020), pp. 12–23.

Goldstein, Jonah, and Jeremy Rayner, 'The Politics of Identity in Late Modern Society', *Theory and Society* 23.3 (1994), pp. 367–84. Online at https://link.springer.com/article/10.1007%2FBF00993835; doi: 10.1007/bf00993835.

Goleman, Daniel, *Emotional Intelligence: Why It Can Matter More Than I.Q.* (London: Bloomsbury, 1996).

Gondreau, Paul, 'Life of Christ', in *The Cambridge Companion to the Summa Theologiae* (eds Philip McCosker and Denys Turner; *Cambridge Companions to Religion* series, New York, NY: Cambridge University Press, 2016), pp. 240–54.

Gondreau, Paul, *The Passions of Christ's Soul in the Theology of St. Thomas Aquinas* (*Beiträge zur Geschichte der Philosophie und Theologie des Mittelalters* series, Münster: Aschendorff, 2002).

Govrin, Aner, *Ethics and Attachment: How We Make Moral Judgments* (Milton: Taylor & Francis Group, 2018).

Greenacre, Liam, 'An Introduction to the History of Emotions', *The York Historian: the University of York Student History Magazine* (4 November 2019). Online at https://theyorkhistorian.com/2019/11/04/an-introduction-to-the-history-of-emotions.

Griffiths, Paul E., *What Emotions Really Are: The Problem of Psychological Categories* (Chicago: University of Chicago Press, 1997).

Haidt, Jonathan, 'The Emotional Dog and Its Rational Tail: A Social Intuitionist Approach to Moral Judgment', *Psychological Review* 108.4 (2001), pp. 814–34; doi: 10.1037/0033-295X.108.4.814.

Haidt, Jonathan, *The Happiness Hypothesis: Finding Modern Truth in Ancient Wisdom* (New York: Basic Books, 2006).

Haidt, Jonathan, 'Morality', *Perspectives on Psychological Science* 3.1 (2008), pp. 65–72; doi: 10.1111/j.1745-6916.2008.00063.x.

Haidt, Jonathan, 'The New Synthesis in Moral Psychology', *Science* 316.5827 (2007), pp. 998–1002; doi: 10.1126/science.1137651.

Haidt, Jonathan, *The Righteous Mind: Why Good People are Divided by Politics and Religion* (London: Allen Lane, 2012).

Haidt, Jonathan, and Craig Joseph, 'How Moral Foundations Theory Succeeded in Building on Sand: A Response to Suhler and Churchland', *Journal of Cognitive Neuroscience* 23.9 (2011), pp. 2117–22; doi: 10.1162/jocn.2011.21638.

Haidt, Jonathan, and Craig Joseph, 'The Moral Mind: How Five Sets of Innate Intuitions Guide the Development of Many Culture-Specific Virtues, and Perhaps Even Modules', in *The Innate Mind, Volume 3: Foundations and the Future* (eds Stephen Stich, Stephen Laurence and Peter Carruthers, New York: Oxford University Press, 2008), pp. 367–92; doi: 10.1093/acprof:oso/9780195332834.003.0019.

Hare, John E., 'Augustine, Kant, and the Moral Gap', in *The Augustinian Tradition* (ed. Gareth B. Matthews, Berkeley and London: University of California Press, 1999), pp. 251–62.

Hare, John E., *The Moral Gap: Kantian Ethics, Human Limits, and God's Assistance* (Oxford: Clarendon Press, 1996).

Hari, Johann, *Lost Connections: Why You're Depressed and How to Find Hope* (London: Bloomsbury, 2018).

Hart, David Bentley, *The Doors of the Sea: Where was God in the Tsunami?* (Grand Rapids, MI: Eerdmans, 2005).

Hart, David Bentley, *The Experience of God: Being, Consciousness, Bliss* (New Haven: Yale University Press, Kindle edition, 2013).

Hart, David Bentley, 'No Shadow of Turning: On Divine Impassibility', *Pro Ecclesia* 11.2 (2002), pp. 184–206; doi: 10.1177/106385120201100205.

Harvey, A. E., *Strenuous Commands: The Ethic of Jesus* (London: SCM Press, 1990).

Helm, Paul, 'Impassionedness and "So-called Classical Theism"', in *Within the Love of God: Essays on the Doctrine of God in Honour of Paul S. Fiddes* (eds Anthony Clarke and Andrew Moore, Oxford: Oxford University Press, 2014), pp. 144–54; doi: 10.1093/ac prof:oso/9780198709565.003.0011.

Henrich, Joseph, Steven J. Heine, and Ara Norenzayan, 'Beyond WEIRD: Towards a Broad-Based Behavioral Science', *The Behavioral and Brain Sciences* 33.2–3 (2010), pp. 111–210; doi: 10.1017/S0140525X10000725.

Himmelfarb, Gertrude, *The De-Moralization of Society: From Victorian Virtues to Modern Values* (New York: Knopf, 1995).

Holland, Tom, *Dominion: The Making of the Western Mind* (London: Little, Brown, 2019).

Hume, David, *A Treatise of Human Nature* (vol. II, London: J. M. Dent and Sons Ltd, 1911).

Hursthouse, Rosalind, 'Virtue Ethics and the Emotions', in *Virtue Ethics* (ed. Daniel Statman, Edinburgh: Edinburgh University Press, 1997), pp. 99–117.

Hutcheson, Frances, *An Essay on the Nature and Conduct of the Passions and Affections: With Illustrations on the Moral Sense* (ed. Paul McReynolds, Gainsville: Scholars' Facsimiles and Reprints, 1969).

Johnson, Sue M., *Hold Me Tight: Seven Conversations for a Lifetime of Love* (New York: Little & Brown, 2008).

Jordan, Mark D., 'Aquinas's Construction of a Moral Account of the Passions', *Freiburger Zeitschrift für Philosophie und Theologie* 33.1–2 (1986), pp. 71–97.

Jordan, Mark D., *Teaching Bodies: Moral Formation in the Summa of Thomas Aquinas* (New York: Fordham University Press, 2017).

Kant, Immanuel, *Critique of Practical Reason* (trans. Mary J. Gregor, Cambridge: University Press, Cambridge Edition of the Works of Immanuel Kant: *Practical Philosophy*, 1996).

Kant, Immanuel, *Groundwork of the Metaphysics of Morals* (eds Mary J. Gregor and Allen W. Wood; trans. Mary J. Gregor, Cambridge: University Press, Cambridge Edition of the Works of Immanuel Kant: Practical Philosophy, 1996).

Katay, Andrew P., 'Preaching to the Heart: Investigating Theory and Practice Among Sydney Anglican Preachers' (unpublished D.Min. dissertation, Trinity Evangelical Divinity School, 2019).

Kemper, Theodore D., 'Social Models in the Explanation of Emotions', in *Handbook of Emotions* (eds Michael Lewis and Jeannette M. Haviland-Jones, New York and London: Guilford Press, 2nd edn, 2000), pp. 45–58.

Kenny, Anthony, *Aquinas on Mind* (London: Routledge, 1993).

Kretzmann, Norman, and Eleonore Stump, 'Aquinas', in *Routledge Encyclopedia of Philosophy* (ed. Edward Craig, Vol. 1; 10 vols, London: Routledge, 1998), pp. 326–50.

Laird, Martin, 'Under Solomon's Tutelage: The Education of Desire in the Homilies on the Song of Songs', *Modern Theology* 18.4 (2002), pp. 507–25; doi: 10.1111/1468-0025.00201.

LeDoux, Joseph E., and Elizabeth A. Phelps, 'Emotional Networks in the Brain', in *Handbook of Emotions* (eds Michael Lewis and Jeannette M. Haviland-Jones, New York and London: Guilford Press, 3rd edn, 2008), pp. 159–79.

Lewis, C. S., *The Abolition of Man: or, Reflections on Education with Special Reference to the Teaching of English in the Upper Forms of Schools* (University of Durham, *Riddell memorial lectures*; 15th series, London: Geoffrey Bles, 1946).

Lewis, C. S., *The Great Divorce: A Dream* (London: Geoffrey Bles, 1945).

Lewis, Charlton T., and C. Short, *A Latin Dictionary: Founded on the Andrew's Edition of Freund's Latin Dictionary* (Oxford: Clarendon, 1896).

Lewis, Michael, Jeannette M. Haviland-Jones, and Lisa Feldman Barrett, *Handbook of Emotions* (New York: Guilford Press, 3rd edn, 2008).

Lombardo, Nicholas E., O. P., 'Emotion and Desire in the *Summa Theologiae*', in *Aquinas's Summa Theologiae: A Critical Guide* (ed. Jeffrey Hause; *Cambridge Critical Guides* series, Cambridge: Cambridge University Press, 2018), pp. 111–30.

Lombardo, Nicholas E., O. P., *The Logic of Desire: Aquinas on Emotion* (Washington, DC: The Catholic University of America Press, 2011).

Long, D. Stephen, 'Thomas Aquinas' Divine Simplicity as Biblical Hermeneutic', *Modern Theology* 35.3 (2019), pp. 496–507; doi: 10.1111/moth.12510.

Louw, J. P., and Eugene A. Nida, *Greek-English Lexicon of the New Testament: Based on Semantic Domains* (New York: United Bible Societies, 2nd edn, 1989).

Lyons, William, *Emotion* (Aldershot: Gregg Revivals, 1993).

Lyu, Sun Myung, *Righteousness in the Book of Proverbs* (Tübingen: Mohr Siebeck, 2012).

MacIntyre, Alasdair, *After Virtue: A Study in Moral Theory* (Notre Dame, IN: University of Notre Dame Press, 3rd edn, 2007).

MacIntyre, Alasdair, *Three Rival Versions of Moral Enquiry* (London: Duckworth, 1990).

Mandeville, Bernard, 'The Grumbling Hive (1705)', Online at https://mandevillesbees .weebly.com/the-fable-of-the-bees.html.

Marcus, Gary F., *Kluge: The Haphazard Construction of the Human Mind* (London: Faber, 2008).

Mathewes, Charles T., 'Augustinian Anthropology', *Journal of Religious Ethics* 27.2 (1999), pp. 195–221.

Mele, Alfred, 'Moral Psychology', in *Continuum Companion to Ethics* (ed. Christian Miller, New York: Bloomsbury Publishing, 2011), pp. 98–118.

Messer, Neil, *Theological Neuroethics: Christian Ethics Meets the Science of the Human Brain* (*T&T Clark Enquiries in Theological Ethics* series, New York: T&T Clark/Bloomsbury, 2017).

Miles, Margaret R., *Augustine on the Body* (American Academy of Religion Series Number series, vol. 31, Missoula: Scholars Press, 1979).

Miner, Robert C., '*Affectus* and *Passio* in the *Summa Theologiae* of Thomas Aquinas', in *Before Emotion* (ed. Juanita Feros Ruys, et al., New York: Routledge, 2019), pp. 121–30.

Miner, Robert C., *Thomas Aquinas on the Passions: A Study of Summa Theologiae, 1a2ae 22–48* (Cambridge: Cambridge University Press, 2011).

Moltmann, Jürgen, *The Crucified God: The Cross of Christ as the Foundation and Criticism of Christian Theology* (trans. R. A. Wilson and J. Bowden, London: SCM Press, 1974).

Moltmann, Jürgen, 'The Passibility or Impassibility of God', in *Within the Love of God: Essays on the Doctrine of God in Honour of Paul S. Fiddes* (eds Anthony Clarke and Andrew Moore, Oxford: Oxford University Press, 2014), pp. 108–19; doi: 10.1093/ac prof:oso/9780198709565.003.0008.

'Monasteries of the Heart', Online at www.monasteriesoftheheart.org.

Mostert, Christiaan, 'Moltmann's Crucified God', *Journal of Reformed Theology* 7.2 (2013), pp. 160–80; doi: 10.1163/15697312-12341293.

Mozley, J. K., *The Impassibility of God: A Survey of Christian Thought* (Cambridge: University Press, 1926). Online at https://archive.org/details/impassibilityofg0000mozl.

Nietzsche, Friedrich, *The Anti-Christ* (ed. Michael Tanner; trans. Reginald J. Hollingdale, London: Penguin, *Penguin Classics* edn, including *Twilight of the Idols*, 1990).

Nietzsche, Friedrich, *On the Genealogy of Morality* (trans. Carol Diethe, Cambridge: Cambridge University Press, *Cambridge Texts in the History of Political Thought* edn, 1994).

Nietzsche, Friedrich, *Twilight of the Idols* (ed. Michael Tanner; trans. Reginald J. Hollingdale, London: Penguin, *Penguin Classics* edn, including *The Anti-Christ*, 1990).

Nussbaum, Martha C., 'Augustine and Dante on the Ascent of Love', in *The Augustinian Tradition* (ed. Gareth B. Matthews, Berkeley and London: University of California Press, 1999), pp. 61–90.

O'Donovan, Oliver M. T., 'Book Review: Simeon Zahl, *The Holy Spirit and Christian Experience*', *Modern Theology* 38.1 (2022), pp. 144–47; doi: 10.1111/moth.12715.

O'Donovan, Oliver M. T., 'Deliberation, Reflection and Responsibility', in *The Grandeur of Reason: Religion, Tradition and Universalism* (eds Peter M. Candler and Conor Cunningham, London: SCM Press, 2010), pp. 29–46.

O'Donovan, Oliver M. T., *The Desire of the Nations: Rediscovering the Roots of Political Theology* (Cambridge and New York: Cambridge University Press, 1996).

O'Donovan, Oliver M. T., *Entering into Rest* (*Ethics as Theology* series, vol. III, Grand Rapidsm, MI: Eerdmans, 2017).

O'Donovan, Oliver M. T. *Lecture 2, The Missing Frontier: Time, (Gifford Lectures 2021: The Disappearance of Ethics)* (St Andrews, Fife: University of St Andrews, 2021).

O'Donovan, Oliver M. T., *The Problem of Self-Love in St Augustine* (New Haven, CT: Yale University Press, 1980).

O'Donovan, Oliver M. T., *Resurrection and Moral Order: An Outline for Evangelical Ethics* (Leicester: Apollos, 1994).

Oakley, Justin, *Morality and the Emotions* (London: Routledge, 1992).

Oei, Amos Winarto, 'The Impassible God Who "Cried"', *Themelios* 41.2 (2016), pp. 238–47. Online at https://www.thegospelcoalition.org/themelios/article/the-impassible -god-who-cried.

Olsen, Stephanie, and Rob Boddice, 'Styling Emotions History', *Journal of Social History* 51.3 (2018), pp. 476–87; doi: 10.1093/jsh/shx067.

Ortony, Andrew, Gerald Clore, and Allan Collins, *The Cognitive Structure of Emotions* (Cambridge: Cambridge University Press, 1988).

Oxford English Dictionary (2nd edn [CD-ROM, v. 4.0.0.3]; Oxford: Oxford University Press, 2009).

Oxford English Dictionary Online (2nd edn, with prospective 3rd edn revisions; Oxford: Oxford University Press, 2021). Online at https://www.oed.com.

Panksepp, Jaak, 'The Affective Brain and Core Consciousness: How Does Neural Activity Generate Emotional Feelings?', in *Handbook of Emotions* (eds Michael Lewis and Jeannette M. Haviland-Jones, New York and London: Guilford Press, 3rd edn, 2008), pp. 47–67.

Panksepp, Jaak, *Affective Neuroscience: The Foundations of Human and Animal Emotions* (New York and Oxford: Oxford University Press, 1998).

Panksepp, Jaak, 'Emotions as Natural Kinds within the Mammalian Brain', in *Handbook of Emotions* (eds Michael Lewis and Jeannette M. Haviland-Jones, New York and London: Guilford Press, 2nd edn, 2000), pp. 137–56.

Pinckaers, Servais, *The Sources of Christian Ethics* (trans. Mary Thomas Noble, Edinburgh: T&T Clark, 1995).

Porter, Jean, *The Recovery of Virtue* (London: SPCK, 1990).

Puchalski, Christina M., Robert Vitillo, Sharon K. Hull, et al., 'Improving the Spiritual Dimension of Whole Person Care: Reaching National and International Consensus', *Journal of Palliative Medicine* 17.6 (2014), pp. 642–56; doi: 10.1089/jpm.2014.9427.

Pugmire, David, *Rediscovering Emotion* (Edinburgh: Edinburgh University Press, 1998).

Putnam, Ruth A., 'Perceiving Facts and Values', *Philosophy* 73 (1998), pp. 5–19.

Ramsey, Paul, 'Human Sexuality in the History of Redemption', *Journal of Religious Ethics* 16.1 (1988), pp. 56–86.

Reed, Esther D., 'Book Review: Robin Gill, Moral Passion and Christian Ethics', *Studies in Christian Ethics* 32.3 (2019), pp. 416–17; doi: 10.1177/0953946819843467d.

Reiner, Peter B., 'The Rise of Neuroessentialism', in *The Oxford Handbook of Neuroethics* (eds Judy Illes and Barbara J. Sahakian, Oxford: Oxford University Press, 2011), pp. 306–29.

Rist, John M., *Augustine Deformed: Love, Sin and Freedom in the Western Moral Tradition* (Cambridge: Cambridge University Press, 2014).

Roberts, Robert C., 'Emotions Among the Virtues of the Christian Life', *Journal of Religious Ethics* 20 (1992), pp. 37–68.

Roberts, Robert C., 'Thomas Aquinas on the Morality of the Emotions', *History of Philosophy Quarterly* 9.3 (1992), pp. 287–305.

Roberts, Robert C., 'What an Emotion Is—a Sketch', *Philosophical Review* 97.2 (1988), pp. 183–209.

Ross, W. D., and Philip Stratton-Lake, *The Right and the Good* (*British Moral Philosophers* series, Oxford: Clarendon Press, 2002).

Rowland, Tracey, *Catholic Theology* (*Doing Theology* series, London: Bloomsbury, 2017).

Russell, James A., and Lisa Feldman Barrett, 'Editorial', *Emotion Review* 1.1 (2009), p. 2; doi: 10.1177/1754073908097174.

Ruys, Juanita Feros, Michael W. Champion, and Kirk Essary, *Before Emotion: The Language of Feeling, 400–1800* (*Routledge Studies in Medieval Literature and Culture* series, vol. 14, New York: Taylor & Francis and Routledge, 2019).

Sarot, Marcel, 'God, Emotion, and Corporeality: A Thomist Perspective', *The Thomist* 58.1 (1994), pp. 61–92; doi: 10.1353/tho.1994.0043.

Sarot, Marcel, 'Patripassianism, Theopaschitism and the Suffering of God', *Religious Studies* 26.3 (1990), pp. 363–75.

Satel, Sally, and Scott O. Lilienfeld, *Brainwashed: The Seductive Appeal of Mindless Neuroscience* (New York: Basic Books, Kindle edn, 2013).

Scarantino, Andrea, and Paul Griffiths, 'Don't Give Up on Basic Emotions', *Emotion Review* 3.4 (2011), pp. 444–54; doi: 10.1177/1754073911410745.

Schlabach, Gerald W., 'Augustine's Hermeneutic of Humility: An Alternative to Moral Imperialism and Moral Relativism', *Journal of Religious Ethics* 22 (1994), pp. 299–330.

Scrutton, Anastasia, 'Emotion in Augustine of Hippo and Thomas Aquinas: A Way Forward for the Im/passibility Debate?', *International Journal of Systematic Theology* 7.2 (2005), pp. 169–77.

Seligman, Martin E. P., Peter Albert Railton, Roy F. Baumeister, et al., *Homo Prospectus* (Oxford: Oxford University Press, 2016).

Service, Jacqueline, 'Divine Self-Enrichment and Human Well-Being: A Systematic Theological Inquiry, with Special Reference to Development and Humanitarian Aid' (unpublished Ph.D. dissertation, Charles Sturt University, 2018). Online at https://researchoutput.csu.edu.au, accessed 28 September 2021.

Service, Jacqueline, *Triune Wellbeing: The Kenotic-Enrichment of the Eternal Trinity* (Lanham, MD: Fortress Academic, forthcoming).

Solomon, Robert C., *The Passions: Emotions and the Meaning of Life* (Indianapolis, IN: Hackett, 2nd edn, 1993).

Solomon, Robert C., 'The Philosophy of Emotions', in *Handbook of Emotions* (eds Michael Lewis and Jeannette M. Haviland-Jones, New York and London: Guilford Press, 3rd edn, 2008), pp. 3–16.

Sorabji, Richard, *Emotion and Peace of Mind: From Stoic Agitation to Christian Temptation* (Oxford: Clarendon Press, 2000).

Sorley, W. R., 'Berkeley and Contemporary Philosophy', in *The Cambridge History of English Literature* (eds Adolphus W. Ward and Alfred R. Waller, Vol. 9; 18 vols; Cambridge: University Press, 1907–27), pp. 279–304.

Spezio, Michael L., 'The Neuroscience of Emotion and Reasoning in Social Contexts: Implications for Moral Theology', in *Faith, Rationality, and the Passions* (ed. Sarah Coakley, Malden, MA: Wiley-Blackwell, 2012), pp. 223–40.

St Nicodemus of the Holy Mountain, and St Makarios of Corinth (eds), *The Philokalia: The Complete Text* (trans. G. E. H. Palmer, Philip Sherrard and Kallistos Ware, Vol. I, London: Faber & Faber, 1979).

Stark, Rodney, *For the Glory of God: How Monotheism Led to Reformations, Science, Witch-hunts, and the End of Slavery* (Princeton, NJ: Princeton University Press, 2003).

Stearns, Peter N., and Carol Z. Stearns, 'Emotionology: Clarifying the History of Emotions and Emotional Standards', *American Historical Review* 90 (1985), pp. 813–36.

Stevenson, Angus (ed.), *Oxford Dictionary of English* (Oxford: Oxford University Press, 3rd edn, 2015). Online at www.oxfordreference.com; doi: 10.1093/acref/9780199571123.001.0001.

Stevenson, Charles L., *Ethics and Language* (New Haven, CT: Yale University Press, 1944).

Stewart, Anne W., *Poetic Ethics in Proverbs: Wisdom Literature and the Shaping of the Moral Self* (Cambridge: Cambridge University Press, 2016).

Stocker, Michael, *Valuing Emotions* (Cambridge: Cambridge University Press, 1996).

Stump, Eleonore, 'The Non-Aristotelian Character of Aquinas's Ethics', in *Faith, Rationality, and the Passions* (ed. Sarah Coakley, Malden, MA: Wiley-Blackwell, 2012), pp. 91–106.

Suhler, Christopher L., and Patricia Churchland, 'Can Innate, Modular "Foundations" Explain Morality? Challenges for Haidt's Moral Foundations Theory', *Journal of Cognitive Neuroscience* 23.9 (2011), pp. 2103–16; doi: 10.1162/jocn.2011.21637.

Suhler, Christopher L., and Patricia Churchland, 'The Neurobiological Basis of Morality', in *The Oxford Handbook of Neuroethics* (eds Judy Illes and Barbara J. Sahakian, Oxford: Oxford University Press, 2011), pp. 99–145.

Tacey, David, 'Contemporary Spirituality', in *Oxford Textbook of Spirituality in Healthcare* (eds M. Cobb, C. M. Puchalski and B. D. Rumbold, Oxford: Oxford University Press, 2012), pp. 473–79.

Taylor, Charles, *A Secular Age* (Cambridge, MA: Belknap Press of Harvard University Press, 2007).

Taylor, Charles, *Sources of the Self: The Making of the Modern Identity* (Cambridge: Cambridge University Press, 1989).

Thomson, Heather, 'On the Humble God', *St Mark's Review* 236 (2016), pp. 86–90.

Tiberius, Valerie, *Moral Psychology: A Contemporary Introduction* (London: Taylor & Francis Group, 2014).

Vlachos, Hierotheos S., *Orthodox Psychotherapy (The Science of the Fathers)* (trans. Esther Williams, Levadia, Greece: Birth of the Theotokos Monastery, 1994).

Voyer, Benjamin G., 'Toward a Multidisciplinary Moral Psychology', in *Moral Psychology: A Multidisciplinary Guide* (eds Benjamin G. Voyer and Tor Tarantola, Cham, Switzerland: Springer International Publishing AG, 2017), pp. 1–3.

Westermann, Claus, *Roots of Wisdom: The Oldest Proverbs of Israel and Other Peoples* (Louiseville, KY: Westminster John Knox Press, 1995).

Williams, Rowan, *Looking East in Winter: Contemporary Thought and the Eastern Christian Tradition* (London: Bloomsbury, Kindle edn, 2021).

Williamson, Marianne, *A Politics of Love: A Handbook for a New American Revolution* (New York: HarperCollins, Kindle edn, 2019).

Wirzba, Norman, 'Creaturely Humility', in *The Joy of Humility: The Beginning and End of the Virtues* (ed. Drew Collins, Ryan McAnnally-Linz and Evan C. Rosa, Waco, TX: Baylor University Press, 2020), pp. 107–21.

Wittman, Tyler R., 'Belonging to Another: Christ, Moral Nature, and the Shape of Humility', *Studies in Christian ethics* 33.3 (2020), pp. 392–410; doi: 10.1177/0953946818822276.

Wolterstorff, Nicholas, 'Suffering Love', in *Philosophy and the Christian Faith* (ed. Thomas V. Morris: , Notre Dame, IN: University of Notre Dame Press, 1988), pp. 196–237.

Woodberry, Robert D., 'The Missionary Roots of Liberal Democracy', *The American Political Science Review* 106.2 (2012), pp. 244–74; doi: 10.1017/S0003055412000093.

Yoder, Christine Roy, 'The Objects of Our Affection: Emotions and the Moral Life in Proverbs 1–9', in *Shaking Heaven and Earth: Essays in Honor of Walter Brueggemann and Charles B. Cousar* (eds Christine Roy Yoder, Kathleen M. O'Connor, E. Elizabeth Johnson, et al., Louisville, KY: Westminster John Knox Press, 2005), pp. 73–88.

Zahl, Simeon, *The Holy Spirit and Christian Experience* (Oxford: Oxford University Press, 2020).

INDEX OF SCRIPTURE REFERENCES

INDEX OF SUBJECTS

Specific descriptors of particular affections, emotions, moods, passions, vices, virtues etc.

INDEX OF AUTHORS AND NAMES

Lightning Source UK Ltd.
Milton Keynes UK
UKHW020016170123
415455UK00005B/263